Pater to Forster

transitions

General Editor: Julian Wolfreys

Published Titles
ORWELL TO THE PRESENT: LITERATURE IN ENGLAND, 1945–2000   John Brannigan
CHAUCER TO SHAKESPEARE, 1337–1580   SunHee Kim Gertz
POPE TO BURNEY, 1714–1779   Moyra Haslett
PATER TO FORSTER, 1873–1924   Ruth Robbins
BURKE TO BYRON, BARBAULD TO BAILLIE, 1790–1830   Jane Stabler
MILTON TO POPE, 1650–1720 Kay   Gilliland Stevenson
SIDNEY TO MILTON, 1580–1660   Marion Wynne-Davies

BATAILLE   Fred Botting and Scott Wilson
NEW HISTORICISM AND CULTURAL MATERIALISM   John Brannigan
POSTMODERN NARRATIVE THEORY   Mark Currie
FORMALIST CRITICISM AND READER-RESPONSE THEORY   Todd F. Davis and Kenneth
    Womack
QUEER THEORIES   Donald E. Hall
MARXIST LITERARY AND CULTURAL THEORY   Moyra Haslett
LOUIS ALTHUSSER   Warren Montag
RACE   Brian Niro
JACQUES LACAN   Jean-Michel Rabaté
LITERARY FEMINISMS   Ruth Robbins
DECONSTRUCTION•DERRIDA   Julian Wolfreys

Forthcoming Titles
IMAGE TO APOCALYPSE, 1910–1945   Jane Goldman
DICKENS TO HARDY, 1837–1884   Julian Wolfreys

TERRY EAGLETON   David Alderson
JULIA KRISTEVA AND LITERARY THEORY   Megan Becker-Leckrone
NATIONAL IDENTITY   John Brannigan
HÉLÈNE CIXOUS: WRITING AND SEXUAL DIFFERENCE   Abigail Bray
HOMI BHABHA   Eleanor Byrne
GENDER   Claire Colebrook
IDEOLOGY   James Decker
POSTMODERNISM•POSTMODERNITY   Martin McQuillan
ROLAND BARTHES   Martin McQuillan
MODERNITY   David Punter
PSYCHOANALYSIS AND LITERATURE   Nicholas Rand
SUBJECTIVITY   Ruth Robbins
POSTCOLONIAL THEORY   Malini Johan Schueller
TRANSGRESSION   Julian Wolfreys

---

transitions Series
Series Standing Order ISBN 0–333–73684–6
(*outside North America only*)

You can receive future titles in this series as they are published by
placing a standing order. Please contact your bookseller or, in case of
difficulty, write to us at the address below with your name and address,
the title of the series and the ISBN quoted above.

Customer Services Department, Macmillan Distribution Ltd
Houndmills, Basingstoke, Hampshire RG21 6XS, England

---

transitions

Pater to Forster, 1873–1924

Ruth Robbins

First published 2003 by
PALGRAVE MACMILLAN
Houndmills, Basingstoke, Hampshire RG21 6XS and
175 Fifth Avenue, New York, N.Y. 10010
Companies and representatives throughout the world

PALGRAVE MACMILLAN is the global academic imprint of the Palgrave
Macmillan division of St. Martin's Press, LLC and of Palgrave Macmillan Ltd.
Macmillan® is a registered trademark in the United States, United Kingdom
and other countries. Palgrave is a registered trademark in the European
Union and other countries.

ISBN 0–333–69614–X hardback
ISBN 0–333–69615–8 paperback

This book is printed on paper suitable for recycling and made from fully
managed and sustained forest sources.

A catalogue record for this book is available from the British Library.

Library of Congress Cataloging-in-Publication Data
Robbins, Ruth, 1965–
      Pater to Forster, 1873–1924 / Ruth Robbins.
         p. cm. – (Transitions)
      Includes bibliographical references and index.
         ISBN 0–333–69614–X – ISBN 0–333–69615–8 (pbk.)
         1. English literature – 19th century – History and criticism. 2. Forster, E. M.
      (Edward Morgan), 1879–1970 – Criticism and interpretation. 3. Pater, Walter,
      1839–1894 – Criticism and interpretation. 4. English literature – 20th
      century – History and criticism. I. Title. II. Transitions (Palgrave Macmillan
      (Firm))

      PR461.R63 2003
      820.9′008–dc21   2003045602

10   9   8   7   6   5   4   3   2   1
12   11   10   09   08   07   06   05   04   03

Printed in China

For my parents,
Cath and Stan Robbins

Contents

General Editor's Preface   ix
A Note on Texts Used   xi
Acknowledgements   xii

Introduction: Ways of Seeing   1
- The moral imperative of clear vision   5
- Clouded vision? Subjectivity and impressionism   9
- Dark visions   16
- Ears or eyes?   24

1. The Persistence of Realism   30
- The strained case of George Gissing   39
- H. G. Wells and the quarter-educated   48
- Galsworthy the materialist   55
- Aesthetics and the market, or the artist and the artisan;
  or Mr Bennett and Mrs Woolf   62

2. Rhymers and Reasoners: Poetry in Transition   74
- Country   80
- Woman   86
- City   92

3. The Strange Case of Mr Wilde: or, 1895 and all that   105
- Doubles and double vision   118
- 1895: or, looking both ways?   125

4. Masculine Romance, Cultural Capital and Crisis   128
- The Gothic and obscure vision   134
- Degeneration: The context of late-nineteenth-century
  monstrosity   138
- Telling clearly …? The eyewitness and cultural capital   145

- *Dracula*: (cultural) capital and
  (epistemological) crisis   149
- The good ended happily ...?   155

5. New Women for Old: Politics and Fictional Forms in
    New Woman Writing   159
    - Defining the New Woman   159
    - Olive Schreiner   165
    - Sarah Grand: seeing things purely   173
    - George Egerton and impurity   179
    - The New Woman beyond the nineties   187

6. Conclusions? *Rainbow's* End: The Janus Period   192
    - Time and character in *The Rainbow*   195
    - Forster's connections   202

Selective Chronology 1865–1925   210
Annotated Bibliography   222
Bibliography   228
Index   241

General Editor's Preface

Transitions: *transition–*, n. of action. 1. A passing or passage from one condition, action or (rarely) place, to another. 2. Passage in thought, speech, or writing, from one subject to another. 3. **a**. The passing from one note to another. **b**. The passing from one key to another, modulation. 4. The passage from an earlier to a later stage of development or formation ... change from an earlier style to a later; a style of intermediate or mixed character ... the historical passage of language from one well-defined stage to another.

The aim of *transitions* is to explore passages and movements in language, literature and culture from Chaucer to the present day. The series also seeks to examine the ways in which the very idea of transition affects the reader's sense of period so as to address anew questions of literary history and periodization. The writers in this series unfold the cultural and historical mediations of literature during what are commonly recognized as crucial moments in the development of English literature, addressing, as the OED puts it, the 'historical passage of language from one well-defined stage to another'.

Recognizing the need to contextualize literary study, the authors offer close readings of canonical and now marginalized or overlooked literary texts from all genres, bringing to this study the rigour of historical knowledge and the sophistication of theoretically informed evaluations of writers and movements from the last 700 years. At the same time as each writer, whether Chaucer or Shakespeare, Milton or Pope, Byron, Dickens, George Eliot, Virginia Woolf or Salman Rushdie, is shown to produce his or her texts within a discernible historical, cultural, ideological and philosophical milieu, the text is read from the vantage point of recent theoretical interests and concerns. The purpose in bringing theoretical knowledge to the reading of a wide range of works is to demonstrate how the literature is always open to transition, whether in the instant of its production or in succeeding moments of its critical reception.

The series desires to enable the reader to transform her/his own reading and writing transactions by comprehending past developments.

Each book in the second tranche of the series offers a pedagogical guide to the poetics and politics of particular eras, as well as to the subsequent critical comprehension of periods and periodization. As well as transforming the cultural and literary past by interpreting its transition from the perspective of the critical and theoretical present, each study enacts transitional readings of a number of literary texts, all of which are themselves conceivable as having effected transition at the moments of their first appearance. The readings offered in these books seek, through close critical reading, historical contextualization and theoretical engagement, to demonstrate certain possibilities in reading to the student reader.

It is hoped that the student will find this series liberating because the series seeks to move beyond rigid definitions of period. What is important is the sense of passage, of motion. Rather than providing a definitive model of literature's past, *transitions* aims to place you in an active dialogue with the writing and culture of other eras, so as to comprehend not only how the present reads the past, but how the past can read the present.

Julian Wolfreys

A Note on Texts Used

This book is aimed primarily at student readers. For that reason, wherever possible, I have made use of good, in-print, modern editions of the texts I discuss. In some cases this has not been possible, and the dates in the references will alert the reader to those texts which have not been recently reprinted. Dates of original publication are noted in the text, and again in the bibliographical references for your information. This process can have the effect of making references look odd – D. H. Lawrence was not still publishing in 1995, but the current Penguin edition of *The Rainbow* was produced in that year. In relation to the discussion of poetry I have made extensive use of anthologized collections because I wanted my readers to be able to read the texts for themselves. An anthology implies a certain organization of material, and a certain view of that material which is the editors' view, rather than the poets'. Editions of this kind go in and out of date, and what for example, the 1890s meant in 1970 and what they mean now are rather different things. I hereby warn readers therefore that if they want to know in more detail what 'really happened', they need to go and look for themselves in the original books. I am acting in good faith – but that's no reason why you should trust me.

Acknowledgements

Thank you to my colleagues at University College Northampton. To George Savona, Peter Brooker and Chris Ringrose, who arranged a period of study leave, and to the rest of the English Division, who spread out to close the gap, my thanks. Conversations with Laurence Marriott and the references he supplied have been extremely useful – thank you.

Julian Wolfreys is still the best of editors and the best of friends. This book's current shape owes more to him than I can possibly say. Thanks are more than due and are warmly offered. The staff of the University of Warwick Library and of UCN Learning Resources Centre have aided me much more than they know; my thanks to them. Our thanks are also due to our husband, Richard Andrews, who remains just what the doctor ordered.

King Lear, father of three daughters, was very exercised by filial ingratitude. Lest anyone should think that I have it in me to be 'sharper than a serpent's tooth', this book is dedicated to my parents, Cath and Stan Robbins.

Introduction: Ways of Seeing

In a very famous moment in the history of art, the Victorian critic, John Ruskin (1819–1900), arbiter of public taste and commentator on the morality of art, visited the Grosvenor Gallery in London in the summer of 1877. Amongst the exhibits he saw there were paintings by British-born artist Edward Burne-Jones (1833–98) and the American James Abbott McNeill Whistler (1834–1903). Burne-Jones, who had begun his career as a Pre-Raphaelite painter, depicting mythic and medieval subjects with an almost photographic realism in technique, was unsurprisingly highly praised by Ruskin for his eight exhibits at the Grosvenor. From the beginning of the Pre-Raphaelite movement in the late 1840s, Ruskin had championed the cause and had been one of key formers of a public taste that eventually learned to love what had earlier been disapprovingly called 'the fleshly school' of painting and poetry on account of its sensuous treatment of sensuous subject matter. The Pre-Raphaelite virtue in Ruskin's eyes was that the painters painted in ways which were intensely realistic and produced highly worked canvases that were testament to their craft as well as their art. Because of this realism of technique, the message of a given painting was immediately and obviously legible, and this was for Ruskin the point of a work of art.

About Whistler's paintings, however, Ruskin was scathing. In an edition of his own publication, *Fors Clavigera*, an irregular periodical that he published at his own expense, he wrote:

> For Mr. Whistler's own sake, no less than for the protection of the purchaser, Sir Coutts Lindsay [owner of the Grosvenor] ought not have admitted works into the gallery in which the ill-educated conceit of the artist so nearly approached the aspect of wilful imposture. I have seen, and heard, much of Cockney impudence before now; but never expected to hear a coxcomb to ask two hundred guineas for flinging a pot of paint in the public's face. (Ruskin, quoted in Merrill 1992, 47)

That commentary clearly suggests, amongst other things, that Whistler is not an artist but a conman. His paintings are not art, Ruskin suggests, because there is none of the labour of art to be seen in the finished product; he does not apply paint – he merely throws it at the canvas, and by extension at the public, who might just be fooled into buying it for two hundred guineas, if they are silly enough to pay to be insulted. The painting that especially aroused his ire was an oil painting entitled *Nocturne in Black and Gold*, a title later amended with the addition of *The Falling Rocket*. It is a London landscape – a view over the Thames towards the Cremorne pleasure gardens, depicting a night scene with fireworks. William Michael Rossetti, who saw it exhibited at the Dudley Gallery in 1875 called it 'extremely good' and described it thus:

> The scene is probably the Cremorne Gardens; the heavy rich darkness of the clump of trees to the left, contrasted with the opaque obscurity of the sky, itself enhanced by the falling shower of fire-flakes, is felt and realized with great truth. Straight across the trees, not high above the ground, shoots and fizzes the last and fiercest light of the expiring rocket. (Rossetti in Spencer 1991, 19)

That word 'probably' is an instructive one: even a well-practised art critic cannot be quite sure of what he is seeing.

When Whistler saw Ruskin's views in print, he sued for libel in the hope of substantial damages. Ruskin was too ill to defend the case and did not appear in court at the trial which took place on 25–26 November 1878, and Whistler won his case – but the jury signalled their contempt for him by awarding only a farthing (a quarter of a penny and the smallest monetary amount possible) in damages. But the point about Whistler's painting, Ruskin's commentary on it, and the lawsuit they produced is that this was an argument about ways of seeing the world, especially ways of seeing the world through art. *Nocturne in Black and Gold* is an impressionist painting. It presents a momentary event – the explosion of a firework over the Thames and a pleasure garden by night. Because it presents an intense but very evanescent moment taking place in darkness, by definition it does not present the scene 'clearly'. As Lynda Nead has suggested, the trial 'was a contest of two opposing aesthetic theories and two … artistic reputations' (Nead 2000, 143). In itself, a painting which offered no immediately inter-pretable image – a painting which, as it were, told no story, and which had no simply paraphrasable content – was an assault on mainstream Victorian values in painting and, indeed, the other arts. Moreover,

Whistler's choice of title for his picture compounded the offence and made his resistance to narrative clarity all the more pointed, for the painting's original title made no claim whatsoever to describe the content within the frame. Moreover, it deliberately confused the issue, mixing up the senses of hearing (a Nocturne is a piece of music) and sight (a picture is meant to be seen) with a synaesthetic flourish.

Ironically, since Ruskin was a major champion of the virtually impressionist canvases of J. M. W. Turner (1775–1851), it is strange that he viewed more recent impressionistic manifestations with extreme distaste as exemplifying all that was wrong with modernity. The poet A. E. Housman narrates in a letter to his stepmother, also in 1877 (29 November), how, in a lecture at Oxford where Housman was then a student, and where Ruskin was Slade Professor of art, Ruskin had given a brilliant demonstration of the horror of modernity. He took a Turner canvas depicting a view of Leicester Abbey across the river – the frame was glassed over. Ruskin stood in front of the painting and declaimed:

> 'You ... may go to Leicester to see what is like now. I never shall. But I can make a pretty good guess.' Then he caught up a paintbrush. 'These step-ping stones of course have been done away with, and are replaced by a be-au-ti-ful iron bridge.' Then he dashed in the iron bridge on the glass of the picture. 'The colour of the stream is supplied on one side by the indigo factory.' Forthwith one side of the stream became indigo. 'On the other side by the soap factory.' Soap dashed in. 'They mix in the middle – like curds,' he said, working them together with a sort of malicious deliberation. (Housman 1988, 450)

He added to his picture factories, houses, smoke and flame, and turned to receive the rapturous applause of his undergraduate audience at his version of impressionism superimposed over Turner's. This episode implies that Ruskin disapproved not only of Whistler's extreme version of impressionism, nor only of his painting's lack of 'finish', but also of the subject matter he had depicted in the *Nocturne in Black and Gold*. Taking aesthetic pleasure in a cityscape was all well and good so long as the city had an element of nostalgic pastoral about it. Modernity, on the other hand, was not fit to be represented.

In a moment of certainly unintentional synchronicity, also in 1877, Walter Pater had published an essay entitled 'The School of Giorgione' in the *Fortnightly Review* (October 1877). This essay later became part of the third edition of *The Renaissance: Studies in Art and Poetry* (1888), as *Studies in the History of the Renaissance* had been retitled and has been described as 'the theoretical center of the argument implicit

throughout *The Renaissance* that the fine arts should receive no ideological interpretation' (Stein 1975, 222). The essay opens with a number
of statements about the meaning of aesthetic criticism in which Pater is
at pains to insist that such criticism must pay more attention to the
formal properties of the work of art, rather than focusing simplistically
on its 'content', as most Victorian critics took it for granted that one
should:

> One of the functions of aesthetic criticism is ... to estimate the degree in
> which a given work of art fulfils its responsibilities to its special material;
> to note in a picture that true pictorial charm, which neither a mere poet-
> ical thought or sentiment on the one hand, nor a mere result of commu-
> nicable technical skill in colour or design, on the other; to define in a
> poem that true poetic quality, which is neither descriptive nor meditative
> merely, but comes of an inventive handling of rhythmical language, the
> element of song in the singing; to note in music the musical charm, that
> essential music which presents no words, no matter of sentiment or
> thought, separable from the special form in which it is conveyed to us.
> (Pater ed. Hill 1980, 102–3)

What Pater is resisting here is a whole tradition of art and literary criticism which took the abstractable content – the story, the message, the
meaning of the work – as central to its evaluation. The traditions of
nineteenth-century art criticism are 'ekphrastic'; that is to say, the
critic's role is to describe what he sees in such ways as he can *extract a
narrative which points a moral,* and to this extent, art criticism shared
much with literary criticism which was also concerned with content
and with a relatively simplistic didacticism. Pater's text, with its long,
complex sentences and exaggerated care in the process of writing,
represents a criticism in which the critic himself is an artist, and in
which textual morality is not part of the critical project. Slightly later
in the essay he made a very famous statement with which Whistler
would certainly have been in sympathy, though I suspect that Ruskin
would have disapproved:

> *All art constantly aspires to the art of music.* For while in all other kinds
> of art it is possible to distinguish the matter from the form, and the
> understanding can always make this distinction, yet it is the constant
> effort of art to obliterate it. (Pater ed. Hill 1980, 106; italics in original)

Now whilst musicians and composers would probably argue that one
can in fact separate the content from the form in music, Pater's analogy

is nonetheless clear to the non-specialist. Aesthetic criticism has to do with the *feelings* evoked by a given work of art or poem. Pater certainly knew, for he was a tutor in classics at Oxford, that the word aesthetic derives from the Greek *aistetikos*, meaning 'feeling' in the sense of physical sensation as well as in the sense of emotion.[1] It is this absolute connection between form and content to which Whistler also alluded when he called several of his paintings 'Nocturnes', 'Arrangements' and 'Symphonies' – musical terms intended to evoke emotional rather than the intellectual (and specifically moral) responses favoured by mainstream criticism. In his emphasis on form, however, Pater like Whistler in a different medium, was attacking some dearly held critical truths of the Victorian age. To understand something about what was new in ways of seeing the world in the late nineteenth and early twentieth centuries, therefore, we must go back a little in time to before the beginning of this book's period.

The moral imperative of clear vision

As one reads the reviews of the major and minor novels of the mid-Victorian period, certain critical principles become very obvious. The function of criticism above all is to achieve an opinion about the text's moral message. Where twentieth-century criticism, which draws much of its impetus from Modernist aesthetics, often placed enormous value on ambiguity and, eventually in Derridean thought, on *undecidability*, the Victorians preferred to know for certain what message a book could offer to its reader. One of the most striking cases is Emily Brontë's *Wuthering Heights* (1847): for most Victorian reviewers the novel was coarse and vulgar and offered no easily legible moral; twentieth-century criticism, on the other hand, has valued precisely its refusal to make concessions to the conventional proprieties of its own age.[2] One of the prerequisites for pursuing moral criticism is clear vision, for unless the critic can see clearly he (and sometimes she) cannot pronounce clearly on the text's message. Clear vision demands self-evident content, for it is in content that moral messages are planted. The critic must be able to paraphrase what happens in a novel or poem, or to tell the story that a painting illustrates, if he is to be able to pronounce on the decency of its tendencies. When Miss Prism, the foolish governess in Oscar Wilde's *The Importance of Being Earnest* is asked whether her lost three-volume novel ended happily, Wilde makes her the spokesperson for the conventions he himself wishes to debunk. In Miss Prism's novel, 'The good ended happily, and the bad unhappily. That it what Fiction means' (Wilde, 376). This is a good and right-up-to-the minute joke in 1895, the year that the three-volume novel finally disappeared as the mainstay of Victorian circulating library fiction, but it is not very far from the views of fiction expounded by most reviews in the mid- to late-nineteenth century. Ruskin himself, fairly consistently throughout his critical oeuvre, expounds views that are not so far away from those of Miss Prism. In October 1881, for example, he wrote in *The Nineteenth Century*, under the title 'Fiction – Fair and Foul – 2': 'All healthy and helpful literature sets simple bars between right and wrong; assumes the possibility, in men and women, of having healthy minds in healthy bodies, and loses no time in the diagnosis of fever which signifies the ungoverned appetite of any appetite or passion' (Ruskin in Goodwin, 167). Good, wholesome stuff: that is what fiction should be – and the bars between right and wrong are 'simple', easily read, and fundamentally communicable.

Ruskin's art criticism requires the same clarity. In his praise for William Holman Hunt's *The Awakening Conscience* (1853), it is the legibility of the painting's message that he approves. Hunt's painting represents a young woman, a kept woman, leaping from her place on her lover's lap, as though she has rather suddenly realized the error of her ways. Of this image, Ruskin wrote in a letter to the *Times* on 24 May 1854:

> The poor girl has been sitting with her seducer; some chance words of the song 'Oft in the Stilly Night' [the music on the piano stand in the picture] have struck upon the numbed places of her heart; she has started up in agony; he, not seeing her face, goes on singing, striking the keys carelessly with his gloved hand ... .
>
> There is not a single object in that room – common, modern, vulgar ... but it becomes tragical *if rightly read* ... the torn and dying bird upon the floor; the gilded tapestry ... the picture above the fireplace with its single drooping figure – the woman taken in adultery; nay, the very hem of the girl's dress ... *has story in it.* (Ruskin, quoted in Marsh 1987, 82, my emphasis)

Ruskin typically 'reads' this picture as if it is a story; more specifically he reads it within the conventions of literary as well as pictorial realism. It is not only the central human figures in the image that have meaning. Every detail of the room in which they sit has its part to play in telling the story of the kept woman and her lecherous lover. The cheap piano, a discarded glove, the showy mirrors, a cat killing a bird under the table, are all part of the story, and all aid the viewer to *read* the image. The technique of the painting, of which Ruskin so strongly approves, is that the message is self-evident to those trained in right reading. Both image and message are *clear* and available to be explained clearly by the intelligent reader.

The letter to the *Times* is Ruskin indulging in incidental art-criticism, but that trope of seeing clearly is central to most of his critical work. In the third volume of his series *Modern Painters* (1856), he wrote: 'The more I think of it I find this conclusion more impressed upon me, – that the greatest thing a human soul ever does in this world is to *see* something, and tell what it *saw* in a plain way' (Ruskin in Warner and Hough 1983, I, 15, original emphasis). Clear vision, and the clear articulation of that clear vision, is the foundation of criticism and of art itself. And despite the many differences between them, this is also a figure found repeatedly in the writings of critic, poet and social commentator, Matthew Arnold (1822–88). His most famous critical statement, from 'The Function of Criticism at the Present Time' (1865) shares Ruskin's commitment to clear vision: criticism demands 'the endeavour, in all branches of knowledge, theology, philosophy, history, art, science, *to see the object as in itself it really is*' (Arnold 1993, 174, my emphasis). Moreover, as well as seeing the object clearly, it is also necessary, as Arnold puts in his essay 'On the Modern Element in Literature', to see things steadily and see them whole (Arnold 1993, 136);[3] to see the world, in other words, in ways that emphasize clarity, patterning, and the possibility of making verbal sense of what you see. Thus in 1853, in the Preface to the first edition of his *Poems*, Arnold writes: 'What is *not* interesting, is … that which is general, indeterminate, and faint, instead of being particular, precise, and firm' (Arnold 1993, 116), and he castigates vagueness, impressionism, and the failure of modern poetry and art to produce a total coherent vision: 'We have poems which seem to exist merely for the sake of single lines and passages; not for the sake of producing any total impression. We have critics who seem to direct their attention merely to detached expressions, to the language about the action, not to the action itself' (Arnold 1993, 120–1). Not only does this mode of criticism demand clear vision, it also focuses the critic's attention on content – the action – over form, the object described over the 'detached expressions of the language'.

But what one can also see in these statements about the necessity for clear vision is that both Ruskin and Arnold are anxious about whether such vision actually exists. Their statements demand that it should as a matter of obvious commonsense; on the other hand, the very fact that this apparently self-evident truth needs to be stated, and stated repeatedly, would tend to imply that it is not quite self-evident. George Eliot states the problems of clear vision very forcefully in a number of the metafictional interludes of her fiction, 'In Which the Story Pauses a Little', as one of the chapters of *Adam Bede* (1859) is entitled. In an address to her 'lady readers', Eliot's shorthand for the unsophisticated reader who prefers merely conventional propriety to broader truth in literary fiction, she asserts that she is no 'clever novelist', but one who is obliged to 'creep servilely after nature and fact'. Her narrator has no 'lofty vocation' to represent the world as neatly moralistic; her aspiration is rather:

> to give no more than a faithful account of men and things as they have mirrored themselves in my mind. The mirror is doubtless defective; the outlines will sometimes be disturbed; the reflection faint or confused; but I feel as much bound to tell you, as if precisely as I can, what that reflection is, as if I were in the witness-box narrating my experience on oath. (Eliot [1859] 1980, 221)

This statement gives with one hand and takes away with the other. On the one hand, there is the metaphor of the mirror, an image intended to evoke the concept of clear vision, and Arnoldian objectivity: where, if not in a mirror, can one 'see the object as in itself it really is'? On the other, however, Eliot, in a move that seems to predict much twentieth-century theory, makes it clear that the mirror might be a space of misrecognition and of subjective failure.[4] The emphasis in her statement is hard to disentangle – does it fall on the mirror, or on the mind, on the objective realm of reflected images, or on the subjective impression those images might make in a 'defective' mirror? And despite the attempt to argue that whatever is written is produced in good faith, the doubt about clear vision has already been planted.

In her later novel *Middlemarch* (1870–71), a similar point is made by slightly different means, again in a direct address to the reader. Eliot's narrator insists on the illusory nature of objectivity:

> An eminent philosopher among my friends, who can dignify even your ugly furniture by lifting it into the serene light of science, has shown me this pregnant little fact. Your pier-glass or extensive surface of polished steel made to be rubbed by a housemaid, will be minutely and multi-tudinously scratched in all directions; but place now against it a lighted candle as a centre of illumination, and lo! the scratches will seem to arrange themselves in a fine series of concentric circles round that little

sun. It is demonstrable that the scratches are going everywhere impartially, and it is only your candle which produces the flattering illusion of a concentric arrangement, its light falling with an exclusive optical selection. These things are a parable. The scratches are events, and the candle is the egotism of any person now absent.... (Eliot [1871] 1994, 264)

There is much that might be said about this passage. The tone is obviously mocking, and the implied addressee – someone both wealthy and philistine enough to have 'ugly' furniture and a housemaid to deal with it – is cast as unwilling to accept a truth unpalatable to the conventional morality of bourgeois existence. In life, Eliot tells us, events are random, not arranged into the discernible patterns which are supposed to enable us to judge clearly what the moral meaning of the events might be. Clear sight, even when aided by the artificial illumination of a candle, is illusory. Egotism clouds vision; our view of reality is subjective and renders the ideal of objectivity null and void; moreover, it is science, more usually associated precisely with objectivity and clear vision, which tells us this fact. All the same, Eliot goes on, we do not behave as if this is true; we act as if the patterns are still there.

Clouded vision? Subjectivity and impressionism

Pater's *Studies in the History of the Renaissance* is a key text for understanding how the alleged (but certainly mythical) certainties of the past were put aside in favour of new ways of seeing in the late nineteenth century. Interestingly, however, it is also a transitional text, which depends for its force precisely on its connection to the Victorian context against which it reacts and in which it was produced. Its very first page alludes to Ruskin and mischievously quotes Arnold against himself, establishing both Pater's relationship with Victorian ways of seeing and his subversion of them. As Laurel Brake has noted, 'The address to Ruskin and Arnold in *Studies*... is cumulative and palpable from the Preface onward' (Brake 1994a, 23). *The Renaissance* begins, Donald L. Hill suggests, with a specific attack, on Ruskin's attempts to define beauty as an abstract concept (Pater ed. Hill 1980, 294), though the attack is veiled since Ruskin is not named:

Many attempts have been made ... to define beauty in the abstract, to express it in the most general forms, to find some universal formula for it. The value of these attempts has most often been in the suggestive and penetrative things said by the way. Such discussions help us very little

> to ... discriminate between what is more and what is less excellent in
> them, or to use words like beauty, excellence, art, poetry, with a more
> precise meaning than they would otherwise have. Beauty ... *is relative*;
> and the definition of it becomes unmeaning in proportion to its
> abstractness. (Pater ed. Hill 1980, xix, my emphasis)

For Ruskin in Pater's construction of him, beauty had been self-evident
and universal. Anyone could see it and judge it immediately. Pater,
however, argues differently. There is no universal formula for beauty;
beauty is relative, and if it is relative, it is also subjective rather than
objective, leading to his less concealed – though nonetheless subtle –
attack on Arnold's critical position. Arnold is not named, but he is
directly quoted and creatively misunderstood:

> 'To see the object as in itself it really is,' has been justly said to be the aim
> of all true criticism whatever; and in aesthetic criticism the first step
> towards seeing one's object as it really is, is to know one's impression as
> it really is, to discriminate it, to realise it distinctly .... What is this song
> or picture, this engaging personality presented in life or in a book to *me*?
> Does it give me pleasure? and if so, what sort or degree of pleasure?
> (Pater ed. Hill 1980, xix–xx, emphasis in original)

Where Matthew Arnold had made objectivity the primary critical virtue,
and where George Eliot had suggested with some anxiety that she was
reporting the world as it had mirrored itself *in her mind*, making the
limitations of subjectivity part of the complex problem of representation, Pater very quietly makes subjectivity central to both criticism and
artistic creation. In his quotation from Arnold, he borrows Arnold's
authority; at the same time, however, he utterly subverts the point that
Arnold was making, virtually reversing it whilst apparently agreeing
with it.

As Chris Baldick argues in *The Social Mission of English Criticism*
(1983), part of the 'mission' of critical work in the Victorian period was
that it would produce a social and political consensus about both life
and art; that it would uphold communal rather than purely individual
values. Pater stands against this hegemonic tradition in his emphasis
on personal *pleasure* and on impressionism over objectivity. The
Paterian critic does not seek the reflection of appropriate community
ideals in the work of art or literature; he (this is a masculine mode of
criticism) seeks his own personality in the works he values.

More than that, the Paterian critic not only seeks his personal preference and pleasure in the art-work, he also *expresses* his personality

in his critical writing. Throughout the essays that make up *The Renaissance*, Pater pursues his own interests in androgynous figures, in the sensuality of art, and in emotional and physical as well as intellectual responses to artistic stimuli. There are multiple examples of this throughout the text, where Pater insists on ambiguity as the essential quality of the art he values. Of the sculptors of the fifteenth century, for example, he writes:

> They are haters of all heaviness and emphasis, of strongly-opposed light and shade, and seek their means of delineation among those last refinements of shadow, which are almost invisible except in a strong light, and which the finest pencil can hardly follow. The whole essence of their work is *expression*, the passing of a smile over the face of a child, the ripple of the air on a still day over the curtain of a window ajar. (Pater ed. Hill 1980, 50, emphasis in original)

This is a world away from the kind of art which is *seen clearly*. It is also distanced from the clarity of vision demanded by Ruskin: and Pater does not tell what he saw in a clear way. Most famously perhaps, in the chapter on Leonardo da Vinci, Pater focuses on ambiguity with a telling emphasis. What he values in Leonardo's art is not its black-and-white legibility, but its shades of grey, and in the most famous passage of the book the chapter reaches its crescendo in a description of *La Gioconda* (The Mona Lisa) which dwells on not only the famous enigmatic smile in the painting, but also on the radical violence masked by the apparently calm surface of the painting. Pater reads the painting as the expression of several centuries of artistic experience, combining the sensual pagan world of ancient Greece with Mediaeval piety and purity, and the casual cruelties of Renaissance Italy:

> She is older than the rocks among which she sits; like the vampire she has been dead many times, and learned the secrets of the grave; and has been a diver in deep seas, and keeps their fallen day about her; and trafficked for strange webs with Eastern merchants; and, as Leda, was the mother of Helen of Troy, and, as Saint Anne, the mother of Mary; and all this has been to her but as the sound of lyres and flutes, and lives only in the delicacy with which it has moulded the changing lineaments and tinged the eyelids and hands. (Pater ed. Hill 1980, 99)

In my experience, this is not quite what most viewers see in the Mona Lisa. Pater's description tells us at least as much about his critical persona as it does about the painting. In this passage, Pagan mythology

(Leda) and Christian iconography (St Anne) are combined – this is how Pater defined the Renaissance; it is a movement in the arts that brought together of Greek body and Christian spirituality. The Mona Lisa, Pater argues implicitly, has the same face in Leonardo's depictions of these other figures from the two traditions. More subtly, he suggests by mere juxtaposition, she also has the same face as Leonardo's depiction of St John the Baptist, 'one of the few naked figures Leonardo painted – whose delicate brown flesh and woman's hair no one would go out into the wilderness to seek, and whose treacherous smile would have us understand something far beyond the outward gesture or circumstance' (93). The John the Baptist painting, like *La Gioconda* has a strange smile; like the more famous painting it is not easily 'read' and what one sees in the image is a reflection of the personality and the desires of the viewer.

For some, this was not a good proceeding in criticism. W. J. Courthorpe in his review of *The Renaissance*, entitled 'Modern Criticism' (published in *The Quarterly Review* in July 1874) was decidedly hostile to Pater's critical method, and through his commentary it is possible to reconstruct some of the conventions of what criticism 'ought' to be. He first castigated Pater by implication, quoting Aristotle's view 'that those who wrote in this manner sought to conceal the poverty of their thought by the showiness of their style'. In other words, like Ruskin, he believed that one should tell what one saw in a *plain* way. He then went on to quote the 'Mona Lisa' passage as an example of what he meant by showy style, before commenting:

> Now all this is plain, downright, unmistakable poetry. The picture is made the thesis which serves to display the writer's extensive reading and the finery of his style. Of reasoning in the ordinary sense there is positively none. 'The eyelids are a little weary,' therefore it is quite plain that 'all the ends of the earth are come upon her head' ... The lady appears to Mr. Pater to have a somewhat sensual expression. A fact which fully warrants a critical rhetorician in concluding that she is an unconscious incarnation of all the vices which he has found preserved in the literature of the Renaissance ... there is no justification for calling that criticism which is in fact pure romance. (Courthorpe in Seiler 1980, 93)

Poetry here is clearly used as an insult. There is no place for poetic or creative prose in criticism which demands clarity above all things and rational rather than emotional connection as its structuring device. In addition, though, Courthorpe implicitly finds Pater's choice of subject matter distasteful. The Mona Lisa is not the problem; it is Pater's insistence on seeing in her sensuality and 'vice' that he objects to. A clean-minded man, as well as a clear-sighted one, would see no such thing. Underlying this whole discussion is the feeling that everyone knows what *La Gioconda* is all about and we need no 'romance' to explain her significance.

The Mona Lisa passage nonetheless is one of the most famous moments of prose writing of the nineteenth century. Oscar Wilde quoted it extensively in his recorded conversations, as well as in print, in his essay 'The Critic as Artist: Part One', first published as 'The True Function and Value of Criticism' in the *Nineteenth Century* in July 1890.[5] In that essay, he evokes the appeal of Pater's style: 'Who ... cares,' says Gilbert, the bearer of Wilde's opinions in the essay, 'whether Mr. Pater has put into the portrait of the Mona Lisa something that Leonardo never dreamed of?' The important thing is that the description has added something to the viewer's experience of the painting, proliferating subjective impressions of the objective existence of the work of art. Whenever Gilbert goes to the Louvre, he quotes Pater to himself and *feels* more: 'And it is for this very reason that the criticism which I have quoted is criticism of the highest kind. It treats the work of art simply as a starting-point for a new creation' (Wilde 1994, 1126–7). In other words, it allows the critic to be a poet. The influence of the passage passed beyond the limits of that century. When W. B. Yeats edited the *Oxford Book of Modern Verse* in 1936, he included this passage, divided into lines as a free verse poem. This was certainly an idiosyncratic thing to do, but it tells us that for some readers, Pater's prose felt like poetry. His style is anything but transparent, and utterly refuses to tell what Pater has seen in a clear way. Isobel Armstrong has noted Pater's keywords – 'Intense, fervent, sharp, enthusiasm, excitement, delight, blitheness' amongst others – and describes his style as being characterized by 'nervously subtle arpeggios' (Armstrong 1993, 388). These are subjective words that describe an individual's highly personal, emotional response to aesthetic stimulus, and to life itself. They are also words which imply sensuality rather than intellectual or moral criticism.

The most influential passages of Pater's *Renaissance* came from what was to become its notorious 'Conclusion'. The 'Conclusion' is a partly re-written version of Pater's review 'Poems by William Morris' which had originally been published in the *Westminster Review* in October 1868, and that original incarnation, anonymously published in an unsigned review, had caused very little stir. As Laurel Brake argues, however, its appearance in volume form with the author's name on the

front cover 'was bold, dangerous, and retrospectively imprudent, comparable in both its compulsiveness and its outcomes to Oscar Wilde's
decision in 1895 to appear in court in the second trial' (Brake 1994a,
19–20). This is perhaps a slight overstatement: the result of Pater's
indiscretion was a stymied academic career rather than a term of
imprisonment and utter disgrace. But I'm very much in sympathy with
the spirit of Brake's commentary nonetheless. For what Pater produced
in the 'Conclusion' to *The Renaissance* was a very quietly expressed
revolution in the conventional terms and conditions of Victorian criticism. For, as Brake argues, Pater resisted 'the constraints of "morality"
on art (as many Victorian writers did)' by calling into question both the
ideal, and the very possibility, of the transparency and objectivity of
representation. For Pater, rather than a shared, communal sense of
reality, available to all right-minded free-born Englishmen, the real
world is entirely subjective and impressionistic:

> Experience … reduced to a swarm of impressions, is ringed round for
> each one of us by that thick wall of personality through which no real
> voice has ever pierced on its way to us, or from us to that which we can
> only conjecture to be without. Every one of those impressions is the
> impression of the individual in his isolation, each mind keeping as a
> prisoner its own dream of a world. (Pater [1873] ed. Hill 1980, 187–8)[6]

This is virtually a statement of solipsism, the belief – or fear – that the
world has no objective existence outside the mind of the individual. To
see clearly and tell what one saw in a clear way, or, indeed, to see the
object as it really is, demands at the very least a faith that the world 'out
there' is in some sense the same for all of us; it requires a faith in the
objective existence of the objects to be seen. Pater suggests that we
cannot be nearly so sure either of the world out there, or of ourselves
within that world.

Despite the apparently melancholy tone and the threat implied by
that 'swarm' of impressions (so undomestic and uncomfortable when
compared to Eliot's more homely image of random scratches on philistine furniture), the impressionism and subjectivity of the world's
existence is not a matter for despair. The impressions we derive from
the world may be fleeting and evanescent, like Whistler's falling rocket
over the Cremorne Gardens, but for Pater this does not mean that
there is no meaning or significance in the emotions and sense impressions we derive from the world: it merely means that significance is
located elsewhere than has traditionally been thought to be the case.

Instead of seeking the permanence of an Arnoldian touchstone or the certainties of any kind of clear vision, we might, alternatively, embrace and celebrate transience as part of the human condition and modify our expectations accordingly. Pater's argument moves, then, from solipsism to a kind of qualified hedonism. Life, philosophy and art exist for the purpose of 'rousing' the human spirit to 'a life of constant and eager observation'. The pursuit of that experience is what counts – 'Not the fruit of experience, but experience itself, is the end', says Pater. In other words, we judge the quality of experience not by its results, as a moral or didactic criticism would ('The good ended happily...'); we judge by what we felt 'for that moment only' (188).

The 'Conclusion' offers a philosophy of life which remains strangely attractive, perhaps because it is the nearest thing that serious writing in the late nineteenth century could get to the hedonism of 'sex, drugs and rock and roll'. Pater very quietly suggests that to live by conventional propriety is a failure – 'our failure is to form habits' (189). Furthermore, he suggests that his readers must seek their heightened existence in a variety of places: in 'the stirring of the senses, strange dyes, strange colours and curious odours, or work of artist's hands, or the face of one's friend' (189). The emphasis is on sense impressions, on art, and in that final item of the list, in a very evasively expressed sexual desire, a desire which takes place between men. The best kind of life is not lived through such masculine pursuits as conquest, politics, economic production, and sexual reproduction, but through feelings – of the body as much as of the mind. Richard Dellamorra argues convincingly that Pater was an intellectually seductive figure (Dellamorra 1990, 49) who gathered a coterie of young men around him at Oxford University – men including the poet Gerard Manley Hopkins and, of course, Oscar Wilde. That seductiveness, however, was perceived as morally dangerous since seduction, of course, is not a rational process in which one sees the world objectively; rather it is an emotional process, depending entirely on subjectivity and, in part, on the surrender of one's personality to the influence of another person. Such self-surrender offended against the construction of contemporary masculinity, which was supposed to be rational, strong and self-possessed. And since the young men who participated in Pater's seductions were *young men*, alongside the fact that there are clear elements of homoerotic coding with its repeated fascination for androgynous masculinity in the writing of *The Renaissance*, the writer and the text raised many issues of concern to the powers that ran the University. We do not know exactly what happened to Pater in the 1870s, though there seems to have been some sort of muted scandal, which led to his being consistently passed over for promotion for the next twenty years, and which brought him the enmity of Benjamin Jowett (1817–93), the master of Balliol College.[7] We also know that Pater himself was rather shocked by the ways in which his writings were (mis)interpreted by some of his own 'disciples'. When *Studies in the History of the Renaissance* ran to a second edition in 1877, retitled, *The Renaissance: Studies in Art and Poetry*, Pater made many changes: the most important of these was his omission of the Conclusion, which was not restored until the third edition of 1888, when Pater wrote that it had been suppressed lest 'it might possibly mislead some of the young men into whose hands it might fall'. Well, some of the young men (and it was usually young men) were 'misled', most notoriously and self-consciously, Oscar Wilde. But the clouded vision of the *Renaissance* with its swarms of impressions and its articulation of the impossibility of clarity nonetheless had important effects.

Dark visions

It was all very well for Ruskin in his lecture on Turner to lament and rail against the conditions of modernity; but those conditions were there to stay. And in any case, Victorian nostalgia for a better past notwithstanding, the world has always been too complicated to see it clearly and see it whole. That complexity was particularly obvious to the late Victorians. In many of the fictions and some of the poetry of the late nineteenth century there is a strong sense of dismay at the impossibility of clear vision. The world of Arthur Conan Doyle's Sherlock Holmes stories, for example, is often shrouded in fog or mist, and Dr Watson, lacking Holmes's acumen, is at a loss to repeat his mentor's methods for seeing facts clearly. The city in general, and London in particular, becomes a gothic space, with labyrinthine streets and casual violence. In Arthur Morrison's *A Child of the Jago* (1896), there is a sketch map of the slums of the East End, but the pattern of the mean streets remains hard to discern and virtually impossible for the outsider to read:

> From where, off Shoreditch High Street, a narrow passage, set across with posts, gave menacing entrance on one end of Old Jago Street, to where the other end *lost itself in the black* beyond Jago Row ... A square of two hundred and fifty yards or less – that was all there was of the Jago. But in that square the human population *swarmed* in thousands. (Morrison 1996, 11, my emphasis)

Here is a place where strange crimes and violence are the stuff of daily life. Within the first few pages, a hapless victim is coshed and robbed, and the inhabitants of the Jago think themselves safe from the workings of the law. The London of Robert Louis Stevenson's *The Strange Case of Dr Jekyll and Mr Hyde* (1886), with its chocolate-coloured fogs and the violence of Mr Hyde at its heart is another example. As Marlow, in Joseph Conrad's *Heart of Darkness* says of London: 'this also ... has been one of the dark places of the earth' (Conrad 1985, 29).

Marlow, of course, is making a kind of moral judgement about the capital of the British empire, and the implication of his remark is not only that England has been a savage place sometime safely distant in the past, but that it continues to be a dark place, which trades – as his tale will go on to show – in human misery and which depends on brute force for the maintenance of power. He compares the Roman Empire with the British Empire, and cannot bear the implications of clear vision: 'the conquest of the earth ... is not a pretty thing when you look into it too much' (31–2); if Marlow sees too clearly, he will lose whatever faith he has left. On the one hand he is committed to the concept of empire, to the 'idea' that sustains it – the 'something [that] you can set up, and bow down before, and offer a sacrifice to' (32);[8] on the other he is disgusted and appalled by the methods by which it is maintained. Half of him believes in the ideal of enlightenment – the ideals that imperial warriors set out to disseminate; the other half of him is disgusted by the futile violence of it all, figured in the African prisoners who have been mistreated till they are scarcely human and the incomprehensibility of a French warship 'firing into a continent' (40). But if the space that is being described is dark (literally foggy and lit only by gaslight, and metaphorically dark because it is morally ambivalent), it can neither be seen clearly, nor told clearly. Conrad's unnamed narrator explicitly tells us that we will get no clear narrative, no unambiguous message from Marlow:

> The yarns of seamen have a direct simplicity, the whole meaning of which lies within the shell of a cracked nut. But Marlow was not typical (if his propensity to spin yarns be excepted), and to him the meaning of an episode was not inside like a kernel but outside, enveloping the tale which brought it out only as a glow brings about a haze, in the likeness of one of those misty haloes that are sometimes made visible by the spectral illumination of moonshine. (Conrad 1985, 30)

The kernel of a nut is something that can be easily seen and understood, once the shell has been cracked. Marlow, however, is not going to tell a story that leads to clear vision. He does not believe in the certainties of such a narrative universe and appears to fear the 'horrors' that will be uncovered by clear vision.

It is rather doubtful that Joseph Conrad was directly influenced by Walter Pater's aestheticism, despite the verbal echoes of the 'Conclusion' in *Heart of Darkness*. But he did theorize the novel in terms that often seem closely related to Pater's concept of impressionism. Conrad also took an active interest in contemporary scientific discovery that supported his nihilistic and solipsistic vision of the universe. He understood something of the theory of atoms, of Lord Kelvin's theories of waves and particle motion, and of the projected end of the world in the death of the sun. He also attended an early demonstration of a Röntgen x-ray machine, writing in a letter afterwards:

> The secret of the universe is the existence of horizontal waves whose varied vibrations are at the bottom of all states of consciousness ... there is no space, time, matter as vulgarly understood, there is only the eternal something that waves and an eternal force that causes the waves – it's not much – and by the virtue of these two eternities exists that Corot and that Whistler. (Conrad ed. Garnett 1928, 143)

He is much more pessimistic, indeed nihilistic, about the value of art – paintings by Corot and Whistler exist only by virtue of the waves of light and atoms. Art offers no salvation, not even the salvation of one's own impressions; it is just another example of the physical laws of the world, and these laws are not consolatory. The waves might make patterns which are more or less predictable, but they are invisible to the naked eye – impossible to see clearly, and difficult to explain, clearly or otherwise.

Conrad is a key writer of the period of transition between one vision of the world and another. He makes use of Victorian genres in that many of his fictions bear some generic similarities to the late-nineteenth-century adventure story. Lord Jim is one such hero, inspired to go to sea by reading romances and stories of masculine heroism; and Marlow as a 'little chap ... had a passion for maps ... and would lose [himself] in all the glories of exploration' (Conrad 1985, 33). Both learn disillusion in face of the realities that romances neither imagine nor describe. At the same time though, in the attitudes of his fiction – both of his characters and in the narrative position – with their pessimism and their evasion of moral certainties, he resists the comparative comforts of Victorian clarity and looks forward to the positions taken up by the writers of the Modernist canon. *The Secret Agent* (1907) in its representation of the sordid world of Mr Verloc is a sustained rebuke of the ideal of heroism immortalized elsewhere in adventure fiction. But Conrad does also belong amongst the writers of adventure fiction, and can just as easily be seen as the last member of one tradition as the instigator of another. It is the sense of Conrad as innovator which is most valorized by the academy, however. As Ian Watt has noted, only Conrad and the equally pessimistic Thomas Hardy were exempted by Virginia Woolf from her 'objections to traditional novels', and especially from the criticisms she levelled at Arnold Bennett, John Galsworthy and H. G. Wells in her notorious essay 'Modern Fiction' (1919) (Watt 1979, 170).

Why was Hardy exempted? After all, his novel-writing career took place entirely within the Victorian period, and certainly his earlier novels were routinely compared with the great Victorian traditional writings of George Eliot in reviews because of their apparently similar subject matter, particularly their quasi-Wordsworthian concentration on rural life. The reasons why Hardy seemed different are complicated but they have to do both with the sense that he was writing against the grain of Victorian proprieties and morals, and with the difference of vision that his choice of subject matter implied. From very early in his novel-writing career, starting with his third book, *Far From the Madding Crowd* (1874), Hardy struggled against the straitjacket of what George Moore was to call in 1885 'Literature at Nurse' – literature fit only for maiden ladies and adolescent girls imposed by the standards of the family magazines in which novels were serialized, and by the circulating library, where they found their largest audiences. As Moore put it, the English novel was subject to 'the illiterate censorship of the librarian' (whom he regarded as a lowly tradesman), and this censorship had led to the English novel being nothing more than 'a sort of advanced school-book, a sort of guide to marriage and the drawing-room' (Moore 1976, 32). As R. G. Cox has noted, Leslie Stephen (1832–1904)[9] was the editor of the *Cornhill Magazine* who had commissioned Hardy to produce *Far From the Madding Crowd* because he had liked *Under the Greenwood Tree* (1872). But as the story began, Stephen began to get cold feet about the subject matter of the later novel, and 'had found it necessary to warn Hardy to treat the seduction of Fanny Robin ... in "a gingerly fashion", out of deference to his more prudish readers' (Cox 1970, xx) on the grounds that the *Cornhill* was a family magazine, and had to appeal to all age groups. The problems of serialization in such magazines would plague Hardy for the rest of his writing career. In the end, Stephen refused to publish

The Return of the Native (1878) at all, because he 'feared that the relations between Eustacia, Wildeve and Thomasin might develop into something "dangerous" for a family magazine' (Hardy, qtd in Cox, xx). Similarly, the vicissitudes suffered by *Tess of the D'Urbervilles* (1891) are very well known: it was originally commissioned by a newspaper syndicate, but rejected when the editors read the early part of Tess's story, which include her seduction/rape, the birth of her illegitimate child, and its death and burial; the mainstream family magazines also rejected it, and when it was published, by *The Graphic*, it was 'in a severely modified form which omits the seduction and the illegitimate child, replacing them by a mock marriage ceremony, and makes Angel Clare convey the dairymaids across the stream not in his arms, but in a wheelbarrow' (Cox, xxviii).

Hardy did not modify his practice to mollify his audiences – indeed his novels became more and more 'scandalous' as his career progressed, and like George Moore, he was highly exercised by the effects of censorship on the dissemination of his fiction, writing in similar vein to Moore in a symposium entitled 'Candour in Fiction' (1890) in the *New Review*:

> The crash of broken commandments is as necessary an accompaniment to the catastrophe of a tragedy as the noise of drum and cymbals to a triumphal march. But the crash of broken commandments shall not be heard; or, if at all, but gently … an arbitrary proclamation has gone forth that certain picked commandments of the ten shall be preserved intact – to wit the first, third, and seventh; that the ninth shall be infringed but gingerly; the sixth only as much as necessary; and the remainder alone as much as you please, in a genteel manner. (Hardy in Ledger and Luckhurst 2000, 118)[10]

Adultery – or indeed any expression of sexuality, especially female sexuality – and swearing required particular policing for Victorian England. Virginia Woolf certainly regarded openness about sexual matters as daringly modern and resolutely un-Victorian, writing of a day in 1908 when Lytton Strachey had identified a mark on her sister's dress as semen as an utterly liberating moment:

> With that one word, all the barriers of reticence and reserve went down. A flood of the sacred fluid seemed to overwhelm us. Sex permeated our conversation. The word bugger was never far from our lips. We discussed copulation with the same excitement and openness that we had discussed the nature of good. It is strange to think how reticent, how reserved we had been and for how long. (Woolf 1985, 213)

Her sympathy for Hardy's will-to-express what was supposed to be unspeakable may well be one explanation for her sympathy with his fiction.

This is, though, a rather trivial reason for Woolf's relatively positive view of Hardy. Better explanations also exist. In particular, the comparison with Eliot made by Hardy's early reviewers is instructive. In *Adam Bede* the clergyman Mr Irwine tries to dispense good moral advice to Arthur Donnithorne about his conduct. He says to the young man:

> Consequences are unpitying. Our deeds carry their terrible consequences, quite apart from any fluctuations that went before – consequences that are hardly ever confined to ourselves. And it is best to fix our minds on that certainty, instead of considering what may be the elements of excuse for us. (Eliot 1980, 217–18)

Mr Irwine is convinced – and Eliot implicitly approves of his position – that consequences are in some sense predictable, and that even if we do not know the precise effects of our actions, we must behave responsibly as if we do: a solipsistic denial of consequences is ethically irresponsible, as the outcomes of Arthur's actions will attest. An action produces an effect, just as a stone thrown into a pond produces ripples. The pattern of the ripples – or the fact that there will be a pattern of ripples – is always already known in Eliot's fictional world, in a way that it is not in Hardy's. No one but Gabriel Oak gives Bathsheba Everdene good advice in *Far From the Madding Crowd* and she always ignores him, but Hardy's narrator occupies a very different position in relation to cause and consequence, to the patterning of events in general, than Eliot's narrator does. When Bathsheba thoughtlessly sends her infamous Valentine, sealed with the 'Marry Me' seal, to Farmer Boldwood, she initiates a series of events that are utterly unpredictable. Boldwood's mystification is described thus:

> The [Valentine] letter must have had an origin and a motive. That the latter was compatible with the smallest magnitude compatible with its existence at all, Boldwood of course did not know. And such an explanation did not strike him as a possibility even. It is foreign to a mystified condition of mind to realize of the mystifier that the very dissimilar processes of approving a course suggested by circumstance, and striking out onto a course from inner impulse and intention only, would look the same in result. The vast difference between starting a train of events and directing into a particular groove a series already started, is rarely apparent to the person confounded by the issue. (Hardy 2000, 87–8)

This is remarkably close to a version of chaos theory. In other words, Hardy stands against the ordered predictability of the Newtonian world where every action produces an opposite and equal reaction. Chaos theory renders the world terrifyingly unstable. In his book *Thomas Hardy: The Offensive Truth*, John Goode argues that unlike George Eliot, who described herself as a meliorist (a qualified optimist), Hardy is far closer to being a nihilist. There is no compromise in Hardy's fiction, no attempt to make the world *seem* a better place, no pandering to the desires of his readership for comfort and faith. Over and over again, indeed, the contemporary reviews attacked him for pessimism, accustomed as they were to the far more consolatory fictions of an earlier generation. The offensive truth, then, is that the world is actually unpatterned, unpredictable and unsafe. The good do not necessarily end happily in Hardy's fictional universe. (The positive ending of Gabriel Oak in Bathsheba Everdene's arms was not part of Hardy's original plan but was imposed upon him by his publishers.) He thus represents a distinct and new way of seeing the world. And although he was often compared with Eliot, he is also different in that he makes no meliorist attempt even to *pretend* that the world is stable.

In addition to seeing the larger world differently, Hardy also sees character differently. There is, in a sense, no explanation offered for the kinds of people his characters have become. In contrast to earlier nineteenth-century realism where – as Eliot suggests – actions and consequences are closely interlinked, and where character is also predictable and stable because it also acts according to certain laws, in Hardy there is no equivalent realist sense of consequentiality. What was central to other kinds of realism – the story for example of an individual's rise (or fall) based on particular material circumstances and inherited characteristics which were shown to us through detailed examinations of family life (*David Copperfield* represents an example of this kind of fiction), is relegated in Hardy to non-narrative status. Some things are simply never told at all. Thus John Goode argues, writing of Michael Henchard, *The Mayor of Casterbridge*:

> We have no indication of the details of Henchard's rise from journeyman to Mayor and are surely not intended to think that being teetotal is a guarantee of such success. The only explanation Hardy ever offers is the admittedly very significant 'one talent of energy'. We are given only a gesture and a quality. It is not within the terms of the novel that the life story should have general significance. (Goode 1988, 79)

What Goode identifies here is a conception of character that is mythically constructed as opposed to character that is socially constructed.

Throughout *The Mayor of Casterbridge*, Hardy quotes Novalis, and one of the key issues he takes from the philosopher is the idea that character is fate, not open to development or modification by experience and circumstance: it comes from outside the self in a far more elemental way than the mere accumulation of social detail would imply. Since Woolf strongly disapproved of the realist method of material and social detail represented particularly by Arnold Bennett (see Chapter 1), this may be another explanation for her qualified approval of Hardy.

We know that Hardy read Pater, though he read the Pater of *Marius the Epicurean* (Pater's only full-length novel, published in 1885) rather than that of *The Renaissance* – he wrote extensive notes on Pater's novel, and Goode suggests that part of its spirit infects *Jude the Obscure* (1895) where 'no philosophy works', just as no philosophy works for Marius (Goode 1988, 158–9). Woolf on the other hand certainly had read Pater's *Renaissance*, and the 'Modern Fiction' essay bears the marks of his influence, even if he is not directly named. Like Pater in the Conclusion to *The Renaissance*, Woolf sees failure in the formation of habits, or in fiction writing, in the conformity of the novelists to the demands of conventional propriety. What Henry James had earlier called 'solidity of specification' and identified as 'the supreme virtue of a novel' (James 1962, 33), by which he meant the rich details which make it possible for the reader to imagine 'characters dressed down to the last button of their coats in the fashion of the hour' (Woolf 1993a, 8) is dismissed as an unhelpful obsession with the unnecessary and the stultifying in Woolf's essay. In a passage that is now justifiably famous, the echoes from Pater are self-evident:

> Examine for a moment an ordinary mind on an ordinary day. The mind receives a myriad impressions – trivial, fantastic, evanescent, or engraved with the sharpness of steel. From all sides they come, an incessant shower of atoms; and as they fall, as they shape themselves into Monday or Tuesday, the accent falls differently from of old; the moment of importance comes not here but there.... Life is not a series of gig-lamps symmetrically arranged; life is a luminous halo, a semi-transparent envelope surrounding us from the beginning of consciousness to the end. Is it not the task of the novelists to convey this varying, this unknown and uncircumscribed spirit, whatever aberration or complexity it may display, with as little mixture of the alien and external as possible? (Woolf 1993a, 8)

This passage echoes the Conclusion to *The Renaissance*; Pater's swarm of impressions becomes Woolf's 'myriad', his exhortation to evade stereotyped responses is her emphasis on the difference of the present from the past, and his sense of the individual 'ringed around by a thick wall of personality' is her sense of being surrounded (less forcibly, admittedly) by haloes and semi-transparent envelopes through which it is difficult to penetrate. In contrast to George Eliot's slightly anxious attempt to see patterns in narrative events in *Middlemarch*, in Woolf's essay, instead of lights producing reflections that make sense of things, the emphasis is on the elusiveness and intangibility of meaning; moreover, for Woolf, in contrast to Eliot, the role of the novelist is to evoke the confusion, not to dispel it through a narrative that renders things clearly. Indeed, slightly later in the essay, she suggests that one of the places in which modern writers must seek their subject matter is 'in the dark places of psychology' (10) – a psychic space that, the writings of Sigmund Freud (then coming into public consciousness) notwithstanding, cannot be seen steadily or whole since it is by its nature fragmented, distorting, illusory and elusive.

Ears or eyes?

Woolf practised in her own fiction what she preached (though a better word might be 'suggested'; her critical writing, like Pater's, is highly suggestive). Her novels and short stories evade paraphrasable content and are resolutely short of the kind of detail favoured by nineteenth-century and Edwardian realists: these are not declarative fictions. In a fairly gentle parody of Woolf from *Aspects of the Novel* (1927), E. M. Forster points out her characteristic mode:

> [She] start[s] with a little object, take[s] a flutter from it, and settle[s] on it again. [She] combine[s] a humorous appreciation of the muddle of life with a keen sense of its beauty. There is [...] a rather deliberate bewilderment, an announcement to all and sundry that [she does] not know where [she] is going [...] the parlour door is never mended, the mark on the wall turns out to be a snail, life is such a muddle, oh dear, the will is so weak, the sensations fidgety ... philosophy ... God ... oh dear, look at the mark ... listen to the door – existence ... is really too ... what were we saying? (Forster 1990, 36–7, ellipses in square brackets mine)

Forster is rather dismissive of Woolf's style. Nonetheless, he prefers her modus operandi to that of the novelist who focuses on what he calls *pattern*. Pattern, Forster admits, is merely a convenient metaphor for describing fiction in pictorial terms, and sometimes it produces very powerful effects; but in *Aspects of the Novel*, Forster disapproves of the falsification of human life that is necessary to make a novel behave like a pattern, and to observe an unwarranted 'unity'. He takes the example of Henry James's novel *The Ambassadors* (1903) to suggest that the imposition of a pattern, rather than an Eliot-like acceptance that the marks on the furniture are random, robs the novel of vivacity: in a James novel, Forster says, 'most of human life has to disappear' and for his taste the sacrifice is too great (Forster 1990, 142). His own ideal novel is one based on the tentatively expressed ideal of 'rhythm'.

Rhythm, of course, is a metaphorical description borrowed from the music to which all art constantly aspires, and in Forster's book it relates partly to the idea of the repeated motif. His own example is from the novels of Marcel Proust which are partly structured around a repeated musical phrase that recurs both at important and at insignificant moments of the plot of *A la recherché du temps perdu*. (There are similar examples in Forster's own fiction, notably the motif of the wasp in *A Passage to India*.) The key difference between pattern and rhythm is one of development: a pattern is a visual image, fixed and complete, comprehensible as it were at a glance. A rhythm is dynamic, taking place in time, developing and altering every time the motif that is its representative reappears. Pattern is all about clear sight and fixity; but for Forster – and the parallel with Pater's thought is self-evident – 'in music fiction is likely to find its nearest parallel' (149), and he exhorts a future for the novel in which it will aspire to the condition of music:

> Music ... does offer in its final expression a type of beauty which fiction might achieve in its own way. Expansion. That is the idea that the novelist must cling to. Not completion. Not rounding off but opening out. When the symphony is over *we feel* that the notes and tunes composing it have been liberated, they have found in the rhythm of the whole their individual freedom. Cannot the novel do that? (Forster 1990, 149–50, my emphasis)

It is a rhetorical question to which the answer might well be 'no'. But the aspiration to uncover literary forms that escape from visual metaphors of construction, and to escape from the tyranny of paraphrasable content ('Yes,' writes Forster, 'oh dear yes – the novel tells a story ... and I wish that it was not so' [40]), marks a will to resist the conceptual hold of Victorian clear vision. In *Howards End* (1910), clear vision belongs to the Wilcox family, and is consequently less valued than a certain tolerance of confusion. The narrator comments: '[Margaret] could not concentrate on details ... It is impossible to see modern life steadily and see it whole and she had chosen to see it whole. Mr Wilcox saw steadily' (Forster 1989a, 165). But Wilcox only sees steadily by not seeing a good half of what passes before him at all. On the other hand, of course, that very act of resistance, the necessity of mounting such explanations as Woolf and Forster offer, does rather suggest that the ideal of clear vision did not go away. Indeed, in Forster's *The Longest Journey* (1907) the aspiring writer Rickie Elliot has been unsuccessful in finding a publisher for his stories. He is all for music in his fiction – 'music has wings' (Forster 1989b, 141) – because it allows the writer to suggest rather than explain in bullying detail. His repugnant wife Agnes comments:

> couldn't you make your stories more obvious? I don't see any harm in that. Uncle Willie floundered hopelessly .... *I had to explain and then he was delighted.* Of course, to write down to the public would be quite another thing and horrible. You have certain ideas, and you must express them. *But couldn't you express them more clearly?* (Forster 1989b, 141, my emphasis)

In this novel, clear vision is philistine vision. Hints and nuances are where artistic integrity lie – but hints and nuances do not sell, and have to be explained away to a floundering public. Or again, in *Howards End*, Helen Schlegel's response to Beethoven's music is to turn it into literature, making stories out of the musical themes and rhythms, to the exasperation of her sister who exclaims in a statement that is both Paterian and anti-Paterian:

> Helen's one aim is to translate tunes into the language of painting, and pictures into the language of music. It's very ingenious, and she says several pretty things in the process, but what's gained, I'd like to know? ... If Monet's really Debussy, and Debussy's really Monet, neither gentleman is worth his salt – that's my opinion. (Forster 1989a, 52)

Margaret wants the special and particular qualities of each of the arts to be appreciated for their own sake; but she also recognizes the synaesthetic sensitivity of her sister as a creative expression of her personality – Tibby's entirely technical appreciation of music makes her 'simply furious' because it takes personality out of the question entirely (52). Helen asks 'what is this music to *me*?' Margaret does not quite approve of the solipsism of such a question, desiring Helen – and everyone else – to 'connect'. Her point is that everyone has an ethical responsibility at least to try to penetrate the thick wall of subjectivity and to avoid total impressionism, and it is her viewpoint that the novel supports.

The chapters that follow do not chart a history in which Pater actually influenced everyone who came after him because that would be patently untrue. He was influential, but in relatively narrow and privileged circles. Any writer who had a social commitment to the world beyond literature – whether the wishy-washy liberalism of Forster's desire to 'connect', or the more radical political positions adopted by New Women writers, or the Socialism of Wells, or the aesthetic humanism of Bennett – would tend to refuse a view of Art as existing for its own sake or as the mere expression of a special personality. In seeking a new kind of vision, in valuing an alternative to art's social mission, however, Pater was both profoundly Victorian and profoundly anti-Victorian, and the underlying suggestion of this book is that the ambivalence this suggests had a very long post-Victorian afterlife. Pater wanted, like Arnold, to find value in something other than the mechanical universe and in something more than the cash nexus, but chose a different route in his articulation of the relationship between Art and Life. Other seekers sought those relationships in other places.

Pater's new way of seeing is one early example of the crises of Modernism. To think such things in the cloistered halls of Oxford however is one thing; to confront an illiberal social reality amongst the crowds of an industrial city is another. Literary Modernism is many things. It is a reaction to a crisis of faith deriving from Darwinian thought and from Nietzschean nihilism; it is an aesthetic response – often characterized by withdrawal and wilful isolation – to the conditions of modernity; it is a reaction to the post-Freudian discovery that man can no longer know even himself, and to the post-Marxist view that social conditions are neither God-given nor unchangeable; and it is a crisis in language, an epistemological terror that words no longer adequately reflect the world they are alleged to describe. But the high Modernists were not the only people to feel these things, and to respond to them. The qualified realist fictions of the late-Victorian and Edwardian novelists described in Chapter 1 are one alternative representation of modernity, and it is no less valuable for not being 'Modernist'. The disembodied voices, the nostalgia and melancholy of poetry, described in Chapter 2 is another. The interlude chapter on Oscar Wilde discusses Wilde's subversive response – which was also a response to Pater; if anyone was influenced by him, Wilde was – to the conventions of representation of his own society, pointing out their limitations through parody and play. Chapter 4 argues that the epistemological crisis more usually associated with high modernism can be discerned in that most unlikely of places, the masculine romance, or adventure story. Chapter 5 considers the New Woman, often anguished because painfully excluded from her social and artistic aspirations by the social status quo, and seeking new forms of representation not as a retreat from the world, but as an attempt to make it really new. And finally, the loosely modernist fictions of Lawrence and Forster are also shown to be realist fictions in Chapter 6, nostalgic for the Victorian past at least as much as they strive to forge a new future.

Notes

1. 'What is the opposite of aesthetic?' asked Professor John Stokes in a class where I was a student sometime in the mid-1980s. The answer is 'anaesthetic' – the state of non-feeling, of inability to feel. And that makes the point pretty effectively that aesthetics have to do with feelings – not just emotions, but perhaps more particularly, physical sensations.
2. To follow this up, see Miriam Allott, ed., *Emily Brontë: Wuthering Heights: A Casebook*. Revised Edition. Basingtoke: Macmillan, 1992. The contemporary reviews emphasize critical disgust with the novel because it is hard to follow its moral message. Admiring critics, like George Henry Lewes, go to enormous and very contorted lengths to find a moral in the text. By way of contrast, the twentieth-century critics largely dismiss morality as a critical criterion, and focus on the text's form and structure.
3. In the essay, Arnold is quoting one of his own poems, 'To a Friend', and in the poem, he describes Sophocles as one 'whose even balanced soul/ ... Saw life steadily and saw it whole' (Arnold 1993, 23). He compares this stability of vision with the blurred and unclear vision of his own age, to the advantage of the Ancient Greeks.
4. My reference is here is to the theories of Jacques Lacan, specifically his description of the mirror phase of childhood development. Lacan suggests that the child, when first born, experiences himself as continuous with the world. Only after he has either literally or figuratively seen himself in a mirror does he recognize his own image, and understand that he is a coherent unitary self. Because the image in the mirror is an *image*, however, not a reality, a signified rather than a real object, Lacan labels this recognition a misrecognition. It is, nonetheless, the mistake which enables the child to develop his own subjectivity.
5. Wilde's title, of course, like Pater's book, alludes mischievously to Arnold's 'The Function of Criticism at the Present Time'.
6. Hill's edition of Pater provides a concordance of the various emendations Pater made through the publication history of the articles that make up *The Renaissance*. In most cases I have quoted the 1893 text – the last version printed in Pater's lifetime. On this occasion, however, I've used Hill to reconstruct the 1873 text. The phrase 'swarm of impressions' was later

altered in subsequent editions to 'group of impressions', a much less threatening image. The sense of threat, however, matters to the impression made by the first edition of *Studies in the History of the Renaissance*.

7. In his biography of Oscar Wilde, Richard Ellmann describes how Pater was damaged by a scandal involving one of Wilde's acquaintances, William Money Hardinge, in 1875 a student at Balliol. Pater had written letters to Hardinge signed 'Yours lovingly'. The private letters in themselves were not the problem, but there appears to have been an atmosphere of homoeroticism current at the time at Oxford of which the authorities strongly disapproved. Hardinge was the subject of complaints from other students and tutors and was eventually sent down by Benjamin Jowett for blasphemy and impiety on the basis that he had circulated homoerotic poetry. When Pater's letters to Hardinge came to light, Jowett was deeply shocked and broke off good relations with the author of *The Renaissance*. See Ellmann 1988, 58.

8. It is of course, worth noting that Marlow's depiction of the 'idea' or ideals that sustained the British and other European empires, is like a 'savage' fetish in that it demands human sacrifice and suffering and unquestioning obedience.

9. Coincidentally, but interestingly nonetheless, Leslie Stephen was later to be the father of Virginia Woolf.

10. The commandments Hardy refers to are: 1. The commandment that there is only one God; 3. The forbidding of swearing; 7. The commandment against adultery; 9. The commandment against bearing false witness. The sixth commandment forbids killing.

I The Persistence of Realism

Most people in this world seem to live 'in character'; they have a beginning, a middle and an end, and the three are congruous with one another and true to the rules of their type. *You can speak of them as being this sort of people or that.* They are ... no more (and no less) than 'character actors'. They have a class, they have a place, they know what is becoming in them and what is due to them. (Wells 1978, 9, my emphasis)

She would not say of any one in the world now that they were this or that. She felt very young, at the same time unspeakably aged. She sliced like a knife through everything; at the same time was outside, looking in ... She knew nothing; no language, no history ... and *she would not say* of Peter, she would not say of herself, *I am this, I am that.* (Woolf 1992b, 8–9, my emphasis)

In the juxtaposition of the above quotations from H. G. Wells and Virginia Woolf there is an interesting point of comparison as well as one of contrast. George Ponderevo, speaker of the Wells passage, believes in the possibility of simple characterization in the first lines of the novel, though he goes on to except himself from the rule of pinning a person down in a phrase. His experience has been different from the common run of folk, and so his character and his points of view are more valuable, at least in his opinion. Woolf's Mrs Dalloway who focalizes the second quotation is apparently more generous: she would not say of *any one* now that they could be summed up in a single phrase; she would not say it of Peter, and she would not say of it herself. Later in the novel, however, she would quite precisely sum up in simple phrases the characters she does not like – Miss Kilman (whose very name is a summing up of misanthropy and whose appearance is an indictment of her character), Sir William Bradshaw ('Richard agreed with her ... "didn't like his taste, didn't like his smell"' [Woolf 1992b, 201]), and Lady Bruton (also *brutally* defined by a name). And even Peter Walsh is caricatured in his repeated gesture of playing with his penknife, a gesture that speaks volumes for post-Freudian readers about violence and sexuality barely repressed by a veneer of civilization.

Character is often called the lifeblood of fiction. In 'Mr Bennett and Mrs Brown' indeed, Woolf quotes Arnold Bennett to the effect that 'The foundation of good fiction is character creating and nothing else' (Bennett qtd in Woolf 1992a, 69). And as I have argued elsewhere, character is a term that has to do with writing and representation at least as much as with the lived experiences of real people. Character is stamped through the individual like lettering in a stick of rock. The word 'character' proposes a human being who is stable and consistent, and who is therefore knowable. The word is used to describe figures in literature precisely because it implies that written personalities are 'easily read', just as character in its meaning of the letters of the alphabet are also to be easily read (Robbins 1996, 112). The conventions for reading character inherited from the great tradition of Victorian fiction were also easily understood. You could judge character by results. Or, in a more subtle formulation from Henry James: 'What is character but the determination of incident? What is incident but the illustration of character?' (James 1962, 34). Characters are known by their deeds, and can be judged thereby. Or, again, characters can be known by their surroundings, their clothing, their tastes, their socio-economic positions, and other such external things. For William James, brother of novelist Henry and pre-Freudian psychologist, it was common sense that there was continuity between the external objects of a man's life and the internal life he led (James I 1950, 291–2). And this view was commonplace in fiction too, at least until the Modernists began to question the materialist basis of human existence. The questioning, however, did not entirely do away with the fact that psychology and sociology are related disciplines and their effects are felt in related ways, whether by real people or by characters in fiction.

What I want to describe here is the persistence of the conventions and proprieties of realism from the Victorian age to the Edwardian one and beyond. In a realist world view, certain propositions are taken for granted as the basis of the fictional universe they are used to recreate – and by extension, they claim to recreate the fictional universe in the image of the real universe. At its most basic, realism involves the following claims:

1 The world is a knowable place, rationally constructed along Newtonian lines of cause and effect; consequently the world – whether fictional or real – is susceptible to totalizing explanations that can be provided through the narrative process.

2   Narrative therefore produces patterns (as we saw in the Introduction with Forster's concepts of 'pattern' and 'rhythm') which enable the reader to understand the world as 'designed' and give us the capacity to make sense of a world which might otherwise appear purely random or contingent. Reality may be complicated, but it is not beyond explanation.

3   A narrative that makes sense of the world makes it possible for readers to judge the world. In other words, the sense of patterning gives a sense of perspective, a feeling of secure ground from which we are able to form logical opinions.

4   Characters within realist fictions are, like the world they inhabit, 'knowable'. They are formed by diverse influences, including – in some versions – heredity, environment and education or upbringing, as well as whatever innate temperament or personality they have at birth. They behave therefore in broadly predictable ways. Their personalities determine what they will do in given circumstances; and by extension, circumstances will determine what a given character is able to do, or imagine doing, as in the quotation from Henry James (James 1962, 34).

5   The social world matters intensely to characters in realist fictions as it does to real people. The place occupied by a character in the world is of the greatest importance in formulating what that character is and what s/he can become. Birth, education, and experience make character what it is; and since most people also believe that these things are true in real life too, continuity between reality and fiction is imaginatively constructed by realist fiction. This continuity can result in empathetic identification with characters within the fictional world: the reader is asked to consider what s/he would do in the same circumstances, for example. To this extent, although character represents individuality, it must not be extraordinarily eccentric because it also is heavily invested with the limitations of the type. If characters do not behave typically, readers can learn nothing from their representation.

6   As is proper to a mode that really came to fruition in the mid-nineteenth century, the notion of clear patterning (or seeing the world clearly) is mirrored in the realist text's form (it tells about the world 'in a clear way'). Narrative is transparent and draws little attention to itself, requiring readers to forget that they are 'only reading a story'.

These propositions involve the reader in a complex negotiation with the text. On the one hand, judgement is demanded by a mode that sees the world clearly and sees it whole; on the other, empathy and identification might well cloud clear vision. It is that complexity of response that anti-realist criticism perhaps dismisses. Much has been written about realism – and the pages of late-nineteenth-century journals are filled with commentaries, both negative and positive about its aesthetic value. I am not using the term here in quite the way the Victorians and Edwardians might have done because I want to use it as a neutrally descriptive term that tells us something about fiction written under its aegis, not as a term of value judgement, which was the inescapable focus of much nineteenth-century commentary. I want to reclaim the word as a useful term that properly describes some of the important writings of the transitional phase between the Victorians and the Modernists.

In *The English Novel from Dickens to Lawrence*, Raymond Williams suggests that 1895 is a key date for British literature. Williams focuses on Thomas Hardy's publication in that year of *Jude the Obscure* to a torrent of critical abuse, to the extent that Hardy gave up writing fiction in favour of poetry, and thus an era of Victorian fiction came to an end. But whilst Williams sees that there is a cut-off point in 1895, he also argues that there was a central continuity from Hardy to Lawrence, a continuity, that is, between the broadly realist tradition in which Hardy wrote, and the qualified Modernist aesthetics of Lawrence's *The Rainbow* (1915). Conventional literary history, however, often implies that between Hardy's last fiction and Lawrence's first major novel, *Sons and Lovers* (1913), 'there is in effect … a missing generation' (Williams 1984, 119). There are of course names that belong to that generation; it is the period of 'James and Conrad; the early novels of Forster; and then of course that composite figure H. G. A. J. Wells–Bennett–Galsworthy' (120). Williams's point is that the privileged position given to the writers broadly understood as Modernist writers – Conrad, Joyce, Woolf, Mansfield, and with heavy qualifications, Lawrence and Forster – by the mainstream of the critical academy, has tended to obliterate the other broadly realist tradition of fiction writing in the period. He identifies the central opposition between the two traditions as an emphasis on ' "individual" or "psychological" fiction on the one hand and "social" or "sociological" fiction on the other' (119–20).

What this chapter seeks to suggest is that this opposition is based on a misunderstanding of how the writers in the less privileged position in that binary opposition – the realists – set out to compose their fiction. Where Woolf was sure that the future of fiction lay in excavating 'the dark places of psychology', and that psychology was largely an internal and individual matter, Wells–Bennett–Galsworthy amongst others understood psychology as being at least in part externally constructed, by circumstance and material conditions as much as by essence or innate personality. While Virginia Woolf had said that 'in or about December 1910 human character changed' (Woolf 1992a, 70), nevertheless in the same essay she takes for granted that one would naturally have servants. Change was only *visible* if one was privileged. Unlike Woolf, H. G. Wells was only too aware that character was constituted by material and cultural circumstances. His mother had been a housekeeper on a country estate, and Wells knew that the life of the servant class was not all sweetness and light even after the turn of the century, making great play in *Kipps* (1905) of the fact that even modern houses were not built for the convenience of those who did the hard labour of running them. Kipps's wife Ann, who has been in service, announces as they hunt for their first home that they must not have a house with a basement kitchen: '[A basement] is a downstairs where there's not 'arf enough light and everything has got to be carried – up and down, up and down, all day – coals and everything. And [our house has] got to 'ave a water-tap and sink and things upstairs. You'd 'ardly believe, Artie, if you 'adn't been in service, 'ow cruel and silly some 'ouses are built' (Wells 1993a, 246). Wells's narrator treats Kipps and his wife with amused patronage, commenting that the home they seek exists only in 'dreamland or 1975 A.D.' (254). Nonetheless, he is making an important comment about the ways in which material existence significantly determines the kind of spiritual and emotional life it is possible to have. The limitations of Kipps are not simply temperamental or personal. They are a function of the limited life that has been available to him. Now, whilst I am sure that Woolf would have treated her servants well, the calm assumption that her readers have servants implies that she did not really *see* the life she is so blasé about, as H. G. Wells, whatever his limitations, did.

Woolf's major fictions are all resolutely set in the very comfortable world of the upper middle classes; her characters are people who have choices because they are not involved in hard material struggles for bare subsistence. Compare and contrast the world view of Woolf's *To the Lighthouse* (1927) with that of Arthur Morrison's *A Child of the Jago* (1896) looks like the kind of examination question that will never be set. Apart from the obviously galvanizing effects of the First World War for Woolf's novel, however, these two texts came to being in wholly different worlds – and the main substance of the differences between them is not historical as such, but is to do with the sociological arenas in which they are each set: the Ramsays are privileged; the Perrotts are not. In William James's terms, understanding personality through ownership, the Ramsays have characters that match their possessions, and the Perrotts do not. This is not to say that only brute existence is possible in the Jago. The child Dicky Perrott is capable of affection and love, nursing his baby sister to sleep in an early chapter of the novel (Morrison 1996, 15). He is willing to be a 'good' boy, in the right circumstances. But the right circumstances never arise. He cannot keep an honest job; he is surrounded by criminality and violence and the only moral lesson he can take from his surroundings is that the biggest villains get the biggest rewards: 'Straight people's fools, *I* reckon,' he tells his mother. 'Kiddo Cook says that, an' 'e's as wide as Broad Street. W'en I grow up I'm goin' to git toffs' clo'es an' be in the 'igh mob. They does big clicks' (16).[1] His only possible ambition is to join the aristocracy of crime (the high mob) and to participate in lucrative theft (big clicks). Dicky's story is about a struggle against overwhelming odds, a battle with material circumstances that he cannot win. In the world of the Jago, a fictionalized version of the worst parts of the East End, casual violence is a way of life, and of death, and Dicky dies its victim, despite the potential he displays for a more fully human existence.

Casual violence also kills Andrew Ramsay in *To the Lighthouse*, of course. His death is announced parenthetically: '[A shell exploded. Twenty or thirty young men were blown up in France, among them Andrew Ramsay, whose death, mercifully, was instantaneous]' (Woolf 1992c, 145). But the point about Andrew Ramsay's death is that it is a long way outside his ordinary experience, rather than part of it, whereas Dicky's death, stabbed in a Jago fight, following hard on the heels of his father's hanging for murder, expresses a whole way of life rather than an exceptional aberration in it. The fact that Dicky is scarcely educated and fundamentally inarticulate does not mean that he has no potential or that his psychological make-up is insignificant, merely that it is clearly not the most significant thing about him.

Morrison of course deliberately sets out to invoke pathos for political ends. His writing has a palpable design on the reader, as he comments in the Preface he wrote to the third edition in 1897:

> [My critics] claim that if I write of the Jago I should do so 'even weep-ing' ... The cant of the charge stares all too plainly from the face of it. It is not that these good people wish me to write 'even weeping'; for how do they know whether I weep or not? No; their wish is, not that I shall weep, but that I shall do their weeping for them ... that I shall make public

parade of sympathy on their behalf, so that they may keep their own
sympathy for themselves, and win comfort from their belief that they
are eased of their just responsibility by vicarious snivelling. (Morrison
1996, 7)

His purpose, in other words, is to insist that 'just responsibility' for the
conditions of the Jago is everyone's concern and their reform is everyone's business. *A Child of the Jago*, like a number of the fictions
produced in the late nineteenth century dealing with the Condition of
England in the 1880s and 1890s,[2] is designed as a call to action. If Dicky
and Josh provoke sympathy, they should also provoke the will to do
something about the abysmal conditions which produced their wasted
lives. This is a profoundly 'Victorian' view of the purpose of fiction –
that it should teach us, or exhort us, to lead better lives. It is also
one of the key motivations of realist writing. This view of the purpose
of fiction was roundly rejected as a basis for literature by writers
like Virginia Woolf. Commenting on D. H. Lawrence's *Letters* in her
diary, she wrote, 'Art is being rid of all preaching things' (Woolf 1997, 326),
and she regarded any form of didacticism as aesthetic failure. This,
though, is a world view that depends on being in a particular comfort
zone; what is wrong with Woolf's position is that it argues for a very
narrow way of seeing, a way of seeing that refuses to follow through
the implications of the fact that the world at large has very specific
effects on the individual psyche. As Edwin Reardon, the failed novelist
of George Gissing's *New Grub Street* (1891) puts it in conversation with
his wife:

> The difference … between a man with money and the man without is
> simply this: the one thinks, 'How shall I use my life?' and the other, 'How
> shall I keep myself alive?' A physiologist ought to be able to discover
> some curious distinction between the brain of a person who has never
> given a moment's thought to the means of subsistence, and that of one
> who has never known a day free from such cares. (Gissing 1985, 232)

One way of thinking about divisions in serious fiction in the forty years
around the turn of the twentieth century is in terms of this distinction:
there is a kind of psychology available to the 'haves' that is not
available to the 'have-nots'. With relatively few exceptions, we could
categorize almost all the writers of this period according to whether
they present characters who are concerned with subsistence as opposed to those who are concerned with Spiritual Existence or Life Itself
(the capitals are part of the rhetoric).

To put it another way, there is a clear class bias in the insistence that psychological fiction involving the excavation of deep motivations for human actions is somehow 'better' than sociological fictions which consider material life as an essential part of the formation of character. This bias has many different roots and explanations. One is the rise of mass literacy. Q. D. Leavis's wonderfully snobbish (yet extremely informative) *Fiction and the Reading Public* (1932) surveys the field of published fiction at the beginning of the twentieth century with mounting dismay at the abysmal taste of the public and at readers' contentment with poor product. Leavis identifies mass literacy as a major contributor to a literary culture in which bad writing is far more successful than good (Leavis 1990, 3). The tone of her critique, and especially her view that the English literary novel has no potential market represents, coming as it does from a representative of the literary-critical establishment, in part explains why the complex psychological fiction of Modernism has been preferred by university departments over the social fictions and the pulp fictions that were far more popular in their own time. Mass market fiction – the bestseller – is characterized by escapism (readers choose it 'to obtain vicarious satisfaction or compensation for life' [48]). The closer relationship between public demand and product in the literary market-place of the nineteenth century had an appalling effect on the quality of the product, Leavis argues. Thus, where Matthew Arnold, writing in the 1850s, had been convinced that a literary education would 'tend to elevate and humanize' the populace, and consecrate an elite culture at the centre of British life (Arnold in Sandford 1889, 19), Leavis feared a very different effect. Her book is peppered with references to reading light fiction as an equivalent to drug addiction and drunkenness, and she comments consistently on the demoralizing effect of popular writing, even amongst those sections of society who should know better:

> It is relevant to note... that the author of detective novels consulted receives [fan] letters chiefly from 'school-boys, scientific men, clergymen, lawyers, and business men generally,' and adds 'I think I am read more by the upper classes than the lower classes, and by men more than women.' The social orders named here as forming the backbone of the detective-story public are those who in the last century would have been the guardians of the public conscience in the matter of mental self-indulgence. (Leavis 1990, 51)

These anxieties tended to promote a literary-critical tradition that valued difficulty and complexity over simplicity, and the inner life expressed in ambiguous ways over the external life, or any kind of escapist fantasy, clearly stated in plain language. Far too may people, Leavis argues, 'admit to reading indiscriminately and rarely if ever re-reading' (51). Too many people do no 'serious' reading at all, and are even disdainful of anything difficult, which they dismiss as 'highbrow'. This state of affairs is a disgrace.

Wells's *Kipps*, however, takes a very different line. Kipps escapes a desperately narrow life, memorably described by a fellow apprentice as a 'life in a blessed drainpipe, and we've got to crawl along it till we die' (Wells 1993a, 34) via that staple of pulp fictions, an unexpected inheritance. His life up till this point has left him ill-educated, emotionally immature and virtually inarticulate. Newly flushed with fortune but embarrassed by his lack of cultured manners, Kipps attempts to acquire educated polish; he is taken under the wing of Chester Coote. Coote – as his name clearly implies – is pretentious and ridiculous, though Kipps does not know this at first. He takes his mentor's advice on proper conversation, manners and dress, and attempts to follow a course of reading set out for him by his new-found friend. Before sending him off to read '(1) [Ruskin's] *Sesame and Lilies*, (2) *Sir George Tressady* [and] (3) an anonymous book on "Vitality" that Coote particularly esteemed' (133), Coote has advised his protégé about the 'virtue in books' (130):

> Nothing enlarges the mind [...] like Travel and Books...And they're both so easy nowadays and so cheap! [...] You'd hardly believe [...] how much you can get out of books. Provided you avoid trashy reading, that is. You ought to make a rule, Kipps, and read one Serious Book a week. Of course we can Learn even from Novels, Nace Novels that is, but it isn't the same as serious reading. I made a rule, One Serious Book and One Novel – no more. There's some of the Serious books I've been reading lately – on that table: *Sartor Resartus*, Mrs Twaddletome's *Pond Life*, *The Scottish Chiefs*, *Life and Letters of Dean Ferrar*. (Wells 1993a, 131, my ellipses in square brackets)

Coote borrows the authority that Q. D. Leavis took for granted, on rather less basis. He has no right to advise Kipps, being extremely ignorant himself – as Wells's rather heavy-handed satire testifies (Mrs Twaddletome's *Pond Life* speaks many more such volumes in Coote's library). In his struggles with Ruskin and with a book on etiquette, Kipps becomes utterly miserable. All he learns is how to behave like an affected snob – a lesson we can pick up immediately from Coote's exaggerated pronunciation of 'Nace Novels' and his unwarranted capitalization of words in speech to make the sound all the more impressive, hence my comment about Life and Existence earlier.

Ironic, then, that Kipps finds true happiness at the end of the novel as a bookseller who scarcely knows his own product except as goods to sell. Books are, for Kipps, mere commodities to read just the once, which is the reason that they are also a reasonable commercial proposition; if one does not re-read, there is a built-in obsolescence in fiction that guarantees ongoing sales. He does not need to read to know that and Wells has some fun in the last paragraphs of the novel with the idea that Kipps is unwittingly selling his own life story as a bookseller in Hythe.

Bearing in mind the social history of the mass expansion of education after 1870, and also the fact that realist modes of writing are both reflections of a world and re-creations of it, underlying much of what I want to say about George Gissing and the triumvirate of Edwardians – Wells, Galsworthy and Bennett – is the question of literacy and its effects. Realist fictions very often make great play of the books that characters within them have read: what someone reads tells us as much about them as what they wear or what they put in their houses, and authors perhaps like the idea that books have real influence on real people. There is a degree of self-reflexivity about the turn-of-the-century novelists' evocations of reality, and which is evidence of a kind of sophistication in their work which is too often dismissed by those who wish to hurry on to read Woolf or Joyce. I want to suggest a 'way of seeing' the history of literary fiction that takes proper account of some of the writers who focused their attention on the social formation of character, rather than insisting that psychology bears no relation to sociology. The usual kind of literary history depends on a predetermined set of aesthetic values – values which are indeed anti-Victorian, but not necessarily the better for all that. They are values which make it difficult to produce a proper estimation of the fictions of, say, George Gissing and the composite figure of 'Wells–Bennett–Galsworthy'.

The strained case of George Gissing

George Gissing (1857–1903) was born in Wakefield to comfortable middle-class parents, but his father died when Gissing was only thirteen years old. Thereafter, his education was financed by scholarships and academic prizes won on the basis of his intellectual brilliance. After an education at a minor provincial public school, he went to

Owens College, Manchester. His academic career – extremely promising at the outset – was cut short in 1876 after he was imprisoned and
disgraced for stealing money to help reform a prostitute, Nell Harrison,
who had engaged his interest. He believed that all Nell lacked for
making a successful life was opportunity, and, 'he was not able to
believe something without acting upon it, immediately, consistently and
wholeheartedly' (Schafer in Michaux 1981, 51). After prison, he went to
the United States, living (though only just) by tutoring and occasional
journalism. Having nearly starved in America, and having considered
suicide by throwing himself into the Niagara Falls – both of which
motifs recur in his fiction – he returned to England in 1877 to make a
career as a man of letters. But on his return, he also married Nell. She
failed to 'reform', becoming a confirmed alcoholic and occasional
prostitute to serve her addiction. Gissing's domestic life was anything
but settled and respectable, and although he lived for long periods
separately from his wife, he continued to support her out of his relatively meagre earnings until her death in 1888. Gissing then proceeded
to make the same mistake again, marrying for a second time a girl of
working-class origins, Edith Underwood, in 1891. Edith bore him two
children, but was incapable of running his house, apparently had
a violent temper (she was eventually institutionalized for insanity in
1902), and was utterly unsuited to the kind of domesticity Gissing – a
true middle-class Victorian at heart – craved and idealized.

In 'Gissing's Feminine Portraiture' (1963), Pierre Coustillas has
argued that Gissing's aesthetic vision was a double vision. Coustillas
surveys the whole field of Gissing's work, concluding that the novelist's
views of women are complex because they are enmeshed in the
double vision of femininity that he had inherited from the Victorians:
'Gissing's feelings towards woman lie between two poles: on the one
hand, intense admiration of sensual origin, an irrepressible aspiration
for absolute happiness... on the other hand, cynicism and a barely
contained craving for violence' (Coustillas in Michaux 1981, 100). The
idealism about femininity, and his disgust with any woman who fails
to live up that ideal is symptomatic of the whole of Gissing's writing
life. In the same spirit, many of his fictions are what might be called
'sociological fictions'; texts such as *The Unclassed* (1884), *Demos* (1886)
and *The Nether World* (1889), deal with the lives of the urban poor.
There is a will to idealize the poor, and at the same time, a cynicism
about improving their conditions, based on the fear that they are
perhaps ineducable. Characters who have ideals – for example, Sidney
Kirkwood in *The Nether World* – are ground down by circumstance,

and forced to give up even their limited visions of a better life. In dealing with the poor, as with women (though the two groups are not, of course mutually exclusive), Gissing is constantly torn between sympathy and contempt. His vision is strained by the contradiction between idealization and realization, and between the belief in personal vision and the practical considerations that might stand in the way of their realization. Consequently, contemporary reviewers were often perplexed by Gissing's fiction. In a review of *The Nether World* written for the *Contemporary Review* in September 1889, F. W. Ferrar asked rhetorically: 'What is the object … of painting such scenes, such characters – such conditions of society and human life reduced to its barest blankest elements of spiritual death, or moral atrophy, of physical degradation?' (Coustillas and Partridge 1972, 144). He concluded that as the novel did 'little or nothing to impress upon us as to the nature of the remedy' (145), it did not fulfil the requirements of such representation. It provided no message, and offered no solution.

In few places is this more apparent than in *New Grub Street* (1891), a novel which veers between unrelieved social realism (most of the reviewers protested against its pessimism [see Coustillas and Partridge 1972]) and defeated idealism. Moreover, it is usually read – with real justification – as a text that has much to tell us about the history of book-writing and publishing, rather than as a novel with much in the way of intrinsic value. As P. J. Keating has suggested, 'First and foremost [*New Grub Street*] is a sociological document; a sociological document of genius written in the form of a novel' (Keating 1968, 9). And, indeed, part of its purpose is to provide an anatomy of literary London, a discussion and description of literature as a business, an industry even, and a market. As such, it represents a number of Q. D. Leavis's views about the dangers of a mass market for literature in fictional form, whilst pointing out that even artistic vision is necessarily constrained by the material practices of literary production. Jasper Milvain, the novel's 'villain' and a successful man of letters, argues passionately that literature is just a business like any other business, and has to be dealt with in the same way (Gissing 1985, 39). Jasper then proceeds to live by the practice he preaches. He has a certain contempt for his audience, whom he identifies as 'the people who like to feel that what they are reading has some special cleverness, but who can't distinguish between stones and paste' (43–4), and he recognizes the limitations of his own talent, realizing that he is incapable of writing a great novel, for example. Not only does he develop an acute sense of business in terms of his own literary products, he also sets his sisters to work on writing for the highly lucrative (and utterly unchallenging) market of fiction for Sunday-School Prize books, advising them: 'Get together half a dozen fair specimens of the Sunday-school prize; study them; discover the essential points of such composition; hit upon new attractions; then go to work methodically, so many pages a day' (43). Such books are written to a formula that anyone should be able to discover, and there is a ready market for them. There is no point in awaiting divine inspiration. Writing works of this kind is just a job like any other, requiring a certain amount of training and application, and nothing else.

What the novel proposes throughout is that those who treat writing as a business will succeed. The comic figure of Whelpdale whose own fiction has consistently been rejected by publishers eventually sets himself up in business as a 'literary adviser'. 'Now that's one of the finest jokes I ever heard. A man who can't get anyone to publish his own books,' says Milvain, 'makes a living by telling other people how to write!' (195). Once begun as an entrepreneur, Whelpdale truly becomes successful in journalism, helping to found a magazine named *Chit-chat* (a thinly veiled parody of George Newnes's *Tit-Bits*, founded in 1881). Describing his venture to Jasper and Dora, he says:

> I would have the paper address itself to the quarter-educated; that is to say, the great new generation of that is being turned out by the Board schools, the young men and women who can just read, but are incapable of sustained attention. People of this kind want something to occupy them in trains, and on buses and trams. As a rule they care for no newspapers but Sunday ones; what they want is the lightest and frothiest of chit-chatty information – bits of stories, bits of description, bits of scandal, bits of jokes, bits of statistics, bits of foolery. … Everything must be very short, two inches at the utmost; their attention can't sustain itself beyond two inches. Even chat is too solid for them: they want chit-chat. (Gissing 1985, 496–7)

This incident rehearses in fictional form the argument made by Q. D. Leavis in *Fiction and the Reading Public*. As Dora comments, 'Surely these poor silly people oughtn't to be encouraged in their weakness' (497); lowly journalism is not what the ideal of mass education had been for. But whereas Leavis is outraged by the creation of a new literary market on the basis of the newly educated masses – the result of the Forster Education Act of 1870, who were first coming to maturity in the early 1880s when New Grub Street is set – Whelpdale, supported by Jasper, sees nothing here but a business opportunity. Whelpdale, signalled by his ridiculous name, is a Dickensian caricature who is treated with amused tolerance; at least in this world of the bottom line, he will be able to support his wife through peddling his trashy magazine. He is redeemed by the genuine love and admiration he feels for Dora, whereas Milvain is the object of a more sustained satire of moral outrage. In part this is justified by Gissing's creation of Jasper as a man not averse to 'caddishness'. He treats Marian Yule extremely badly, primarily because it turns out that her inheritance (significantly derived from the manufacture of paper) is not adequate to his wants. But Jasper's real sin is his cynically clear vision about the nature of literary business, and his ability to adapt to the market, making no pretence of literary idealism, and focussing entirely on the cash nexus. Milvain marries Amy Reardon at the end of the novel, and Gissing clearly presents this final marriage of the text as a marriage of true minds. Amy is Jasper's equal in practical materialism: they deserve each other.

Milvain, however, is at least extremely self aware. He knows – and admits to others – that the necessity of earning a living will lead him into a degree of selfishness of which he is not proud. 'Selfishness – that's one of my faults. It isn't a brutal kind of selfishness; [but] the thought of it often troubles me. If I were rich, I should be a generous and good man,' he tells Marian in words that are not so very dissimilar to those of Edwin Reardon quoted above (149). He recognizes that his personality is the result of material and historical circumstances which form him in a particular mould, and to which he must adapt. That self-awareness is presented by Gissing as part of Milvain's cold-bloodedness, in part because it is part of Gissing's satire to insist that the alleged decline in literary standards is a disgrace, in part because worldly success is something he views with deep ambivalence. The novel loads the dice against readers having any sympathy or admiration for Jasper. As Q. D. Leavis once observed, 'when any nineteenth-century novelist names a character Jasper I think we may safely conclude that that character is intended to be the villain' (Leavis in Michaux 1981, 180). But in reality, the only difference between Milvain and the other characters in the novel is that he makes use of his self-consciousness and energy for material gain, where they allow their characters to form their destinies.

In marked contrast to Milvain's success is the parade of literary failures who populate the rest of the novel. They cover a range of literary aspirations, from Alfred Yule, who writes about severe subjects for the monthly periodicals, and whose ambitions to be an editor have been consistently disappointed, to Harold Biffen, who turns to realist fiction because there is no outlet in the modern world for him to make his enthusiasm for Greek literature pay. (As it happens, he cannot make realism pay either.) All the literary failures strive hopelessly against the current conditions of the market rather than adapting to them. Biffen, for example, is presented throughout as both marvellous and ineffectual; because he is a very attractive character, his defeat is all the more bitter. Biffen, as Gissing had done before him, scrapes a bare living by tutoring working men in the classics and by economizing on basics like food, whilst attempting to write a novel entitled *Mr Bailey, Grocer.* His project, he tells Edwin Reardon is to produce

> an absolute realism in the sphere of the ignobly decent.... I don't know any writer who has treated ordinary vulgar-life with fidelity and seriousness ... I want to deal with the essentially unheroic, with the day-to-day life of that vast majority of people who are at the mercy of paltry circumstance. ... An instance, now. As I came along ... half an hour ago a man and a girl were walking close in front of me, love-making; I passed them slowly and heard a good deal of their talk ... Now, such a love scene as that has never been written down: it was entirely decent, yet vulgar to the *n*th power ... I am going to reproduce it verbatim, without one single impertinent suggestion of any point of view save that of honest reporting. The result will be something unutterably tedious. Precisely. That is the stamp of the ignobly decent life. If it were anything *but* tedious it would be untrue. (Gissing 1985, 174)

He will not order life, or give it patterns and explanations; he will simply see life and record it as it happens. He is not concerned with what Reardon calls 'the *art* of fiction' (176), but only with a faithful copy of life. He will not laugh at misfortunes or make them melodramatic as Dickens had done; nor will he depict them as tragic heroes and heroines, as Zola would. He will merely describe what there is.

For all the severely realist outlook of his work, however, Biffen is a romantic at heart. He performs the only act of (mock) heroism in the novel, when he rescues his manuscript about the Grocer from a house fire; and he dies a suicide just as a romantic hero would – though with more (ignoble) decency to others, dying alone in a park where he can make no mess to inconvenience those who find him. The reasons for his death are complex. From the outset the Reardons and Jasper Milvain have identified him as someone who lives far too close to the edge. 'That poor man will die of starvation some day,' Amy comments to her husband (178). But although his poverty is extreme and his outlook as a 'realist' novelist extremely pessimistic, Biffen's despair and suicide come about because of misplaced romanticism. In a cynical conversation with Edwin Reardon after Reardon's marriage has broken up, he discusses the ideal of marriage and companionship. Reardon has just suggested that he would have been better off marrying a 'some simple, kind-hearted work-girl' (404) in preference to his middle-class wife. The reader of the novel or of any potted biography of its author, of course, knows that this is a mistaken view. We have Gissing's own marriages and that of Alfred Yule in mind. By the same token Biffen tells Reardon that such a marriage would have been doomed:

> the girl would have married you in firm persuasion that you were a 'gentleman' in temporary difficulties, and that before long you would have plenty of money to dispose of. Disappointed in this hope, she would have grown sharp-tempered, querulous, selfish. All your endeavours to make her understand you would only have resulted in widening an impassable gulf. She would have misconstrued your every sentence, found food for suspicion in every harmless joke, tormented you with the vulgarest forms of jealousy. The effect upon your nature would have been degrading. (Gissing 1985, 404–5)

This is not only a remarkably accurate diagnosis of the failure of Alfred Yule's marriage; it is also a very clear, if unconscious, statement of the actual problem of Edwin Reardon's, since although the girl in question, Amy, is middle class, she is materialistic and unsuited to be the wife of an idealistic artist struggling in a garret. Just like the hypothetical working girl, she has also married in the firm persuasion that Edwin Reardon is made for better things.

Biffen admits to having nearly made such a mistake himself, in that he almost married a working girl at some point prior to the opening of *New Grub Street*. Taking a realistic attitude to his poverty and prospects, he never tries to find female companionship again. But in a bout of desperately hopeless affection, he falls romantically in love with Amy Reardon, recognizing despite his infatuation that she will never reciprocate. At the end of his resources – financial resources, but importantly also his emotional resources after he encounters the happily engaged Whelpdale – he goes to the British Library to read about poisons, and kills himself in a park because a life without female affection is 'meaningless' (526). What's striking about the figure of Biffen is that for most of the novel he is a figure from a comedy, a cheerful person who lightens the gloom for other characters, who are always able to enjoy a joke at his good-natured expense. But the genre that surrounds him shifts from comedy to melodrama. He is a very intriguing instance of Gissing's strained way of seeing, where the idealist always comes a cropper and the good resolutely do not end happily.

Gissing's rendering of Reardon is also ambiguous. He is generally presented as the struggling artist figure, misunderstood by the world and his wife, and buffeted by circumstances. But he is also a petulant child who does not really behave particularly well. And the fact that he has both talent and ideals is hardly an excuse for his high-handed attitudes and utter incapacity to take a more practical line with his life. The world, as he half-acknowledges, does not owe him a living: 'The world has no pity on a man who can't do or produce something it thinks worth money ... For all that, it's hard that I must be kicked aside as useless just because I don't know a trade' (230–1). Reardon persists in seeing writing as vocation rather than as a job. But Reardon is also presented with sympathy. The writer who cannot write and who must fudge to deal with his conditions is – for readers at least – a sympathetic figure. Mrs Carter, Amy's acquaintance, sums up the attitude of reverence that is part of the myth of the artist, approaching his desk on tiptoe to look at the work in progress (166). Moreover, Reardon really is hemmed in by the literary machinery of his age. As a novelist he has to produce work in the format required by publishers, the three-volume novel, described perceptively by Milvain as a 'triple-headed monster, sucking the blood of the English novelist' (235).

The three-volume form had been the major form of publication for fiction since the time of Sir Walter Scott, and the cost to the casual potential buyer of fiction was prohibitive – a three-decker retailed at 31s 6d, whilst even at the end of the century, the average working man earned rather less than 20 shillings a week. Why produce a product that cost more than even quite wealthy buyers could readily afford? The answer was that books were not produced for individual buyers. Publishers counted on selling virtually the entire print-run of their fiction to Circulating Libraries such as Mudie's Select library. Three volumes were more profitable to the libraries because each borrower would pay for the loan of each volume of the text, making a single volume unattractive in comparison. Publishers had a guaranteed market for their fiction, and scarcely needed, therefore, to market their product aggressively. Everyone – except the novelist – won. Novelists, as *New Grub Street* amply demonstrates, made their money from selling the copyright of their texts outright to the publisher. If the book did not prove popular, the author made an unearned profit. If the book was popular, however, and was subsequently reprinted in cheaper editions for the public to buy, for example at the railway station outlets of W. H. Smith and Sons, the author saw no further profit from his work. In addition, the three-volume form had an effect on *what* got published. Writing in the 1880s, the novelist George Moore was infuriated by the fact that some of his writing had been effectively banned by the libraries because of its sexual content. In his *Literature at Nurse* pamphlet (1885), Moore complained that since Mudie's had to provide fiction that was entirely suitable for a family audience, there was no space for any discussion of sexual or political issues, which were resolutely kept out of Mudie's Select selection.

Furthermore, as Robert Altick describes, the three-volume novel placed a strain on the novel form itself. He comments that 'the exigencies of three-decker publication ... were largely responsible for what some modern readers consider the verbosity, inordinate length, qualitative unevenness, and sometimes sheer formlessness of much Victorian fiction' (Altick 1999, 295). In *New Grub Street*, it is the very fact of how much material must go into a novel that is part of Edwin Reardon's problem. He struggles valiantly to write so many lines per day and gets stuck during his writing of the second volume: 'Messieurs and Mesdames the critics are wont to point out the weakness of second volumes; they are generally right, simply because a story which would have made a tolerable book ... refuses to fill three books' (161). Reardon is reduced to shameless padding: 'He kept as much as possible to dialogue; the space is filled so much more quickly, and at a pinch one can make people talk about the paltriest incidents of life' (154). And the effect of the pressure to write to order has a detrimental effect on his prose: 'He would write a sentence beginning thus: "She took a book with a look of—;" or thus: "A revision of this decision would have made him an object of derision" ' (154). Gissing is anxious to represent Reardon's struggles as almost heroic, and he nearly persuades the reader that the disaster of his life is a tragedy.

New Grub Street is, as the anonymous reviewer for *Murray's Magazine* (June, 1891) put it, a text that bears some of the stamp of Harold Biffen's view of ignoble decency, where circumstance and contingency have more effect on outcomes than talent or intention. Gissing would like to suggest that Edwin Reardon, writer of psychological fictions, is the hero. But the ambiguity of his strained vision is better understood as a way of seeing that demands that readers see material conditions and their effects as central to human life, rather than elevating unrealized and unrealizable ideals as the sole focus of fiction.

H. G. Wells and the quarter-educated

H. G. Wells (1866–1946) had two careers as a novelist. In the 1890s, he wrote a series of fictions usually known as scientific romances which are the progenitors of the modern genre of science fiction; they include *The Time Machine* (1895), *The Island of Doctor Moreau* (1896), *The Invisible Man* (1897) and *The War of the Worlds* (1898). After 1900, when he published *Love and Mr Lewisham*, his fiction took a more realistic turn. As Robert P. Weeks has observed, however, there is a connection between Wells's science fictions and his stories of contemporary reality. Weeks calls the Time Traveller Wells's paradigmatic character because he is a man who seeks 'to break out of the physical universe' (Weeks 1976, 26). Instead of building his novels around the acute observation of character in environment, 'Wells's protagonists ... look on their environment as a series of barriers that somehow must be broken through' (28). In the science fictions, the breaking through is achieved by individual efforts. The Time Traveller builds his time machine and boldly goes into the future; the Invisible Man discovers the process by which invisibility can be procured and crosses the barrier between seen and unseen in a quasi-Nietzschean attempt to become an *Ubermensch*; Dr Moreau seeks to break down the boundaries between species; the Martians invade Earth, overcoming the physical barriers of space. It is no accident that the major protagonists of these fictions are all more or less securely middle class, and all have had a sound scientific education which makes their adventures possible.

In his realist fictions of contemporary life, however, for all the elements of fantasy that persist within them (a convenient inheritance in *Kipps* [1905], the miracle 'cures' of quack medicine in *Tono-Bungay*, the wish-fulfilment fantasy of love in *Ann Veronica* [both 1909], and the miracle of irrepressible enthusiasm in *The History of Mr Polly* [1910], for example), the social positions of the protagonists are much less secure. Ann Veronica is middle class, of course, but despite her social status, her education is distinctly lacking and the opportunities mapped out for her by her conventional family are no less claustrophobic than those of Kipps, Polly or Ponderevo. She is a bird in a gilded cage rather than a rat in a drainpipe, but it is a cage nonetheless. The middle-class woman, in other words, shares some of the same disadvantages as the proletarian man. The major difference between them is that she is able to articulate her desires for a different life, and is able in part to persuade her father that he should provide the resources so that her education should continue, options certainly not open to Kipps or Mr Polly. Nonetheless, in their various ways, each of these characters also seeks to break down barriers, and one of the key ways in which they do so is through achieving the education that Wells's middle-class male protagonists from the scientific romances can take for granted – and which they generally misuse.

What Gissing's Whelpdale called the 'quarter-educated' were very much Wells's concern, not least because he was so nearly one of them himself. Describing his own schooldays in his *Experiment in Autobiography* (1934) the sources of Arthur Kipps, Alfred Polly and George Ponderevo's education become apparent in Wells's experience. His own headmaster, Mr Morley, 'was...not of eminent academic attainments; his first prospectus laid stress on "writing in both plain and ornamental style, Arithmetic logically, and History with special reference to Ancient Egypt" ... there was ... great stress on copperplate flourishes, long addition sums and book-keeping' (Wells I, 1984, 85). Wells goes on to describe a school regime in which there was erratic discipline, since the schoolmaster occasionally fell asleep at his desk, a pedagogic method that relied heavily on rote-learning and unpredictable corporal punishment, and very little logic in a curriculum delivered to a classroom full of boys aged between seven and fifteen. Wells is fairer to Morley, however, than he is to Morley's fictional counterparts. The real headmaster might not have been very competent, but he was at least well meaning. Wells's parents had sent him to this school, as Kipps's and Polly's families also do, to avoid sending him to the National Board School, the publicly funded foundations that were the result of the 1870 Education Act. They did so largely on class grounds: the Board Schools were for the poor – and Academies like those of Mr Morley were for 'members of the tenant-farmer, shopkeeper, innkeeper, upper servant stratum' (85). They existed for the purpose of procuring a commercial education for those who would work at the lower end of business. Apart from whatever natural aptitudes he possessed, Wells also insists that the reason his education did not mark him for life (though it produced a cockney accent and a horror of speaking French from which he could never free himself), was that he broke his leg when he was seven, and spent a great deal of his convalescence reading. Q. D. Leavis would perhaps disapprove, but Wells comments quite happily: 'I cannot recall now many of the titles of the books I read, I devoured them so fast, and the title and the author's name in those days seemed a mere inscription on the door to delay me in getting down to business' (77). His consumption of books was undiscriminating, but he does recall voracious excitement over factual books about foreign places, about biology and natural history, and only later about story books of the adventure genre by Captain Mayne Reid, Fenimore Cooper and 'the Wild West generally' (78).

The tolerance with which he looks back on his own education in the autobiography is put aside in the fiction. The school attended by Arthur Kipps is run by a man with a 'bogus diploma' (Wells 1993a, 8), and attracts its pupils with a prospectus that is long on polysyllabic words and short on truth and grammar. Kipps remembers his school-days with anything but affection, their only purpose having been to make him understand the value of holidays. Mr Polly is no better off, beginning at the local Board School which was

> run on severely economical lines to keep down the rates,[3] by a largely untrained staff; he was set sums to do that he did not understand, and that no one made him understand; he was made to read the Catechism and Bible with the utmost industry and an entire disregard of punctuation and significance; caused to imitate writing copies and drawing copies; given object lessons upon sealing wax and silk-worms and potato bugs and ginger and iron and suchlike things; taught various other subjects his mind refused to entertain. (Wells 1993b, 6)

Then, at the age of twelve, Polly is removed from this school to a private school to 'finish off...under the guidance of an elderly gentleman, who...took snuff, wrote copperplate, explained nothing and used a cane with remarkable dexterity and gusto' (6). It is not at all unreasonable to describe these as 'quarter-educations'.

Where for Gissing's Whelpdale the 'quarter-educated' had been a commercial opportunity, and where for Q. D. Leavis they had been a danger to culture, for Wells these people are a criminal series of wasted opportunities. As a reviewer of fiction in the 1890s, as Linda Anderson argues, Wells's commitment had been to texts that 'focussed attention on society...He applauded the attempt to bring lower class experience into literature, and to widen the scope of the novel beyond the values and experiences of the middle class' (Anderson 1998, 112). He reviewed Gissing's *New Grub Street*, Thomas Hardy's *Jude the Obscure* 1895) and Arthur Morrison's *A Child of the Jago* with general approval, calling Morrison's novel 'the most important naturalistic novel of the period', and praising Hardy for tackling the problems of the working man who wishes to gain an education, and for giving a sound representation of 'the voice of the educated proletarian, speaking more distinctly than it has ever spoken before in English literature' (Cox 1970, 283).[4] At the same time, though, he suggested that there was a problem with such fiction in that it tended to be written from the perspective of the middle-class writer who was really remote from the sufferings he described. This problem also infects Wells's own realist fiction. It is certainly true that Wells patronizes his lower-middle-class characters, which is probably an unavoidable technical problem in the attempt to write sympathetically and articulately about those who are circumstantially incapable of speaking and writing on their own behalf. His evocations of this order of life are indeed distanced from the protagonists by satire and humour, and that might well be a kind of self-protective camouflage intended to disguise his proximity to their fate. Like Dickens, whom he greatly admired, Wells makes use of comedy to make his wider political point.

In Wells's aesthetic vision, there are clearly circumstances when escapism – the escapism of popular fiction – is not a dirty word. Thus, despite being seriously hampered by inadequate education, both Kipps and Mr Polly read for pleasure, though they do this with different levels of success. Wells has his characters read fiction for other purposes also. In part he is making the case for the value of entertainment, amusement and escapism, for who would not wish to escape from the lives led by Kipps and Polly? The rich fantasy life of Mr Polly in particular is responsible for everything that is good in that life. So long as books do not deal with the areas of life that school has killed for him, Mr Polly loves to read:

> He began to read stories voraciously, and books of travel, provided they were also adventurous. He got these chiefly from the local institute, and he also 'took in' irregularly, but thoroughly, one of those inspiring weeklies that dull people used to call 'penny dreadfuls',[5] admirable weeklies crammed with imagination. At fourteen, when he emerged from the valley of the shadow of education, there survived something, indeed it survived still … at five-and-thirty, that pointed … to the idea that there was interest and happiness in the world. (Wells 1993b, 7)

In Wells's fiction, what a character reads is an indication of that character's bearing and development; however, Wells's characters are not just going through a phase in their choice of reading. What Kipps or Mr Polly read at the age of fourteen is a pretty good indication of their taste for life. The adolescent fictional adventures read by Mr Polly inform his adult life. With his newfangled bicycle as his trusty steed, Mr Polly rides through English countryside like a latter-day Don Quixote until he meets 'Romance' in the form of a schoolgirl called Christabel. 'You make me feel like one of those old knights … who rode about the country looking for dragons and beautiful maidens in chivalresque adventures,' he tells her (Wells 1993b, 66). Trapped into marriage with Miriam Larkins, he evades the tedium of his life as a gentleman's outfitter in books, travelling round the country to sales where he buys up anything in book form, and reads it – 'except theology' (101):

> and as he read, his little unsuccessful circumstances vanished and the wonder of life returned to him; the routine of reluctant getting up, opening the shop, pretending to dust it with zest, breakfasting with a shop egg underdone or overdone ... and coffee made Miriam's way ... all these things vanished as the auditorium of a theatre vanishes when the stage is lit. (Wells 1993b, 101)

Although the manner of his buying of books makes his reading undiscriminating, Mr Polly really does know the difference between good and bad writing even if he cannot say what it is, and has a fascination for well-polished prose: 'He read Fenimore Cooper and *Tom Cringle's Log* side by side with Joseph Conrad ... until his heart ached to see those sun-soaked lands before he died. Conrad's prose had a pleasure for him that he was never able to define, a peculiar deep-coloured effect' (102). Fiction, in other words, gives him escapist aspiration towards those far-flung climes on the other side of the world, and an aesthetic pleasure that he cannot analyse – but that he feels nonetheless. And his sheer pleasure in words – their sound and their feel on his tongue, as he mutters malapropisms of occasionally startling and ironic accuracy – implies that even the prosaic Mr Polly has an unrealized poetry in him.

There is a profoundly anti-Victorian irresponsibility about *The History of Mr Polly*. The story turns in the end on Polly's discovery that 'If the world does not please you, *you can change it*' (137, emphasis in original). This does not mean political revolution; to Mr Polly, it simply means reclaiming the pleasure in life by leaving behind all the things that he has come to hate – his shop and his wife. Having at first decided to kill himself and set fire to the shop so that his wife would get the insurance, Mr Polly becomes an unwilling hero: the fire is too successful and threatens to burn to death his neighbour's elderly mother whom Mr Polly then rescues. Having taken that first step, he decides to clear out of his home and go tramping. He comes to rest at the Potwell Inn, an Edenic place for a man who has suffered agonies from indigestion brought on by his wife's bad cooking. The inn is presided over by a plump woman who attracts him, and who needs him to help her to run the place. It is also threatened by the evil Uncle Jim, a man who has been 'reformed' in a prison on distinctly vicious lines. Mr Polly defeats Jim more by luck than good judgement, and is permitted to inhabit his Eden happily ever after. It does not matter to Wells that Polly's pleasure is based on arson and fraud since the ends justify the means: personal happiness in these circumstances is a defeat of the system at large, and the system is bad. This ending points out – as Wells's endings often do – the limitations of a strict application of realist principles. Mr Polly has no right to assume within those principles that his life will end happily; nor does Kipps or indeed Ann Veronica. Wells habitually alters the frame of reference, as if in recognition that adherence to realism means defeat for his characters. The endings partake of fantasy not reality because the persistence of realism leaves no space for happiness if strictly observed.

The History of Mr Polly is fun to read and was probably fun to write. But Wells was not just a journeyman novelist who turned a profit and had no aesthetic vision. The long relationship he enjoyed, and then endured, with Henry James, documented in many letters and reviews, is testament to a fairly coherent critical and creative position. *The Record of their Friendship* edited by Edel and Ray makes fascinating reading in its expression of two very different personalities and two diametrically opposed views of what fiction is for. The editors summarize the grounds of their discussions as involving 'two formulae for fiction'. As a socialist:

> Wells … believed in *la littérature engagée*, a usable, functional art appropriate to the world [he] wished to fashion out of the old. James preferred … to take life as it comes, to deal with it in its *status quo*, with measure, balance and moderation. There was enough for the artist to do in the act of seeing, feeling arriving at awareness – without making of his creations instruments for social instruction and guidance. (Edel and Ray 1959, 11)

This is, of course, a different way of stating the distinction between sociological and psychological fiction that Raymond Williams identified. On the evidence collected by Ray and Edel, Wells in fact made a pretty good case for social engagement as a necessary part of fiction, though his editors do not always credit him with the force of his ideas. His essay 'The Contemporary Novel' (1914), originally a talk for the *Times* Book Club in 1911, might not have quite the same kind of rhetorical force as Woolf's 'Mr Bennett and Mrs Brown' or 'Modern Fiction', but it does have an interesting argument to make. Wells begins by constructing the typical reader as a 'Weary Giant', 'a man, burthened, toiling, worn':

> He has been in his office from ten to four, with perhaps only two hours interval for lunch ... Now at last comes the little precious interval of leisure, and the Weary Giant takes up a book. Perhaps he is vexed: he may have been bunkered, his line may have been entangled in the trees, his favourite investment may have slumped, or the judge have had indignation and been extremely rude to him. He wants to forget the troublesome realities of life. He wants to be taken out of himself, to be cheered, consoled, amused – above all, amused. He doesn't want ideas, he doesn't want facts; above all he doesn't want – *Problems*. He wants to dream of the bright, thin, gay excitements of the phantom world – in which he can be hero – of horses ridden and lace worn and princesses rescued and won. He wants pictures of funny slums, and entertaining paupers ... He wants romance without its defiance, and humour without its sting; and the business of the novelist, he holds, is to supply this cooling refreshment. (Wells in Edel and Ray 1959, 132–3)

So far, so Q. D. Leavis: how outrageous to wish only to be entertained. In some ways, this reader is Mr Polly, who may not be a giant, weary or otherwise, but who also wants to be consoled, to escape from everyday life in his reading, and to become the vicarious hero of unlikely romances. But there is an essential difference of course, in the class of the Weary Giant and the class of the failed draper. Mr Polly's working day is considerably longer than six hours; he gets precious little exercise (and none on a golf course), and his lunch is not worth eating, let alone spending two hours over. Moreover, in *The History of Mr Polly*, romance is largely absent except to be deflated, and humour certainly does have its sting.

Wells's prescription for the novel, whilst admitting that refreshment and entertainment are important, is, as befits a socialist writer, a quasi-Marxist argument which takes it for granted that there is a relationship between reality and fiction that is not all one way. It is not simply that fiction should reflect reality in all its phases; in addition, fiction can recreate reality in its own image. The novel, writes Wells:

> is to be the social mediator, the vehicle of understanding, the instrument of self-examination, the parade of morals and the exchange of customs, the *factory* of customs, the criticism of laws and institutions and of social dogmas and ideas ... I do not mean for a moment that the novelist is

going to set up as a ... sort of priest with a pen, who will *make* men and women believe and do this and that. The novel is not a new sort of pulpit ... But the novelist is going to be the most potent of artists, because he is going to present conduct, *devise* beautiful conduct, discuss conduct, analyse conduct, *suggest* conduct, illuminate it through and through. He will not teach, but discuss, point out, plead, and display. (Wells in Edel and Ray 1959, 154–5, my emphases)

The novelist, then, will not make people behave in certain ways; but he (or even she) will make people think. Imagining and presenting alternative realities is a way of making them possible, of opening up new conceptions. Thus the novelist in Wells's discussion is like the paradigmatic character of his fiction: he seeks to break down boundaries in the way that people behave towards one another. The emphasis on 'conduct' is interesting here since conduct and propriety were watchwords of Victorian morality, and that emphasis is apparently a world away from the 'dark places of psychology'. But the ways in which we behave to each other are surely related to the ways in which we think both about ourselves and about others.

In these terms, then, what is the message of *The History of Mr Polly* or of *Kipps*? The obvious message is that there are people forced to lead very narrow lives on the basis of poor education, inhumane working conditions and poverty: this is not news. There is quietly expressed outrage about those wasted lives; and there is a will to argue that these lives are as valuable as anyone else's. Wells does not always get the tone right: he does patronize his creations. But in making them central – as a writer like Woolf or Joyce never would – and in pursuing fantasy-endings over grimly realistic ones – as Arthur Morrison and George Gissing refused to do – he writes a qualified optimism for a better world.

Galsworthy the materialist

Alone amongst the triumvirate of so-called Edwardian novelists, John Galsworthy (1867–1933) chooses the milieu of the comfortable middle classes as the setting for his most famous work, *The Forsyte Saga*. In social terms, at least, this could be the world of a Henry James or Virginia Woolf novel. It is certainly related to the fictions of Forster, with the Forsytes and the Wilcoxes (from *Howards End*) having a great deal in common. Moreover, although *The Forsyte Saga* is a social world away from the settings described by D. H. Lawrence, like *The Rainbow* (1915), where 'The Brangwens had lived for generations at Marsh

Farm' (Lawrence 1995, 9), the origins of the Forsytes are similarly plebeian and lost in the mists of time; like the Brangwens, too, the modern generations of Forsytes are greatly influenced by the historical changes of the nineteenth century, though the precise nature of those influences on each of the two families differs as their social class differs. *The Rainbow* is as much a family saga as *The Forsyte Saga* is. As such, in terms of the distinction between sociological fiction about the economically impoverished and psychological fiction about the upper middle classes, one would expect Galsworthy to sit firmly with the psychologists. But, as John Stokes has observed, Galsworthy brings together 'emotional impetuosity with a concrete vision of the market' (Stokes 1992, 2), and the psychology of his fiction is firmly couched in opulent materiality. Thus, throughout the three volumes of *The Forsyte Saga* (*The Man of Property*, 1906, *In Chancery*, 1920 and *To Let*, 1921) the psychology of the comfortable upper middle classes is probed, using the symbol of property as the outward sign of inner feeling. The perspective of the narrator is that of 'Young' Jolyon Forsyte, only son of the oldest member of the family, also named Jolyon. Like Galsworthy himself, Young Jolyon is born on the inside of the hegemonic property-owning class; and like Galsworthy, Young Jolyon becomes an outsider through the twinned pursuits of illicit sexual desire, and artistic voca-tion. Their perspective is that of ironic judgement. They know the Forsyte world intimately and remain part of the Forsyte species despite their apparent escape from its narrowness. Young Jolyon, a water-colour artist is given sage financial advice about his art; he should paint in a manner that could be easily 'read' by his potential public, and he would thereby gain a sale. The words of the critic 'bore good fruit with young Jolyon; they were contrary to all that he believed in, to all that he theoretically held good in his Art, but some strange, deep instinct moved him against his will to turn them to profit' (Galsworthy 1978, 251). This sums up something about Galsworthy's aesthetics too. He might stand against the philistine values of the Forsyte-type, but he also panders to their taste in the making of his fiction.

Soames Forsyte, the eponymous man of property of the saga's first volume, stands as a typical representative of his class. He is formulated in the phrase 'The Man of Property' by Old Jolyon Forsyte, the patriarch of the family; and that sense of property defines not only an individual characteristic of Soames, but also the characteristic trait of all the Forsytes:

> There was old Jolyon in Stanhope Places; the Jameses in Park Lane;
> Swithin in the lonely glory of orange and blue chambers in Hyde Park

> Mansions…the Soameses in their nest of Knightsbridge; the Rogers in Prince's Gardens (Roger was that remarkable Forsyte who had conceived and carried out the notion of bringing up his four sons to a new profession. 'Collect house property – nothing like it!' he would say; '*I* never did anything else!'). (Galsworthy 1978, 25)

This is a roll-call of the more expensive areas of London which are the natural habitat of the Forsytes species. All the Forsytes are defined by their sense of property, by the solid materiality of their comfortable existence. Old Jolyon, however, instinctively understands that Soames's sense of ownership is an obsession that goes beyond the bounds of decency.

As the Man of Property, Soames collects art for the sheer pleasure of ownership rather than for aesthetic reasons; most importantly, however, his sense of property extends beyond proper boundaries to his beautiful wife whose 'power of attraction he regarded as part of her value as his property' (59): 'Could a man own anything prettier than this dining-table with its deep tints, the starry, soft-petalled roses, the ruby-coloured glass, and quaint silver furnishing; could a man own anything prettier than the woman who sat at it?' (70). The story of the Soameses' failed relationship takes place against the backdrop of the multiple changes that characterized the fin de siècle – social, histori-cal, familial and personal changes. The fact that Irene and Soames married in 1883, for example, is highly significant to the story, for in 1883 the Married Woman's Property Act of 1882 finally came into force, meaning that married women could own their own property and beginning the process of separating married women from the legal status of *femme couverte*.[6] The Act is explicitly and implicitly referred to at various points throughout the three volumes. Nicholas Forsyte, for example, 'had married a good deal of money, of which, it being then the golden age before the Married Woman's Property Act, he had mercifully been enabled to make a successful use' (27). Legislative change has not, however, produced the cultural change it is commonly supposed to. Irene is not property but Soames does not adapt to that fact buoyed up, perhaps, by the continuity that is preserved against the backdrop of change. The older generation holds on to its values in the same way as it holds on to its possessions.[7] And whatever the his-torical shifts, family life is always made up of small quarrels and jostlings for position so that there is a sense of the continuity of human nature in the context of the larger movements of human affairs.

The action proper begins with Soames's decision to build for himself a country house as a gilded cage in which to keep his wife: 'To get Irene out of London, away from opportunities of going about and seeing people, away from her friends and those who put ideas in her head!' (61). He hires an architect, Philip Bosinney, to design the house for him. The house is to be a statement of his importance, and a setting for his collection of *objets d'art*, including Irene. Irene, however, falls in love with Bosinney and has an affair with him. In an attempt to reassert his property rights over his wife, Soames rapes her; she tells Bosinney what has happened, and the architect, in a state of impotent horror, walks under a bus in a London fog and is killed. *The Man of Property* ends with Irene's enforced return to her husband since she has no money and nowhere else to go. Material circumstances, that is, dictate her final action in the first part of the saga.

The interwoven family stories that make up the saga are not in themselves particularly remarkable. Nor does Galsworthy involve himself in conscious experimentation with the form of fiction. When Woolf accused the Edwardians of making do with the old tools of the nineteenth-century novelists for the new circumstances of modernity, regarding their refusal to adapt as a failure, Galsworthy is probably the most 'guilty' of the parties. This is certainly fiction based in pattern rather than the nebulous realm of rhythm. The action of the main plot is mediated through a series of family gatherings, both formal and informal where gossip is exchanged. Just like the minor characters in George Eliot's fiction, the extended Forsyte family have a choric role, commenting on the action as it unfolds just offstage. In addition, Galsworthy learned from the Naturalists an emphasis on the 'type' rather than on a fully realized and essentialist individuality, dramatized on his emphasis on the Forsytes as a species. Metaphors of animal and bird species abound throughout, from the first page where a Forsyte family gathering is described as a 'charming and instructive sight – an upper-middle-class family in full plumage' (11). The family's instinctive distrust of Bosinney the architect comes from their sense that he does not belong to their species: 'Like cattle when a dog comes into the field, they stood head to head and shoulder to shoulder, prepared to run upon and trample the invade to death' (15–16). It is the partial outsider, young Jolyon, who is able to articulate what they are and what they feel, giving an ironic description of the Forsyte species as only a partial outsider can – he calls himself a 'mongrel' and 'the missing link' (202):

> a 'Forsyte' is a man who decidedly more or less the slave of property. He knows a good thing, he knows a safe thing, and his grip on property – it

doesn't matter whether it be wives, houses, money or reputation – is his hall-mark... I should like... to lecture on it: 'Properties and quality of a Forsyte. This little animal, disturbed by the ridicule of his own sort, is unaffected by in his motions by the laughter of strange creatures... Hereditarily disposed to myopia, he recognizes only the persons and habitats of his own species, amongst which he passes an existence of competitive tranquillity.' (Galsworthy 1978, 202)

The concept of the Forsytes as a species is played out in various ways. It is no accident, for example, that some of the key scenes of *The Man of Property* take place at London Zoo (on a day when it costs a shilling to get in, so that 'there would not be all those horrid common people' [161]) and at Kew Gardens, places of course, where species are there to be examined for the public's edification. The concept of heredity and environment making character is derived from the Naturalists of French literature. Zola had famously described the novel as an experimental place, where environment, heredity and temperament would be added together like so many chemicals in a test-tube to produce predictable results in human behaviour (see Zola in Becker 1963, 162–96). That is not to say, however, that Galsworthy's evocation of the habitat of the Forsytes is utterly deterministic (for young Jolyon breaks out), nor that it is psychologically naïve, nor that it is badly written.

In a world where *things* matter – where objects are the marker of character – and in a novel which explicitly advertises itself as being about 'property', it is no surprise that psychology is expressed by those things, which then take on an almost animated existence of their own. The drawing-room at Uncle Timothy's house, for example, is stuffed to bursting with material objects: 'for Timothy and his sisters... considered that a room was not quite "nice" unless it was "properly" furnished. It held, therefore, eleven chairs, a sofa, three tables, two cabinets, innumerable knick-knacks, and part of a large grand piano' (167). That is the proper 'habitat' of a Victorian Forsyte – an advertisement through conspicuous consumption, of personal wealth which is the marker of personal worth. It is also a satire on an older generation. The over-stuffed houses of the Victorians, it is implied, are a sign of their general intellectual stuffiness. This is the psychology of William James, not the psychology of Sigmund Freud, a commonsense psychology that equates the clearly visible and legible with proper knowledge character. David Trotter has argued that this is a severely limited mode of writing, which imposes an equally limited mode of reading through the relentless emphasis on reading the details (Trotter 1993, 87–8). This may be partly true, but there are also elements of subtlety and complexity in Galsworthy's presentation of his types.

Soames Forsyte, for example, also partakes of that more subterranean psychology associated with modernity. He is a character as it were, in transition, between two modes of being, an externalized personality, and an internalized one: and the split in him is registered in relation to his reading habits. Soames we are told is a voracious consumer of fiction, a Wellsian 'weary giant'. For example, he considers his failing marriage in relation to the novels he has read, and to the 'Problem' plays (that is, plays about adultery and its aftermath) he has seen on the London stage:

> Like most novel readers of his generation…literature coloured his view of life; and he had imbibed the belief that it was only a matter of time. In the end the husband always gained the affection of his wife. Even in those cases – a class of book he was not very fond of – which ended in tragedy, the wife always died with poignant regrets on her lips, or if it were the husband who died – unpleasant thought – threw herself on his body in an agony of remorse.
>
> He often took Irene to the theatre, instinctively choosing the modern Society plays with the modern Society conjugal problem, so fortunately different from any conjugal problem in real life. He found that they too always ended in the same way. (Galsworthy 1978, 71)

Soames uses literature to find the endorsement of views he already holds rather than to have those views challenged. *The Man of Property* ironically ends with a scene that is superficially similar to the ones that he prefers in fiction, with his wife returning to him after the death of her lover, so that one can see that Galsworthy is self-consciously appealing to that market of weary-giant readers made up of the world's Soameses. At the same time, however, Soames 'often sympathized with the lover' (71) who threatened the fictional marriage – and so, of course, does the reader of Soames's story, for Bosinney is presented sympathetically as Soames is not. Thus, on the one hand, Soames Forsyte exercises the position of judgement of the reader of realism, judging by results; on the other, he becomes embroiled in emotional responses that do not sit easily with his intellectual position. This ambiguity is shared by Galsworthy's own readers. The brutal husbands who force their wives into submission both attract and repel readers like Soames, precisely because they would like to be among them but dislike their brutality. But Soames still cannot make Irene love him whether he behaves brutally or not. The limitations of his position as a man of property make it impossible for him to see beyond the question of property in his emotional life.

Soames, then, is insufficiently self-conscious to make sense of his own actions. The split in his personality between a transparent sense of cause and effect and his barely known emotional life is mirrored in the techniques used to describe his mental state. The morning after the rape provides a case in point.

> The morning after a certain night on which Soames at last asserted his rights and acted like a man, he breakfasted alone … He ate steadily, but at times a sensation as though he could not swallow attacked him. Had he been right to yield to his overmastering hunger of the night before, and break down the resistance which he had suffered now too long from this woman who was his lawful and solemnly constituted helpmate? (Galsworthy 1978, 264)

There is no secure perspective in this passage, written both from Soames's point of view in his cliché-ridden language of emotional illiteracy, and from a perspective which requires the reader to judge his actions. It is reasonable to assume that most people would regard rape as a criminal act, even though no actual law has been broken.[8] If we are to see this description as an evocation of Soames's state of mind, what we see is ambivalence. On the one hand, the euphemistic elusive treatment of what Soames has done implies shame, as does his difficulty in swallowing his breakfast. One hunger of the body – sexual desire – has been displaced onto another, the desire for food; Soames knows he should not have indulged the former and consequently has trouble with the latter. On the other hand, the tone of the phrases 'asserted his rights and acted like a man' and 'his lawful and solemnly constituted helpmate' stands for the way in which Soames wishes to represent his act to himself. He wants to reassure himself that he has done the right thing. Euphemism and cliché are pursued as cloaks for immorality and as a comfort that he need not feel remorse. He tries to convince himself that it does not matter: 'The incident was not really of great moment; women made a fuss about it in books; but in the cool judgement of right-thinking men … he had but done his best to sustain the sanctity of marriage, to prevent her from abandoning her duty' (265). These are the watchwords of his class – cool judgement, right-thinking men, the sanctity of marriage, duty – and he uses them to salve his conscience as automatic responses to any problem. Here, he rejects the teaching of books that elsewhere – when it suits him – he finds so useful. But 'the sound of smothered sobbing still haunted him' and not even the automatic gesture of reading the *Times* can make it go away. Surely a solely materialistic being would not feel like that, and this is evidence that Galsworthy's way of seeing is not so psychologically naïve as it is sometimes presented as being.

Aesthetics and the market, or the artist and the artisan; or Mr Bennett and Mrs Woolf

I've been trying what I really could do in one day if I worked my hardest. Now just listen; it deserves to be chronicled for the encouragement of aspiring youth. I got up at 7.30, and whilst I breakfasted I read through a volume I had to review. By 10.30 the review was written – three-quarters of a column in the *Evening Budget*... from 10.30 to 11, I smoked a cigar and reflected ... At eleven I was ready to write my Saturday *causerie* for *Will o' the Wisp*; it took till close upon one o'clock, which was rather too long. I can't afford more than an hour and a half for that job. At one, I rushed out to a dirty little eating-house ... Was back again by a quarter to two, having in the meantime sketched a paper for *The West End*. Pipe in mouth, I settled down to leisurely artistic work; by five, half the paper was done; the other half remains for tomorrow. From five to half-past, I read four newspapers and two magazines, and from half-past to a quarter to six, I sketched down several ideas that had come to me whilst reading. At six I was again in the dirty eating-house ... Home once more at 6.45, and for two hours wrote steadily at a long affair I have in hand for *The Current*. (Gissing 1985, 213)

It was my practice to be at my table every morning at 5.30 am, and it was also my practice to allow myself no mercy ... All those I think who have lived as literary men ... will agree with me that three hours a day will produce as much as a man ought to write. But then, he should so have trained himself that he shall be able to work continuously during those three hours, – so have tutored his mind that it shall not be necessary for him to sit nibbling his pen and gazing at the wall before him till he should have found the words which he wants to express his ideas. It had ... become my custom ... to write with my watch before me and to require from myself 250 words every quarter of an hour. I have found that the 250 words have been forthcoming as regularly as my clock went... This division of time allowed me to produce ten pages of an ordinary novel volume a day, and if kept up through ten months would have given as its results three novels of three volumes each in the year. (Trollope 1996, 174–5)

Thursday November 2nd, 1899. To-day I wrote five articles; two reviews, two articles on 'The Black Tulip' play, and my weekly household notes ...

December 31st 1899. this year I have written 335, 340 words, grand total. 228 articles and stories (including 4 instalments of a serial of 30,000 – 7,500 words each) have actually been published.

Also my book of plays – 'Polite Farces'
I have written six or eight short stories not yet published or sold.
Also the greater part of 55,000 word serial – 'Love and Life' – for Tillotson's, which begins publication about April next year.
Also the whole draft (80,000 words) of my Staffordshire novel, 'Anna Tellwright'.
My total earnings were £592 3s. 1d. of which sum I have yet to receive £72 10s. (Bennett I 1932, 116, 120)

These three quotations had to be reproduced at length in order for the scale of what they each describe to become apparent. The first is Jasper Milvain describing his day's work in *New Grub Street*; the second is Anthony Trollope, discoursing about his own process for writing in his posthumously published *An Autobiography*; the third is from the diary of Arnold Bennett, in 1899 at the very start of the writing career that was to become a publishing phenomenon of the early twentieth century. Both Gissing and Bennett read Trollope's *Autobiography* with rather different results. Gissing disapproved of the cheerfully cold-blooded description of Trollope's working methods and dismissal of writer's block, and gives similar sentiments to the villain of his novel; and Bennett seems to have approved since his description of his own working practice, his meticulous recording of what he wrote, and his account keeping of how much he got for it (also to be found in Trollope) looks very like the work of a man who was taking that epitome of the successful Victorian novelist as his role model.

Alongside the questions of what readers read novels for, the case of Arnold Bennett asks us to consider why writers write: is novel-writing an art and a vocation, or is it just a job of work to be paid by so many pence per column inch or per page as Trollope's persona is constructed to suggest? Is the novelist an Artist, the capitalization signalling his (and it usually is a masculine position) struggle with and contempt for the world, or is he merely an artisan? Trollope suggested the latter with a notably gung-ho attitude, and Gissing feared that it was so. The Modernist generation favoured the former. Comparing Gissing's *New Grub Street* with Charles Dickens's *David Copperfield* (1849–50), and William Thackeray's *Pendennis* (1850) with *A Portrait of the Artist as a Young Man* (1916), P. J. Keating was struck by the fact that:

> Neither David Copperfield nor Arthur Pendennis seem to feel that being a writer is anything to make much of a fuss about. It is a profession which can bring both financial rewards and a place in society. It demands talent and a degree of worldly experience, but not creative agony. Such an attitude is meaningless to Stephen Dedalus. Society is

something to escape from, and the very thought that one's work might bring public acclamation is enough to brand one as an inferior artist. (Keating 1968, 13)

This is perhaps a slight overstatement. Joyce certainly treats Stephen Dedalus with an ironic distance that comes from mockery, suggesting that Stephen is perhaps making too much fuss about artistic and philosophical integrity; and just like the Edwardian novelists, Joyce also makes great play of the intrusion of material circumstance on his 'hero's' delusions of grandeur, where every flight of fancy is – Icarus-like, of course – deflated by its juxtaposition with mundane considerations. But in the stories we tell ourselves about literature and its making, the favoured fiction that we retell and retail is that of the uncompromising Artist, preferably struggling in a garret against enormous odds. The man who can tot up a third of a million published and paid-for words over the course of a year may not be physically grubby as his attic-bound brother is, but he is marked as morally inferior. Surely no one can write so much and be any good, the preferred story suggests.

Ironic, then, that one of the chief purveyors of the Artist myth is Virginia Woolf, who had after all a distinctly materialistic side. The whole of *A Room of One's Own* is based on the argument that material conditions – a decent education, a room in which to write, and the leisure to do so, bought with the sum of five hundred pounds a year – are essential for the woman artist to do her work properly. This sum was, of course, left to Woolf in her aunt's will, and she comments:

> The news of my legacy reached me one night about the same time that the act was passed that gave votes to women. A solicitor's letter fell into the post-box and when I opened it I found that she had left me five hundred pounds a year for ever. Of the two – the vote and the money – the money, I own, seemed infinitely more important. (Woolf 1993c, 33–4)

Rachel Bowlby quite rightly warns us not to take the voice in which this passage is written as that of Woolf herself; the book is spoken by a persona, not a person. Nonetheless, the money has produced, the persona admits, a spiritual change in her life. The freedom from hard-to-obtain, uncongenial work means that she need no longer flatter those she does not like, nor fear those who do not like her. Money has bought the liberty which makes it possible to write calmly and without bitterness, one of the ways in which Woolf defined true artistry. At the same time, however, *A Room of One's Own* also notes that the great achievements of literature by men in the last two hundred years have nearly all been on the basis of wealth and the kind of education that wealth can buy. Browning's poetry is the result, says Woolf, of Browning's family being 'well to do': 'if he had not been well to do, he could no more have attained to write *Saul* or *The Ring and the Book* than Ruskin would have attained to writing *Modern Painters* if his father had not dealt prosperously in business' (Woolf 1993c, 96–7). What, though, of those of us who do not have relatives who could leave us a year's salary in a will – a very large majority? The position of the middle-class woman writer is not, after all, so very different from the position of the proletarian male writer, though the polemics of Woolf's discussion rather disguise that fact.

The passage I quoted above from Bennett's diary was selected because 1899 was the year in which Bennett himself first passed the magical figure of five hundred pounds earned by his pen, which represented a good middle-class income for a single man at this time. The myth of the Artist's struggles versus the sordid manoeuvrings of the artisan–entrepreneur have served Arnold Bennett particularly badly. A man with neither the cultural capital of an Oxbridge education nor the real capital of cash reserves ripe for inheritance from a wealthy family, Bennett took a very pragmatic attitude to writing – one that is much closer to Jasper Milvain's than to Edwin Reardon's. If he wanted to make a decent living by his pen, he had to do so by sheer graft. If he did not want to go hungry in the meantime, he had to pursue a course of discipline as rigorous as anything described by Trollope. And because his five hundred pounds a year had not been left to him 'for ever', and had to be earned again annually, Bennett as much as any Victorian novelist was on a treadmill of production in the literary machine. His diary records phenomenal rates of productivity. The third of a million words he published in 1899 does not include the diary itself but does include short serial pot-boilers for provincial newspapers, reviews and articles in papers and periodicals, short stories for magazines, and plays, and he was also working on the novel that would eventually become *Anna of the Five Towns* (1902). Just because he was writing at speed and for profit, however, does not mean that he was not a self-conscious artist figure as well. Indeed, his diary entries make it clear that the literary hack-work he undertook for his financial well-being was used throughout his career to subsidize what he saw as his more important work. The ephemeral pulp fiction, which was often published anonymously, bought him the time to write the major realist novels on which his reputation ought to rest.

John Carey calls Arnold Bennett the hero of *The Intellectuals and the Masses* and laments the fact that his reputation does not match his achievement:

> His writings represent a systematic dismemberment of the intellectuals' case against the masses. He has never been popular with intellectuals as a result ... his novels are still undervalued by literary academics, syllabus devisers and other official censors. Many students of English literature know of him, if at all, only through Virginia Woolf's scornful estimate in 'Mr Bennett and Mrs Brown', and they naturally, though mistakenly, assume that Bennett, not Woolf, is diminished by that sally. (Carey 1992, 152)

Fair comment. Woolf certainly singled Bennett out for particularly harsh criticism in that essay, and there is a fundamental unfairness in her satirical characterization of Bennett as concerned only with the surface of things. In the essay, she imagines a figure named Mrs Brown, an elderly lady met by chance on a train. If Mr Bennett had seen Mrs Brown, and decided to make her the central figure of a novel his procedure would have been as follows:

> 'Begin by saying that her father kept a shop in Harrogate. Ascertain the rent. Ascertain the wages of shop assistants in the year 1878. Discover what her mother died of. Describe cancer. Describe calico. Describe—' (Woolf 1992a, 82)

But Woolf regards the description of external or material things as unimportant conventions of realist representation. The descriptions, she argues, don't tell us anything real, where 'real' stands for her perception of the psychological, spiritual dimensions of character and culture, not for the material conditions which in some measure produce those dimensions. Woolf's characters are 'deep', Bennett's are 'shallow', at least in her estimation – and shallow is, of course, a term of disapproval.

In fact, though, Bennett's characters are anything but 'shallow'. Writing of the genesis of *The Old Wives' Tale* (1908) in his Preface to the novel, Bennett describes one of the points of origin of his novel, a chance encounter with an elderly woman in a Paris restaurant in the autumn of 1903 – a Madame Lebrun perhaps? Bennett describes her as 'fat, shapeless, ugly and grotesque' and as a source of both irritation and amusement to the other customers in the café as she refuses to settle comfortably with her lumpy parcels. Bennett was not surprised that some of the customers laughed at the old woman, but he describes feeling pained by the mockery of the two pretty young waitresses directed at the difficult older woman:

> I reflected, concerning the grotesque diner: 'The woman was once young, slim, perhaps beautiful; certainly free from these ridiculous mannerisms. Very probably she is unconscious of her singularities. Her case is a tragedy. One ought to be able to make a heart-rending novel out of the history of a woman such as she.' Every stout ageing woman is not grotesque – far from it! – but there is an extreme pathos in the mere fact that every stout ageing woman was once a young girl with the unique charm of youth in her form and movements and in her mind. And the fact that the change from young girl to the stout ageing woman is made up of an infinite number of infinitesimal changes, each unperceived by her, only intensifies the pathos. (Bennett 1990, 32)

In describing the slow processes of physical, mental and emotional changes that make the old woman what she is, Bennett evokes an almost geological notion of time. The alterations in her from young woman to old woman accrete like strata in a process that is imperceptible to the naked eye. What her current state represents is layers and layers of depth caused by age and experience. She is largely unaware of the changes she has undergone, and other people who come across her at different times in her life see only the results of the change, not the process by which they came about. In the laughter of the two young waitresses, Bennett also introduces one of his consistent themes in his major fiction: the generation gaps which consistently make it impossible for the young to sympathize with the old. In his diary in 1897, he commented on the generation gap growing between himself and his father:

> I noticed ... the approaches of middle-age upon him. I felt acutely that he and I were of different generations; that parent and child, be they never so willing, can never come intellectually together, simply because one time of life differs crudely and harshly from another. He has now the physical and mental deliberativeness which characterizes the ageing. I chafe under this slowness, but I need not do so: it is not a sign of decay, but of natural development. (Bennett 1932, 50)

He would make this theme central to *Clayhanger* (1910), where Edwin and his father are temperamentally different because they belong to different eras. But it is also a major part of *The Old Wives' Tale*. As girls,

Sophia and Constance have no inkling of the reality of other people's lives, and are casually indifferent to them. When their servant Maggie gets some new clothes, the narrator comments: 'With the profound and instinctive cruelty of youth [they] had assembled … expressly to deride Maggie in her new clothes. They obscurely thought that a woman so ugly and soiled as Maggie had no right to possess new clothes' (Bennett 1990, 43–4). At the end of the novel, the two ageing women, at the mercy of a succession of incompetent maids have that indifference turned back upon them, and they cannot understand why it should be so. The aim of representing such a figure as the old woman in the café (and the Old Wives in the novel become such figures at the end) is to produce pathos in the service of empathy, empathy being the only way in which the thick wall of personality and egotism described by Pater and recognized by Bennett as part of the human condition can be penetrated. Now this is not Woolf's interest at all as her treatment of Miss Kilman in *Mrs Dalloway* shows. For Bennett the Miss Kilmans come to occupy centre stage and *The Old Wives' Tale* makes the kind of women who would 'pass unnoticed in a crowd' (32) its focus.

The novel tells the story of two sisters brought up in a draper's shop in Bursley (a fictionalized version of Burslem, one of the towns that makes up the 'five towns', the conurbation of Stoke on Trent in the North Midlands of England). It is a comfortable but restricted life and both daughters kick against the limitations imposed upon them by their mother's ideas of propriety and the demands of the shop. Constance, as befits her name, settles down to marry the draper's apprentice-cum-manager, Samuel Povey, while Sophia escapes, albeit temporarily to Paris of the 1860s and 1870s. The two women end their days around 1906 – or roughly speaking, the present day of the novel's publication so that the novel charts a social history – and to some extent a political history – of the last years of the nineteenth century.

Bennett self-consciously modelled his realist fictions on the works of the French realists, Gustave Flaubert and Guy de Maupassant. His interest, like Galsworthy's, is centred on 'typicality' though he presents his types with less self-evident irony. Both Constance and Sophia live lives that are true to type, the result of heredity, environment and education. Despite Sophia's apparently more adventurous and romantic life, in fact, she lives very much as her sister does, and uses the skills of good housekeeping and management learned at her mother's knee to make her fortune in Paris. The novel suggests that no matter what external experience may bring, their early years and training in thrift and industry have formed their characters. It is these skills that Sophia brings to bear against the backdrop of the Franco-Prussian War (1870–71) and the Siege of Paris. In Bennett's description, the Siege is not heroic or galvanizing; rather it is a sordid affair of black-market trading, eating meat from dubious sources (including the Paris Zoological Gardens), and the founding of Sophia's fortunes. Making the large events of official political history into a mere backdrop for individual developments is, of course, precisely what Woolf does, foregrounding her decision through the typographical insistence of presenting the First World War in parenthesis in the middle section of *To the Lighthouse*. Bennett is not so technically innovative, but there is a real sense in which he also brackets off history from the central interest of his story. 'No one,' wrote Woolf, after the 1914–18 war, 'can possibly believe that history as it is written closely resembles history as it is lived' (Woolf 1993a, 3). In his Preface to *The Old Wives' Tale*, Bennett says much the same thing. Realizing that he would have to include the Franco-Prussian War because of the chronology of his fiction, he asked his Parisian landlord and landlady what it had been like:

> I said to the old man, 'By the way, you went through the Siege of Paris, didn't you?' He turned to his old wife and said, uncertainly, 'the Siege of Paris? Yes, we did, didn't we?' The Siege of Paris had only been one incident among many in their lives. Of course they remembered it well, though not vividly... the most useful thing I gained from them was the perception, startling at first, that ordinary people went on living very ordinary lives... and to the vast mass of the population, the siege was not the dramatic, spectacular, thrilling, ecstatic affair that is described in history. (Bennett 1990, 34)

This relative indifference is how Sophia also experiences it; it is an interruption of the process of daily life, a minor irritation rather than a total alteration. Frank Kermode in *The Sense of an Ending* argues that there are two divisions of time that find their way into fiction, which he identifies by the words *kairos* and *chronos*. *Chronos* is roughly speaking the time of 'one damn thing after another' (Kermode 1967, 47), the time of chronology, or of time passing; *kairos* is significant time – the time of the Joycean epiphany, for example, or of Wordsworth's 'spots of time', the 'moments of crisis' which mark the beginnings and ends of phases of existence. This is related to Hayden White's observation that historical narrative is divided into two kinds:

> The *diachronic*, or processionary narratives... and the *synchronic*, or static narratives... In the former, the sense of structural transformation

is uppermost as the principle guiding representation. In the latter, the sense of structural continuity … or stasis … predominates. This distinction points … to a difference of emphasis in treating the relationship between continuity and change in a given representation of the historical process. (White 1973, 10–11)

Fiction might usually be thought of as more invested in *kairos* or diachronic forms of narrative. Bennett focuses on *chronos*, a synchronic representation of time as lived experience, and he is highly committed to this model of time in *The Old Wives' Tale*.

This, as John Lucas has observed, makes it extremely difficult to demonstrate his skill via short quotation and individual incident (Lucas 1974, 12), since every moment has to be read in the context of that slow accumulation of geological detail. One keynote moment will have to suffice. This is the evocation of the state of mind of Constance's baby son, Cyril Povey, aged about ten months:

> the baby rolled about on the hearthrug, which had been covered with a large soft woollen shawl, originally the property of his great-grandmother. He had no cares, no responsibilities. The shawl was so vast that he could not clearly distinguish objects beyond its confines. On it lay an indiarubber ball, an indiarubber doll, a rattle and Fan [the dog]. He vaguely recollected all four items, with their respective properties. The fire was also an old friend. He had occasionally tried to touch it, but a high bright fence always came in between. For ten months he had never spent a day without making experiments on this shifting universe in which he alone remained firm and stationary … He pushed the ball away, and wriggled after it, and captured it with the assurance of practice. He tried to swallow the doll, and it was not until he had tried several times … that he remembered the failure of previous efforts and philosophically desisted. He rolled against the mountainous flank of the mammoth Fan, and clutched at Fan's ear. The whole mass of Fan upheaved and vanished from his view, and was instantly forgotten by him. He seized the doll and tried to swallow it, and repeated the exhibition of his skill with the ball … And so he had existed for centuries: no responsibilities, no appetites; and the shawl was vast. (Bennett 1990, 207–8)

This passage has an intrinsic interest as a proto-Freudian evocation of child psychology. Cyril Povey, for example, plays his own version of the fort/da game described by Freud; he is clearly in the grip of the pre-Oedipal delusion that he is the centre of his own universe; and he is outside (though only temporarily) the realm of measured time. The passage is also physiologically accurate in that small babies do indeed have difficulty in focussing beyond their immediate surroundings.

But the unconscious egotism of the child is also part of a much larger pattern of events in the novel, and is presented in the service of Bennett's philosophy of time and theory of representation. Like a real child, Cyril is involved in the compulsive repetition of small actions – pushing the ball away, trying to swallow the doll. This is almost pure *chronos*, a representation of repeated events that have no intrinsic significance, much as the daily round of real existence is filled with such events. His parents live also in such a world: '[Constance's] life had much in it of laborious tedium – tedium never-ending and monotonous ... both she and Samuel worked consistently hard, rising early, "pushing forward" ... and going to bed early from sheer fatigue; week after week and month after month as season changed imperceptibly into season' (190). In the wider context of the whole novel, then, Cyril's babyish consciousness is also symptomatic of character more generally. Galsworthy described the Forsytes as 'myopic'; Bennett dramatizes the child's myopia and its effects. By extension, the limited lives his parents lead are also somewhat short-sighted, bounded by the Square in the provincial town they inhabit as Cyril's view is bounded by the shawl. The shop they run, inherited from Constance's mother, like the shawl inherited from her great-grandmother, cushions them from material want, but blinds them to the wider world. Cyril's egotism is Constance and Samuel's egotism too. The Poveys live lives of Biffenseque 'ignoble decency', but unlike *Mr Bailey, Grocer*, *The Old Wives' Tale* is not a dull book.

Given her pronouncements about what reality consists of, it is something of a surprise that Virginia Woolf was so hostile to Bennett's procedures in novels such as *The Old Wives' Tale* and *Clayhanger* (1910). In *A Room of One's Own*, Woolf argued, from a broadly feminist position that in literary scholarship, 'it is masculine values that prevail,' she wrote: 'This is an important book, the critic assumes, because it deals with war. This is an insignificant book because it deals with the feelings of women in a drawing-room. A scene in a battle-field is more important than a scene in a shop' (Woolf 1993c, 67). Bennett, like Woolf, deals with both, and like Woolf, he privileges the mundane over the earth-shattering. Moreover, unlike Wells, Bennett has no overt 'programme' of didacticism in his fiction unless it be that empathy is what makes us human. Indeed, he once wrote to Wells about the differences in their world view. In contrast to Wells, he wrote in 1905:

> I have no passion for Justice ... there we come to the 'difference between our minds'. I look down from a height on the show and contemplate a passion for justice much as I contemplate the other ingredients.

Whereas you are simply a passion for justice incarnate. You aren't an artist, except insofar as you disdainfully make use of art for your reforming ends ... Like all great reformers you are inhuman ... You are not really interested in individual humanity. (Bennett in Wilson 1960, 123–4)

In the image of the author looking 'down from a height' at the world he creates, Bennett represents himself as interested in patterns rather than alterations. Like Stephen Dedalus in *A Portrait of the Artist as Young Man*, Bennett's persona 'like the God of creation, remains within or behind or beyond or above his handiwork, invisible, refined out of existence, indifferent, paring his fingernails' (Joyce 1992b, 235). Except, perhaps that he is not indifferent. No one needs to get out their cheque book to complete a Bennett novel, but there is a message in Bennett's fiction, and it is concerned with empathy, with sympathetic identification with character rather than judgement of either character, as with Galsworthy, or of the social circumstances that have formed them, as with Wells. The interest in individual humanity is what counts, and there are worse things to suggest to one's readers.

In the end, though, the real difference between Woolf and the Edwardian novelists of whom she apparently disapproved, is not to do with *what* they tell in their fictions, but to do with *the way that they tell it*. Their visions may each be complex, but they continue to 'tell what they saw in a clear way' as the Victorian novelists had done. No one needs an academic training to read Wells or Bennett or Galsworthy; but most inexperienced readers need at least some help with Woolf and Joyce. 'The Edwardian tools are the wrong ones for us to use,' wrote Woolf in 'Mr Bennett and Mrs Brown' because they lay too much stress 'on the fabric of things' (Woolf 1992a, 82). The new generation, in contrast, felt hemmed in by this materiality and was forced to find a new language in which to express a slightly different reality: 'Signs of this are everywhere apparent. Grammar is violated; syntax disintegrated ...' (84). It is an effort to read the new things as the new novelists and poets grapple towards an adequate way of expressing the reality of Mrs Brown, and this requires the patience of the reader: 'do not expect at present as complete and satisfactory presentment of her. Tolerate the spasmodic and obscure, the fragmentary, the failure' (87). But even Woolf admits a certain nostalgia for the comfortable reading offered by Galsworthy, Wells and Bennett. As she reads the lines of T. S. Eliot's poetry, she writes, 'I cry out, I confess, for the old decorums, and envy the indolence of my ancestors who, instead of spinning madly through mid-air, dreamt quietly in the shade with a book' (85).

To my mind, the pendulum of academic taste has swung too far towards the Georgians, and forgetting to read the Edwardians is to privilege the tastes of the elite at the expense of a more democratic vision in content, certainly, but also in terms of form.

Notes

1. 'As wide as Broad Street' is slang for 'worldly wise', most likely with criminal intent. Toffs are the upper classes.
2. The 1880s and 1890s saw an explosion of sociological reporting on the conditions of the poor in London's East End. Andrew Mearns's *The Bitter Cry of Outcast London* (1883), George Sims's *How the Poor Live* (1883) and William Booth's *In Darkest England and the Way Out* (1890) are just some of the more famous titles of social investigative work undertaken in the period.
3. In the UK, rates were the local taxes levied on householders to pay for local services such as education, lighting and refuse collection.
4. This review appeared anonymously in the *Saturday Review*; it is Anderson who directed my attention to its having been written by Wells.
5. 'Penny dreadfuls' were cheap comic books, mostly containing stories of a sensational, and often violent kind, marketed specifically at working-class adolescent boys. Throughout the 1880s and 1890s, there were campaigns to prevent their apparently pernicious influence on the youth of the day, and Christian organizations in particular tried to publish – with limited success – their own newspapers for the same market, but with a much more pious agenda. To find out more about reading for boys in the late nineteenth century, see Bristow 1991.
6. The phrase literally means 'covered woman' and refers to the legal position of married women at this time; a woman's legal identity was 'covered' by that of her husband, who represented her in all legal matters.
7. Continuity is also signalled by the fact that no fewer than four separate characters have the name Jolyon Forsyte in the three volumes that make up the complete saga. Names similarly represent continuity in Woolf's *Between the Acts* (1941) where 'half the ladies and gentlemen present would have said, "*Adsum*; I'm here in place of my grandfather or great-grandfather"' (1992d, 47), and as they also do in Lawrence's *The Rainbow*, where Tom and Will Brangwens proliferate.
8. British law did not recognize rape within marriage until 1992. Nonetheless, George Forsyte guesses what has happened in his cousin's house from Bosinney's disconnected ravings, and strongly disapproves of him. Soames might have 'rights' as a husband; but he offends against the code of chivalry expected of the English gentleman when he uses violence against his wife.

2 Rhymers and Reasoners: Poetry in Transition

Most of the poetry that we now identify as 'Victorian' through the multiple anthologies that exist to chart the period had been published before 1870, and the period 1880–1914, though 'rich in poetry … was less dominated by evident giants than the high-Victorian period' (Bergonzi 1980, ix). As with fiction in the period, there is the sense of a missing generation between the heights of High Victorianism and the heights of High Modernism, though also as with fiction, that missing generation is heavily populated. The absence of 'giants', however, means that most university students study a particular canon of Victorian poetry followed by a canon of Modernists. Any brief trawl through anthologies designed to map this period produces the impression that there is no 'authorized version' of late nineteenth and early twentieth centuries – no readily agreed canon of 'greatness' between 1870 and 1905, 1910 or 1914: indeed, there is not even much agreement about the dates.[1] The smallness of the lyric poems, and the unsustained achievements of the poets imply a period of minor works.

The lyric has been prevalent for many centuries in poetry; but the late Victorians largely wrote lyrics that emphasized the loss of communal values. They registered their own uncertainties in individual poems that were often impressionistic and subjective in tenor, avoiding grand statements of shared certainties. One of the things that characterizes lyric poetry in Anglophone traditions is self-consciousness in emotion. A poem is a factitious thing, made or 'crafted' (the word poetry derives from the Greek *poeisis*, meaning craft). The inheritance that came from Victorian misreadings of the Romantic poets was to disguise that craftiness by claiming that poems spoke of natural emotions in the language really used by men in their everyday speech. No poem has ever been 'the spontaneous overflow of powerful feelings' (Wordsworth 1988, 297), even if those feelings are also 'recollected in tranquillity'. A poem is always a self-consciously constructed artefact that may or may not express an emotion. There is no simple connection between the words and the feelings, and the late Victorians had learned that from their predecessors, and perhaps particularly from Browning's habits of disguise and impersonation in dramatic monologues and dramatic lyrics. They were becoming increasingly aware that language itself is not God-given, that it is not simply referential, and that it is often purely arbitrary. Throughout the Victorian period poets had wrestled with these facts, and the wrestling continued into the later period.

The poet who perhaps best expresses both the pleasures and the anxieties that a post-Wordsworthian sensibility to language can bring is Gerard Manley Hopkins (1844–89). Hopkins is in many ways the most transitional figure of them all. He lived his entire life as a Victorian subject, but only became known as a major poet thirty years after his death, when his poems were published in 1918. This has led to a great deal of confusion in critical assessments of his work. Because he appeared before the public just as Modernism began to take wing, he has not always been placed in his proper context as a nineteenth-century writer, often being read as a kind of honorary contemporary of T. S. Eliot. At the same time, as a Catholic priest who had to express faith in his poetry if he was to justify writing it all, Hopkins was partially anachronistic even in his own time, a period when religious faith amongst the educated was certainly waning. As Isobel Armstrong observes, 'Hopkins was the last poet to hold a strictly theological account of the logos, the authority of the Word made flesh through the incarnation of Christ' (Armstrong 1993, 420). Or, to put it another way, Hopkins believed that language came from God, and could and should be used above all for the expression of the faith in God's presence. Thus although his poems are startlingly individualistic, they are also expressive of the kinds of communal values, especially a shared faith in God's creation, that eluded other late Victorians.

For this reason, there is no sense in which Hopkins's typical poetic language is that really used by men; nor is he typical of either of the periods – the Victorian or the modern – to which he appears to belong. If poems are prayers, they must make use of the language of ritual, the defamiliarizing effects of a language contorted out of its usual shape. His writing is grammatically, syntactically and semantically bizarre in the service of expressing the immediacy of God's presence to the speaker. The poems give a deeply misleading sense of spontaneity, a fabricated or manufactured authenticity that is utterly dependent on the self-conscious manipulation of linguistic resources. (These words, however, do not necessarily imply dishonesty or insincerity, nor a negative judgement.

They would have done to the Victorians, but I am not a Victorian, and am interested in the visibility and invisibility of Hopkins's craft.) In poems that exuberantly describe his faith in the righteousness and beauty of God's creation, Hopkins's persona dramatically enunciates the belief that even if ordinary language is arbitrary, conventional and non-referential, faith makes language meaningful, and prayerful poetic language therefore can and does recreate God's world. 'God's Grandeur' for example, begins with a simple statement of faith: 'The world is charged by the grandeur of God./It will flame out like shining from shook foil;/It gathers to a greatness like the ooze of oil/Crushed' (Hopkins 1985, 27). This is a poem filled with excited realization that God is present in his world. The excitement, as Richard Dellamorra has observed (Dellamorra 1990, 53), is sexual in its imagery, and homoerotic in its connotations, though those connotations are disguised. The poem is pious on its surface, but it is also an expression of sublimated desire where God takes the place of the beloved in the conventional love poem.[2] The reader alert to nuance – and the classically educated reader – might notice the coding of sublimation; other readers need see only enthusiasm.

The force of the poem's emotion comes from the very deliberate manipulation of some of the less logical linguistic resources at the poet's disposal: onomatopoeia where one gets the (of course, false) impression of sound echoing sense so that language really does feel as if it refers to reality; alliteration and assonance which operate, as it were, hypnotically, suspending logic on a wave of emotion; neologism, where Hopkins coins new words from old to renew the possibility of meaning from the broken husks of old ones; and by an exuberant use of form in which metrical patterns and poetic forms such as the sonnet are stretched to breaking point. Faith, like desire, is not strictly logical, and there is a process of seduction at work in the making of the poem in Hopkins's attempts to persuade or mesmerize himself and his readers into sharing his belief. Whilst his faith in God was secure, so was his faith in language. 'God's Grandeur' remains secure in its pos-session of language *because* it remains secure in its faith: there is a causal relationship between faith and expressivity. Although 'all is seared with trade; bleared, smeared with toil', Victorian preoccupa-tions with the effects of industrialization, the evidence of God's pres-ence in the world is unmistakeable, imaged in the daily return of the morning which comes about *because* of the Holy Ghost's 'bright wings' which protectively enclose the world. This is an intensely realized reli-gious poem which begins and ends with God's continuing creation of the earth which 'flames out' in the morning sun. Man has only to believe and everything will resolve itself.

The intensity of this faith and of its expression, however, has its disadvantages. As Rainer Emig has argued in a discussion of another of Hopkins's most famous poems, 'Pied Beauty':

> The effect of [Hopkins's] condensed imagery is paradoxical. It is striking and original, but it is also alienating and disturbing. It creates the impression of precision, but the neological status of the images prevents their integration into established units of meaning and creates an uncertainty that defeats the precision while creating it. (Emig 1995, 16)

The structure of Hopkins's poetry, of his faith, and of the language in which it is expressed, is precarious. Should any part of the equation fail – especially if there are moments of doubt about God's presence – language is not enough by itself to recreate and re-evoke faith. Towards the end of his life, when Hopkins was unhappy and ill in Dublin, he had a crisis of faith in which his ability to see God at all was severely damaged. The downside of the euphoric pleasure of 'God's Grandeur' can be found in a remarkable poem such as 'Carrion Comfort'. Where in other poems Hopkins used a tortuous syntax to express the miraculous presence of God, and to make his reader *see* that presence *in a new way* (our failure is to form habits), this poem is based on a syntax that almost defeats the principle of communication. The poem's first sentence – 'Not, I'll not, carrion comfort, Despair, not feast on thee,/ Not untwist – slack they may be – these last strands/In me or, most weary cry *I can no more*' (Hopkins 1985, 62) – contains four 'nots'. On the principle that the double negative makes a positive, the simplest paraphrase of the lines should be: I will not despair. But the cumulative effect of those 'nots' has precisely the opposite effect, expressing desperation, not the certainty of faith. This is picked up in the next sentence where the speaker 'can ... not choose not to be', not at all the same thing as choosing 'to be'. The poem might provide the standard theological answer as to why the speaker is suffering: God is testing his faith. It might also argue that the period of near despair is over (it is 'done darkness'). The poem's last words, however, undermine the apparently positive direction of the argument: the speaker has lain 'wrestling with (my God!) my God', words in which he alludes to Christ's penultimate words on the cross – 'My God, My God, Why hast thou forsaken me?' The absence of the question from the poem does not mean that the question has not been asked.

In their despair, Hopkins's so-called 'Terrible Sonnets' speak of the fear of meaninglessness. He had tried to create a world which spoke of a first and last cause of all things, a coherent, stable reality which was coherent and stable despite its multiplicity[3] because of the existence of God. Without the sense of God's presence, all other stabilities fail; where once language anchored the poet into reality, the Terrible Sonnets express the failure of linguistic referentiality. If Wordsworth was a man speaking to men, Hopkins was a man speaking with God; with the loss of faith, his poetry becomes a soliloquy of despair.

As noted in the Introduction, Hopkins had known Pater, and been partially 'seduced' by his thinking whilst he was a student at Oxford in the 1860s. Although he consciously rejected Pater's philosophy in his conversion to Catholicism, there are clear elements of Paterian sensibility in Hopkins's poems. When God withdraws from the world – or is withdrawn through loss of faith – Pater's words in *The Renaissance* seem strangely appropriate: 'the whole scope of observation is dwarfed into the narrow chamber of the individual mind. Experience ... is ringed round ... by that thick wall of personality through which no real voice has ever pierced on its way to us'; impressions are reduced to 'the impression of the individual in his isolation, each mind keeping as a solitary prisoner its own dream of the world' (Pater ed. Hill 1980, 187–8). For Pater, this isolation could be creative; for Hopkins it was disastrous. Emotions and impressions are subjective, and their expression cannot always bring together the consciousness of reader and writer in a common faith, or in communal values, or even into any kind of *commun*ication. For Hopkins this was loss, not opportunity. There can be no seeing things steadily and seeing them whole, nor much telling in a plain way. The pleasures of existence are momentary, and for that moment's sake. Stability and permanence are finally illusions. Hopkins's anguished articulation of that position is one of the reasons that he has often been claimed as a Modernist poet rather than as a Victorian one, for the loss of faith in language is one of the key definitions of Modernism; but we should not forget that loss of faith and the conditions that produced it are Victorian in origin.

Two kinds of story dominate the history of this period. On the one hand, there is the myth of the Yellow Nineties and its aftermath, the story of the writers mythologized by W. B. Yeats in his *Autobiographies* as 'The Tragic Generation' of decadent poets. This is a story of tragedy and wasted talent, of alcoholism, suicide, conversions to Catholicism, and a commitment to the seamier side of life, which ended, depending on which chronology one chooses, with the Wilde Trials in 1895, or, with the turn of the century: after 1900, wrote Yeats in the Introduction to *The Oxford Book of Modern Verse* (1936), 'everybody got down off his stilts; henceforth nobody drank absinthe with his black coffee; nobody went mad; nobody committed suicide; nobody joined the Catholic Church ... or if they did, I have forgotten' (qtd in Beckson 1992, 93). In this version of the period, it is as if tragedy had been a fashion that the bright young things had suffered for, and then got over when the next fashion came along. On the other hand stand the anti-decadent writers – the healthy jingoists who wrote poetry asserting the healthy manliness of British culture, who celebrated empire and warfare, and dealt with life by imbibing copious amounts of good common sense in which British superiority was taken for granted, and language was understood as capable of adequately representing the world.

Neither story makes much space for women writers. And the either/or construction – poets were either decadents or patriots – not only leaves women poets out of the story, but also fails to see the connections between the two groups. Yeats, for example, who certainly associated with the tragic generation poets, and was responsible for giving them that name, was a major founding influence on the Rhymers' Club, a poetic group who met at the Cheshire Cheese pub in Fleet Street from 1890 onwards to discuss each other's poems in an atmosphere conducive to Art with a capital 'A'. But Yeats was also friendly with W. E. Henley (1849–1903), editor of *The Scot's Observer* (later *The National Observer*, and eventually *The New Review*), who is usually associated with a more muscular and masculine frame of mind. Moreover, in a very important article, 'The Decadent Movement in Literature' (1893), the poet and critic who did most to define decadence, Arthur Symons (1865–1945), identified Henley amongst the British Decadents, comparing his work to that of Walter Pater, as well as juxtaposing Henley's poems with the writings of Francophone experimental novelists, poets and playwrights such as Joris-Karl Huysmans, Stéphane Mallarmé, Paul Verlaine and Maurice Maeterlinck (Symons in Nassaar 1999, 223–36). The borders seem rather permeable when the networks of friendships, enmities, influences and quarrels are examined in any detail.

The wealth of materials means that this chapter cannot possibly exhaust the material, nor hope to provide more than a very partial picture. This chapter touches on three basic groupings – the poets of rural nostalgia; those who focussed on the city; and women writers who sometimes also belonged to the other groups, but who had particular difficulties to contend with in the period, whether they wrote of

the country or the city. Many other groups exist, and I make no claim
to having the last word. All three of these groupings, the rural, the
urban and the feminine, have their importance in the story of poetic
modernism, though it is the urban group that has had the longest lasting legacy for as Rita Felski has suggested, the gender of modernity and
of modernism is implicitly masculine (Felski 1995, 1–6) and the preferred landscape of modernism is the city. Women's place in either
landscape therefore, as well as in the literary world of poetry, is
extremely troubled.

Country

In *The Country and the City*, Raymond Williams argues:

> 'Country' and 'city' are very powerful words .... In English, 'country' is
> both a nation and a part of a 'land'; 'the country' can be the whole
> society or its rural area .... On the country has gathered the idea of a nat-
> ural way of life: of peace, innocence, and simple virtue. On the city has
> gathered the idea of an achieved centre of learning, communication,
> light. Powerful hostile associations have also developed: on the city as a
> world of noise, worldliness and ambition; on the country as a place of
> backwardness, ignorance, limitation. A contrast between country and
> city, as fundamental ways of life, reaches back into classical times.
> (Williams 1973, 1)

Despite the potentially negative associations that one might have
about 'the country' meaning rural landscape British literature, history
and culture are powerfully informed by a nostalgic version of the countryside constructed as organic, stable, secure and quasi-Edenic. The
fact that 'country' means both nation state and rural area in the
English language leads directly to the assumption that the state of rural
England and its communities is a direct reflection of the moral state of
the nation itself. Periods of agricultural decline, such as the one that
characterized the 1870s and 1880s, are read as symptomatic of the
failing moral and mental health of the nation. Further, whilst the city
can be understood – and at some points in history has been understood – as a centre of civilizing values, cities are at least as often constructed as centres of corruption. The mass of people that cities collect
into themselves, for instance, can easily become mobs, turning the
urban landscape into a space of barely suppressed potential violence
as in Stevenson's *The Strange Case of Dr Jekyll and Mr Hyde* (1886).

The veneer of fine house fronts only just disguises, in much of the rhetoric of the Victorian period, the brutality of animal man.

In addition, the word 'English' defines a language and a nation state. The meanings of 'country' and 'English' intersected for the Victorians in the word 'culture', which Matthew Arnold had defined for his contemporaries in *Culture and Anarchy* (1869). When 'culture' is used to describe artistic production and, by extension, the society in which that product arises, it is used in a metaphorical sense. Literally, culture means growth. Growth, whether a natural phenomenon or one encouraged by human interventions in plant or animal life, takes place seasonally. There are times of rapid growth (spring and summer), times of fruitfulness and harvest (autumn) and times of no growth at all, or indeed, decline – winter. As Linda Dowling has argued, language generally, and literary language particularly, was conceived of as an emblem of nationhood; the English language is the medium of English culture and English culture is the index of England's status as a nation state. Faith in the English language was to be taken as an index of the moral health of the nation. For many late Victorians the convergence of ideas about culture being subject to phases of both growth and decline, of language as subject to historical alteration for better and for worse, and of the countryside as a dangerously exposed repository for communal values, all of which were described by the word 'English', were symptomatic of a much wider decline in the status of the nation state. Anxieties about language are not just *about* language, in other words. Country, nation and culture are drawn together in a matrix of associations, and a falling away of any one of them leads to a diagnosis of decline or decadence in the others.

In a volume of poems aptly titled *Poems of Past and the Present* published in 1901, Thomas Hardy included one of his most anthologized pieces, 'The Darkling Thrush'. The poem is self-consciously dated '31 December 1900', signalling that it is a poem of transition between the old century and the new, since its date was the very last day of the nineteenth century. The speaker describes a freezing winter's evening in a bleak landscape. It is a time and a place that absolutely lacks joy: 'The tangled bine-stems [that] scored the sky/Like strings of broken lyres' (Hardy 1976, 62) stand as a rebuke to the Romantic tradition of poetry which had remained essential to the majority of poets and critics of the nineteenth century. Where Coleridge and Wordsworth had found inspiration in the natural world, Hardy's poem argues that no Aeolian harp will play a tune here – the lyre-strings are broken. And where Shelley and Keats had both taken birds (the skylark[4] and the nightingale respectively) as emblems for the unconscious 'natural' artistry that was their ideal, Hardy's thrush is almost comically feeble: 'aged…frail, gaunt, and small,/In blast-beruffled plume'. This bird sings as those other poetic birds had done in days of yore; but the poet is not inspired, commenting merely that the cheerful song might express 'Some blessed hope' of which he remains pessimistically 'unaware'. There is no message, moral or otherwise, just a last futile gesture (the bird, it is implied, is dying as it 'fling[s] its soul' into the evening) expressive merely of the bird's uncomplicated nature. The poem is clearly in part about the depressed condition of Thomas Hardy's implied speaker; but in the light of contemporary views about the representative nature of poetry, it is perhaps also about the Condition of England more generally, and about the fears of the unknown future of the twentieth century.

If Hardy eschews Romantic ideas about inspiration in this poem, if his keynote here and elsewhere is bitter pessimism, and his key tone is melancholic, he is nonetheless deeply imbued in the Romantic forms popularized by Wordsworth's *Lyrical Ballads* and defended in the 1800 Preface to the poems. The poems of *Past and Present* are largely ballads; many tell of rural life and of the natural landscape. Many make use, as Wordsworth had done, of an oral peasant tradition re-figured in literary form, and as John Wain has suggested Hardy's poems represent a 'channel whereby a vital popular tradition flows from a remote rural past to our modern world' (Wain 1976, 10). Or rather, they represent the attempt to recover that vital popular tradition for a generation which had lost contact with its roots in the oral, rural community. Hardy's poems are 'haunted' by the past of which they sing, and which they do not quite recuperate or recreate. Poetic language – even when it makes use of archaism, of old poetic forms, of the old stories of rural life – cannot quite bring back that past and the reconstructed security of its values. The apparently uncomplicated lives of the original ballad singers are evoked with nostalgic longing for that past, now irrecoverable in a world where modernity has caught up even with the agricultural labourer.

For most of the nineteenth century, the post-romantic generations of writers had taken Wordsworth as a touchstone for the values that poetry was supposed to express. Whatever their thoughts about some of the individual poems, and despite the fact that Tennyson owed more to Keats, and Browning owed more to Shelley than either did to Wordsworth, the Victorians had bought the myth of rural life that Wordsworth had retailed in the 1800 Preface to *Lyrical Ballads*. The moral seriousness of the poet's role that he identified there was one that sat easily with the moral earnestness of much Victorian thought. And his disgust with the city as a landscape of immorality and dangerous overstimulation seemed strangely prescient to the generations who saw unprecedented urbanization, to the extent that by the 1861 census, for the first time in human history, a clear majority of the population of Britain lived in an industrial, urban economy rather than in an agricultural, rural one. In the Preface, Wordsworth had argued that 'the increasing accumulation of men in cities, where the uniformity of their occupations produces a craving for extraordinary incident, which the rapid communication of intelligence hourly gratifies' was a cause of moral decline (Wordsworth 1988, 284). For that reason, he had turned to 'rural life' as the subject matter of his poems, because in the countryside life had a slower pace, people were unaffected by artificial stimuli, and they remained in touch with nature because their lives were regulated by the passing of the seasons, not by the fashions and shocking events that made city life so dangerous, nor by the mechanistic regulation of clock time in the factory. Wordsworth had faith not just that the content of poetry set in the countryside could act as a restorative to those who were forced to live pent up in the city, but also that the forms of the oral tradition of poetry, the peasant tradition modified by its contact with the poet's literate mind, would calm the jangled nerves of his own modern period. He could believe this in part because his faith in a beneficent God – and God's substitute on earth, Nature – was as yet unshaken by either the material conditions of a brutally urban life, or by the spiritual shift caused by Darwinian thought that later generations had to contend with. Wordsworth might well have found nature 'awful' in the sense of awe-inspiring as well as tranquilly beautiful, writing calmly in *The Prelude* that he had been fostered alike by the beauty of nature and by the fear of her power, but unlike his followers, he did not have to contend with evolutionary evidence of a nature 'red in tooth and claw', an amoral force that preached no moral message of consoling calm. In addition, by the end of the century the binary opposition of country and city as sites representing opposing values were also under threat from suburbanization. The boundaries between country and city were becoming increasingly permeable, as writers as diverse as H. G. Wells, E. M. Forster and D. H. Lawrence attested in their fiction, and as John Davidson's 'A Northern Suburb' describes as the aggressive encroachment of city on country:

> But here the whetted fangs of change
> Daily devour the old demesne –

The busy farm, the quiet grange,
The wayside inn, the village green.
(Davidson in Thornton and Thain 1997, 74)

The organic world of rural England is disappearing under 'gaudy yellow brick and red', as for Lawrence, the countryside of the East Midlands was an industrial landscape, pockmarked by collieries, at least as much as it was a space of rural calm and consolation.

One of the themes of the later Victorians who chose to take the natural world as the *mise-en-scène* of their poetry is that the faith that sustained earlier generations – whether this is religious faith, or merely the reconstruction of a Wordsworth-inspired pantheism – has passed away. For Hardy, in poems such as 'The Impercipient' (published in 1898, but written in the 1860s), there is loss of religious faith. The poetic persona, attending a service at a cathedral, is saddened by his inability to feel the simple faith that those around him clearly have access to. Their beliefs 'seem fantasies to me/And mirage-mists their Shining Land' (Hardy 1976, 44). Spring and the hopes that poetry has traditionally attached to that season have little place in Hardy's work where Autumn and Winter – endings, not beginnings – are much more central. The poems are elegies for lost time, not expressions of the conviction that time can redeem a painful emotion. In 'Neutral Tones' (1898), the tone is anything but neutral. The colours of winter are evoked, and the emotions that come from lost love have become absolutely entwined with those colours: 'keen lessons that love deceives.../... have shaped to me/Your face, and the God-curst sun, and a tree,/And a pond edged with grayish leaves' (20). The once-beloved face, the landscape, the season and the emotion all take their shape from each other, and the poem denies any escape from the circular argument that each of these elements is an absolute condition of each of the others. Spring is a long way off. The beloved 'did not come' in 'A Broken Appointment' (1901); she is a mere ghostly presence in 'The Voice' (1914), and may not even be so much a ghost as merely 'the breeze in its listlessness', suggesting that nature is cruelly deceptive to the emotions as well as physically cruel to the material man. In the ballad-type poems, too, love is about deceit. Young men do young women wrong, or vice versa, and it all ends badly. Poetry has no redemptive function. This is the nihilistic position that John Goode identifies as the 'offensive truth' of Hardy's works.

Similarly, the poems of A. E. Housman insist on loss. This is perhaps in part because the landscape in which the poems are set does not exist. Housman was not a Shropshire Lad himself, but came from Worcestershire, and 'his Shropshire was "not exactly a real place". It was more like "the Cambridge of Lycidas" ' (Bayley 1992, 3), or like the mythical Oxford of Arnold's 'Scholar Gypsy'. As such, it is a landscape that threatens constantly to dissolve. But it is also because Housman can never quite speak the homoerotic desires his persona feels. He associates the landscape with desire, but it is the desires of, and the desire for, doomed young men, and can never be fulfilled. Even when the speaker is surrounded by the evidence of Spring and is in the springtime of his youth, he is always reminded of the coming of Autumn and Winter, presenting Shelley's question in reverse: if it's spring now, winter cannot be far away. The narrowing down of emotion away from joy and into melancholy is expressed by Housman's narrowed vocabulary and the restraint of his prosody's simple sentences. In 'Loveliest of trees' (from *A Shropshire Lad*, 1896), spring is all around him in the blossom of trees 'wearing white for Eastertide', a doubled symbol of hope in conventional terms, for it suggests both a youthful rising of the sap, and the Christian belief in the Resurrection. Nonetheless, the speaker immediately turns to thoughts of his future death: 'Now, of my threescore years and ten,/Twenty will not come again'. The inevitability of time passing implies the inevitability of annihilation, so that even the carefree decision to go 'About the woodlands ... /To see the cherry hung with snow', is tinged with melancholy (Housman 1988, 24). Innocence is horribly caught up in experience at every turn; the precise tone of 'When I was one-and-twenty' is hard to discern, but even if it is a joke, it expresses a fairly bitter humour when the speaker describes getting, and ignoring, good advice not to fall in love; he has now discovered the truth of the warning that he should have kept his 'fancy free':

> When I was one-and-twenty
> I heard him say again,
> 'The heart out of the bosom
> Was never given in vain;
> 'Tis paid with sighs a plenty
> And sold for endless rue.'
> And I am two-and-twenty,
> And oh, 'tis true, 'tis true.
> (Housman 1988, 35)

Consummation either does not happen at all ('And the bridegroom all night through/Never turns him to the bride' [34]), or is unsatisfactory.

There will be no fulfilment here. As George Orwell commented on Housman's poetry in 'Inside the Whale' (1940), 'It is all more or less the same tune' (Orwell 1957, 22). And there is an element of truth in this. Although the poems are often very fine – and some of them are very beautiful – they also express a kind of arrested development (Orwell called them 'adolescent'). In fiction of the period, writers continually came up against the limitations of realism, and sought either new forms to express their ideas, or forced realism into a new shape to say what they wanted to say. By the same token, although I am a fan of Housman, the poems are stymied finally by the limited emotional range that is available when writers cannot break down the old conventions of content (the countryside, unattainable desire) or of form (the lyric ballad).

Woman

Orwell's commentary on Housman goes on: 'the unvarying sexual pessimism (the girl always dies or marries somebody else), seemed like wisdom to boys who were herded together in public schools and were half-inclined to think of women as something unattainable. Whether Housman ever had the same appeal for girls I doubt' (Orwell 1957, 23). What Orwell identifies as Housman's emotional immaturity might better be described as 'Victorian' in the sense that one of the problems that recurs in his poems is the unattainable woman inherited from a Victorian tradition of sexual repression.[5] Just as the countryside had changed – and nostalgia is all very well, but it does not admit of future developments – so too were women changing. Or rather the fact that they were not as they had been constructed by Victorian ideology was becoming increasingly apparent. Woman has usually been the central image of (male-authored) poetry, but has not traditionally been presented (or been able to present herself) as a subjective self in her own right. Yeats, describing the poets of the Rhymers' Club put it slightly differently from Orwell, but it comes to much the same thing. The young poets, he wrote:

> praised a desired woman and hoped that she would find amid their praise her very self, or at worst their very passion ... Woman herself was still in our eyes ... romantic and mysterious, still the priestess of her shrine ... [Lionel] Johnson's favourite phrase, that life is ritual, expressed something that was in some degree in all our thoughts, and how could life be ritual if woman had not her symbolical place? (Yeats 1955, 302)

But what about her real place? What about the idea that Woman, far from being an abstraction or a symbol, was actually a person in her own right, with thoughts and feelings of her own? It is a legacy of the Victorian concepts of femininity derived from uncritical readings of Ruskin and Patmore that for many male poets of the late Victorian period and of the early twentieth century, the ideal image of the Eternal Feminine was more important than the possibility of real women in their actual material and physical circumstances. In the New Woman fiction of the 1880s and 1890s as Chapter 5 suggests, prose writers described the problem of a female subjectivity that was hemmed in by the romantic expectations of masculinity. But the argument was much harder to make in poetry because of the way that poetry itself was understood in the period, and the ways in which it has been understood subsequently.

Most Victorian criticism belonged to an *ad hominem/ad feminam* tradition: the moral character of the author was deduced from the tenor of the writing. Women writers were attacked on the basis of their implied characters: a woman who wrote, especially if she wrote politically, was often dismissed as 'unwomanly' or unfeminine. She was attacked as an artist, but she was also attacked as a woman. Moreover, whilst one stream of late-nineteenth-century fashion followed Pater and valorized the concept of 'art for art's sake', and whilst the subsequent generation of Modernist arts preferred by the academy continued that tradition of valuing self-expression over protest, it was increasingly difficult for women poets who sought to articulate their discontent in poetic form to get an unbiased critical reading. The expression of discontent was for the Victorians unladylike, for the modernists inartistic. Similarly, in a critical tradition that defined the artist as suffering in and for isolation, women poets whose poetry had a communal intention, could not really be poets at all. And finally, there is the question of more recent reception in the university. Based on the academy's values, there is an ongoing problem about how to read poetry with an ostensible political purpose, a problem that has two main subheadings. On the one hand, politically inflected readings by critics committed to feminism are more difficult to accomplish for poetry than for prose because it is in the nature of poetry to be more obscure in its articulation of its message. On the other hand, however, the problem for critics looking at late-nineteenth-century women's poetry has also been that much of that poetry is anything but obscure. Its political messages are sometimes painfully on the surface of the poems, and in a critical world that has come to maturity by valuing

Modernist opacity, such clarity is read as a symptom of poetic failure. Either the poetics are a problem because they are too complicated for simple legibility; or the poems are a problem because they are too apparently simple to be dignified with the name of poetry.

A last problem for contemporary critics looking at the place of the woman poet between say 1880 and 1910 is a practical one. Women poets did publish widely during this period. They published single volumes of their own poems, and they published individual poems in feminist journals and periodicals as well as in the mainstream press. But because they have not been widely anthologized – and no single anthology devoted to women poets of the period has been published – the scholarly apparatus and the contextual background required for their appreciation by new readers is only just being constructed.[6] For women poets too, just as for their male counterparts, there are points of continuity with earlier models of poetry by women and by men. As Margaret Reynolds argues in her Introduction to the *Victorian Women Poets* anthology, in the early part of the century the publication of annuals and memory books provided both a professional forum in which women might publish their poems and a series of models for what poetry by women might look like. In some cases, these models merely replicate the standard norms of feminine propriety leading to a stereotype of feminine poetry based on conventional piety, love, marriage and flowers (Leighton and Reynolds 1995, xxiv–xxxiv). At the same time, however, as Leighton and Reynolds's anthology amply demonstrates, there are also poems of protest against the tradition that sees women as merely muses for a male-defined art; and in some cases, there are attempts to produce distinctively different voices from a female rather than a feminine point of view. In her Introduction, Leighton goes on to examine three of the recurring metaphors of the Victorian woman poet: the mask, the picture and the mirror. The mask, she suggests, is often used playfully as an emblem which subverts the essentialist notion of femininity – gender becomes performance, not biology. The picture, where women sometimes write from the point of view of the model for a male art, and sometimes write from a position outside the frame, reconstructs images of femininity in different forms. The mirror is a space of an often painful self-consciousness (xxvi–xxxvii).

Women poets constructed similar arguments to their contemporaries in prose fiction in their writings, resisting the images of Woman as witch, fairy, angel, whore, or any other figure of masculine fantasy, and demanding that their 'very selves' be accorded cultural space. In Constance Naden's poem 'Love's Mirror', the argument is clear:

> I live with love encompassed round,
> And glowing light that is not mine,
>   And yet am sad; for, truth to tell,
>   It is not I you love so well;
> Some fair Immortal, robed and crowned,
> You hold within your heart's dear shrine.
>
> Cast out the Goddess! let me in;
>   Faulty I am, yet all your own,
>   But this bright phantom you enthrone
> Is such as mortal may not win.
> (Naden in Thornton and Thain 1997, 27)

The beloved loves an image of his own making, not the real woman before him. This is not only limiting for the woman, it is also arrogant of the man – the 'bright phantom', the ideal woman that he has constructed is beyond his capacity to 'win'. The reflected glory of the image returns to the image-maker. The only answer for the woman is iconoclasm, but breaking the conventional images makes it difficult for readers to respond.

It is as difficult to make generalizations about women's poetry of the period as it is to make generalizations about male-authored verse. There are, however, strands of argument that point out the limitations of woman's 'symbolical place'. 'How nice to be a human creature,/Get cross and have a will!' says a doll in a toyshop in May Kendall's 'The Toy Shop' (1894), connecting intertextually to Ibsen's Nora from *A Doll's House*, who was not supposed to have a will of her own, and yet who notoriously shocked Europe when she slammed the door on infantilizing domesticity (Thornton and Thain 1997, 29). The men who think of women as ideal are themselves 'geese', a term very often used of women to describe their inherent silliness, in Edith Nesbit's 'The Goose-Girl' (33), and men certainly have no monopoly of wisdom or of philosophy in Naden's 'Love versus Learning' (1894), where the newly wed bride has just discovered her husband's intellectual shortcomings: 'He's neither a sage nor a bard', she notes, and all his vaunted wisdom, marked by his 'Oxford MA' is merely 'the usual knowledge ... /He formed his opinions at College,/Then why should he think any more?' (37). In a remarkable reversal of the usual gender stereotypes, however, Naden's speaker is caught between her common sense and her desire.

Her husband may be a fool, but he is a good lover, and 'compliments so scientific' as his view that 'love is his law of attraction' 'Recapture my fluttering heart' (38). Desire makes a fool of her as much as it does of him.

Late Victorian women's poetry is perhaps caught up in a paradox. On the evidence of Thornton and Thain's and Leighton and Reynolds's anthologies, it often expresses dissatisfaction with the world as it currently stands, asking its readers to see that world anew, and to remake it in a different image. The goddess is continually being cast out and replaced with a much more human figure. Unlike the rural poetry discussed above, it is often explicitly oriented towards a better future, not towards a lost lamented past. In poetry such as that written by the composite figure of Michael Field, pen name of niece and aunt couple Edith Cooper (1862–1913) and Katharine Bradley (1846–1914), it also expresses a point of view that had never been heard before: female sexual desire is given its own voice; more specifically, Michael Field's speaker very often speaks a desire that is entirely woman-identified, or lesbian in orientation. 'Maids, not to you my mind doth change' speaks woman to women:

> … ye to manifold desire
> Can yield response, ye know
> When for long, museful days I pine,
> The presage at my heart divine;
> To you I never breathe a sign
> Of inward want or woe.
>
> When injuries my spirit bruise,
> Allaying virtue ye infuse
> With unobtrusive skill:
> And if care frets ye come to me
> As fresh as nymph from stream or tree,
> And with your soft vitality
> My weary bosom fill.
> (Field in Leighton and Reynolds 1995, 490)

The woman–woman desire is clearly spoken, but it is also masked by a Greek epigraph from Sappho which lends the poem the respectability that comes with classical civilization. The poem also therefore disguises the speakers and their own desires. It also does so in a language which is largely very straightforward and which makes no formal experiment. The shock of the new in this case depends to a large extent on the contextual knowledge that the speaker is female (the poem is based on a translation from Sappho), and that the poets were lovers, rather than on the poem itself. If the speaker is imagined as male, indeed, the poem partially reinscribes the ideology of the separate spheres in which the female beloved assuages the weary warrior's worldly pain, though the fact that there is more than one beloved maiden (the poem is addressed to 'Maids' in the plural) somewhat alters the Victorian ideal. The desire is present, but only half glimpsed: now you see it, now you don't. That elusiveness of the voice of feminine sexuality is part of the complex contexts for the woman poet.

One of Michael Field's best poems, 'A Palimpsest', dramatizes this elusiveness. A palimpsest is an overwritten text, originally made of wax. The impressions of the first piece of writing might be faintly discernible through subsequent rewritings – or may become completely illegible. This poem articulates much of the ambivalence of the woman poet, forced to respond to masculine models of Woman, yet seeking also to express what a woman might potentially be at some undefined future time:

> ... The rest
> Of our life must be a palimpsest –
> The old writing written there the best.
>
> In the parchment hoary
> Lies a golden story,
> As 'mid secret feather of a dove,
> As 'mid moonbeams shifted through a cloud:
>
> Let us write it over,
> O my lover,
> For the far Time to discover,
> As 'mid secret feathers of a dove,
> As 'mid moonbeams shifted through a cloud!
> (Field 1908, 180)[7]

These woman poets cannot be seen steadily or whole, the poem suggests. The figure of the palimpsest, which is overwritten by subsequent generations, brings together past and future. The best poetry we have written – or the best poetry that has ever been written – the speaking persona suggests, is in the past and it will only be rediscovered by the future – the 'far Time'. The glimpses of the best work afforded to the future will be fleeting, and the golden story will never be completely known. The poem's opening in ellipsis means that the reader has no access to the story's beginning; and the ending belongs to the future. The metaphors of secret feathers and moonbeams advertise the fantasmatic and tenuous nature of the voices that speak from the past;

they also speak in veiled terms of an erotic intimacy that is hinted but not vouchsafed to us. Fulfilment for both reader and writer is infinitely suspended or deferred and it makes for an eroticism that teasingly does not quite rise to the surface.

Comparing a poem like this to Hopkins's effusive self-expression tells us a lot about gender and the gendering of poetry more specifically. The poets who were Michael Field also became Catholics in later life, and that is part of the context of this poem, since religious faith required them to relinquish their sexual desires for each other and to replace them with chastity. The past poetry was better because it was more pleasurable to write and more directly descriptive of pleasure is one possible reading of the palimpsest, implying a real ambiguity at the heart of their conversion. Michael Field's religious poetry is poetry of repression and renunciation, not of sublimated and sexualized fulfilment in faith. Although Leighton argues that a poem such as 'Prologue' (1893, titled 'It was deep April' in Leighton and Reynolds 1995, 497) 'records the two poets' pact of love and work with a free and informal openness which, while it disarms the censor, also discourages a purely innocent reading' (Leighton 1992, 209), disarming the censor – self-censorship as well as misleading other readers – is more important than discouraging innocent readings in a way that is very seldom true of Hopkins's poems. For, as Leighton has already described, Michael Field lived with the ongoing possibility of social and critical rejection because of the collaborative nature of the work, and because of the lesbian erotics of its creators. If for Hardy and Housman consummation belonged to the past, and if for Hopkins it was a persistently sublimated emotion, for Michael Field desire was future oriented: it would be fulfilled when the goddess had been cast out, when social and critical proprieties had passed away, 'no, not there ... no, not yet', as Forster put it in another context (Forster 1989c, 316).

City

> To speak against London is no longer fashionable. The earth as an artistic cult has had its day, and the literature of the near future will probably ignore the country and seek inspiration from the town. (Forster 1989a, 116)

Thus wrote E. M. Forster in *Howards End* (1910), though his prediction is belated since poets had been feverishly writing about London for more than thirty years. As early as 1874 James Thomson had published 'City of Dreadful Night', which describes London as a kind of hellish nightmare vision, though for some later writers it became a dream-scape rather than a place of gothic horror. As Thornton notes, the pop-ularity of London as a subject for poetry in the 1890s can be easily discerned by listing the titles of the numerous volumes which made the city their subject: such titles include 'Amy Levy's *A London Plane-Tree* (1889), W. E. Henley's *London Types* (1898) and *London Voluntaries* (1893), Laurence Binyon's two series of *London Visions* (1896 and 1899), Ernest Rhys's *A London Rose* (1894), John Davidson's *Fleet Street Eclogues* (1893) and Arthur Symons's *London Nights* (1895), to name only those books whose titles advertise their interest' (Thornton and Thain 1997, 68). When T. S. Eliot published *The Waste Land* (1922), an aggressively urban poem describing the aridity of modern city life, he was not 'making it new' so much as referring back to the already estab-lished traditions of urban poetry made by his immediate predecessors.

What such texts announce is that a city is not, in Raymond Williams's memorable phrase, a 'knowable community' (Williams 1984, 14). Actually, it is probably true that villages were not entirely knowable communities either, but Williams's argument in *The English Novel from Dickens to Lawrence* focuses attention on the fact that a city street is more radically unknowable or illegible than a village lane. The peo-ple in it are not people one knows at all, unless one accidentally meets a familiar face. In the city, work and home are separated, often by great distances; in the city, a shifting population means that one need not know one's neighbours at all; its built-up environment, its crowded life, its hurried activities all mean that no one can see it steadily or see it whole. One of the speakers of *The Waste Land* watches the crowds flowing over London Bridge, a group which is not a community, and sees them as the damned (Eliot 1963, 65). The poem expresses despair about contemporary conditions, but it also suggests that those condi-tions are eternal – that they have always existed, and that they are likely to continue to exist, even if they continue to exist in slightly dif-ferent forms. As Edmund Wilson wrote in a contemporary review and attempted explanation of the poem, the waste land of the title is both a mythological place and contemporary London: 'Mr Eliot hears in his own parched cry the voices of all the thirsty men of the past.' The poem's message is despairing: 'not only is life sterile and futile, but men have tasted its sterility and futility a thousand times before' (Wilson in Grant 1982, 140–1). The horror of modernity does not even have the benefit of being original.

Other poets, though, had different views of the urban landscape. W. E. Henley, whose two collections *London Voluntaries* (1893) and

London Types (1897) are often indeed pretty grim in their evocation of the specific urban spaces associated with illness, also writes in a lyrical vein about the beauty of city streets. An early autumn afternoon is described in the 'Scherzando' of *London Voluntaries,* as an astonishing vision, bathed in golden light – ''Tis El Dorado – El Dorado plain,/The Golden City!' (Thornton and Thain 1997, 77). The next movement, 'Largo e mesto' is much less positive, describing the effects of an east wind through the city, a wind that brings 'a cloud unclean/Of excremental humours' and which 'settles down/To the grim job of throttling London Town' (78). But it is not the fault of the city that the city is horrible in this poem; the horror is caused by the wind not the place.

In Henley's more personal poems that describe his own experiences of hospitals and their inhabitants (he had lost a leg as a child, and was threatened with the loss of his other leg in young manhood), it is clear that it is his sickness that is to blame for the often-bitter tone. Amongst the most famous of the poems is one called 'Waiting', which describes a hospital waiting room:

> A square, squat room (a cellar on promotion),
> Drab to the soul, drab to the very daylight;
> Plasters astray in unnatural-looking tinware;
> Scissors and lint and apothecary's jars.
>
> Here, on a bench a skeleton would writhe from,
> Angry and sore, I wait to be admitted:
> Wait till my heart is lead upon my stomach,
> While at their ease two dressers do their chores.
>
> One has a probe – it feels to me a crowbar.
> A small boy sniffs and shudders after bluestone.[8]
> A poor old tramp explains his poor old ulcers.
> Life is (I think) a blunder and a shame.
> (Henley 1898, 4)

The architecture and the incidental articles within it are all grim. The people who populate this place – including the poem's speaker – are by definition sick. That this is the individual's view of his milieu is emphasized in part by his personal interjections into the poem: he waits to be admitted, he thinks that life is a blunder and a shame. Something is out of joint here, signalled by the fact that the poem's remarkably regular rhythm is unmatched by the rhymes that such a rhythm leads readers to expect. In the wider context of the numerous hospital poems however (Henley was hospitalized for over twenty months in the early 1870s whilst doctors battled to save his remaining leg), it is clear that this is a passing mood. In other poems he describes the medical staff, the cleaners, the wound-dressers, and other patients, and the tone of many of those poems is relatively cheerful. 'Children: Private Ward' for example describes two sick little boys who 'eat, and laugh, and sing, and fight, all day', and who 'play/At Operations' (28), making light of their illnesses. Only dying patients, his own pain and the hospital's surroundings provoke Henley's despair. The condition of modernity need not be that life is sterile and futile after all.

Henley's urban poems even when they are lyrical are also realistic. They describe what is there to be seen. Other poets tend towards a more impressionistic vision, sometimes celebrating their impressions, sometimes disapproving of them, but usually aestheticizing them. Oscar Wilde's 'Impression du Matin' (1882) denies any stable point of view. In what is certainly a reference to Whistler's impressionist paintings, he describes a vision of the city at dawn as 'The Thames nocturne of blue and gold/Changed to a Harmony in grey'.[9] The fog of the morning turns the substantial buildings of the cityscape into fantasmatic images – thus the dome of St Paul's cathedral looms 'like a bubble o'er the town'. The morning is a time of hope and life renewed in the poem, except in its final stanza where:

> ... one pale woman all alone,
> The daylight kissing her wan hair,
> Loitered beneath the gas lamps' flare,
> With lips of flame and heart of stone.
> (Wilde 1994, 862)

The modernity of the city is signalled in the presence of the gas lamp, which contrasts with the quasi-pastoral images earlier in the poem, when a barge laden with 'ochre-coloured' hay had docked, and when country wagons had arrived in the city, presumably bringing provisions, and a bird had sung. The lone woman is clearly a prostitute with the flame lips and the hardened heart acting as a kind of shorthand for her profession. Wilde's speaker makes no judgement; he simply observes the fact of her existence, though elsewhere in his urban poetry, notably in 'The Harlot's House', the mechanization of an industrial city has uncanny effects – people become puppets ('like wire-pulled automatons', 'clockwork puppets', 'a horrible marionette' [867]) – and stands as an emblem of the unnaturalness of human relationships in this landscape.

There are, though, also cases of poets who unashamedly celebrated their impressions of the city. In 1892, Arthur Symons published a volume of poems entitled *Silhouettes*. The poems are mostly brief vignettes of city life in which Symons's persona takes an intense pleasure in the artifice of the urban world and in the momentary glimpses of other people, especially the girls he meets in the streets, in cafés, in theatres and music halls, and on public transport such as trains and buses. In 'City Nights 1; In the Train', the speed of transportation is evoked, not with anxiety but with pleasure:

> Night, and the rush of the train,
> A cloud of smoke through the town,
> Scaring the life of the streets;
> And the leap of the heart again,
> Out into the night, and down
> The dazzling vista of streets!
> (Symons in Thornton and Thain 1997, 73)

It is the impression that counts, and there is no attempt to make a message out of it. This was problematic for some reviewers and even for some of Symons's associates. As Yeats recalled, Symons's poems made Lionel Johnson angry 'because [they] would substitute for [intellect] Parisian impressionism, "a London fog, the blurred tawny lamplight, the red omnibus, the dreary rain, the depressing mud, the glaring gin-shop, the slatternly shivering woman, three dexterous stanzas telling you that and nothing more"' (Yeats 1955, 307). This is a pretty good description of Symons's volume. The poems describe cityscapes, and take a frankly sensuous pleasure in the faces of girls who pass by (they may be slatternly, but they seldom shiver), who dance in music halls, and who meet the stage-door Johnnies after the show. There is indeed, an impressionist focus on artifice – on made-up faces, strong perfumes – and on short-lived encounters with girls who smoke the rather daring cigarette. Reviews for this volume were often negative, focussing disapproving attention on Symons's preference for artifice over nature, and – like Johnson – disliking the refusal to make moral or intellectual comment on the world he observed. As John Lucas argues, for Symons:

> The city is simply the condition of modern life. As such, it supplies material for poetry, but only in so far as the poet accepts his role as *flâneur*, the wanderer of the streets which offer a whirl of impressions to be randomly recorded and with no sense that out of them a coherent 'meaning' will emerge. (Lucas 1992, 64)

Symons accepts those conditions – and consequently is not unsettled by their implications.

In response to negative criticism, in the second edition of *Silhouettes* (1896) Symons undertook a defence of his aesthetics in a Preface, writing there:

> Is there any 'reason in nature' why we should write exclusively about the natural blush, if the delicately acquired blush of rouge has any attraction for us? Both exist; both, I think, are charming in their way; and the latter, as a subject, has, at all events, more novelty. If you prefer your 'new-mown hay' in the hayfield, and I, it may be, in a scent-bottle, why may not my individual caprice be allowed to find expression as much as yours? Probably I enjoy the hayfield as much as you do; but I enjoy quite other scents and sensations as well, and I take the former for granted, and write my poem, for a change, about the latter. There is no necessary difference in artistic value between a good poem about a flower in the hedge and a good poem about the scent in the sachet. (Symons in Nassaar 1999, 237)

This is somewhat disingenuous commentary. Symons's poems deliberately set out to *épater le bourgeois*, to shock conventional propriety with their evocations of painted women in (or on) the city streets. His subject matter – in a rather different way from Housman's – has a slightly adolescent feel to it, a schoolboy's fascination with exotic femininity. As Yeats, who shared rooms with Symons in the mid-1890s, notes, he studied the risqué milieu of the music halls 'as he might have studied the age of Chaucer', bringing an apparently scholarly attitude to decidedly unscholarly subjects (Yeats 1955, 304). But the scholarly attitude sometimes slipped, and Yeats also recalls Symons 'throwing himself into a chair after some visit to a music-hall or hippodrome' and announcing, ' "O, Yeats, I was never in love with a serpent-charmer before" ' (335), implying that the search for new sensations was at least as important as any attempt at respectable theorizing. Thus whilst Symons was clearly right in his claim that 'All art … is a form of artifice' (Symons in Nassaar 1999, 236), the particular forms of artifice that he chose to describe were deliberately provocative. Make-up and the scent in the sachet were associated by most readers with the kind of woman who was far from ideal. He casts out the goddess, and replaces her with a complaisant dancing girl. As Laurel Brake observes, Symons's time as editor of the short-lived magazine *The Savoy* (1896) produced 'an aggressively male and heterosexual magazine, full of male discourse, masculine constructions of women and misogyny, bristling (if that is the word) with erotic drawings, and clearly … aimed at male readers' (Brake 1994b, 151). Much the same, with the probable exception of overt misogyny, could be said of his two volumes of 1890s verse, *Silhouettes* and *London Nights* (1895).

Nonetheless, it is possible to read Symons's poems as partially positive for women if only in the sense that they sometimes describe them
as having more than a purely 'symbolical place'. In his poetry sexual
desire is not disembodied or sublimated into some other 'worthier'
goal. It is simply accepted and described. When Symons's friend Yeats
wrote about the figure of the dancer in poems such as 'Michael
Robartes and the Dancer' (1921) or 'Among School Children' (1928),
he argued that femininity was better left ideal. Michael Robartes, for
example, tells the unnamed dancer in his poem that 'your lover's
wage / Is what your looking-glass can show'. The woman should not put
herself 'to college', must not be 'learned like a man', and must accept
that her best self is her bodily self (Yeats 1982, 198). The sense of
woman as symbol for man's desires persists in his work. In 'Among
School Children', a poem about the variety of images available to poets
and artists, Yeats selects various kinds of image: his own image as a
'public smiling man', the images carried by mothers of their children,
by nuns of saints, religious icons and painted images, and rejects each
of them as flawed because they each are referential: that is, they all are
directed beyond themselves to some other meaning which they do not
embody in themselves. In the famous final stanza of that poem, he
privileges the organic image of the tree and the artistic figure of
the dancer as his own ideal images, seeing in them perfect syntheses
of life and art, and of content and form:

> O chestnut tree, great-rooted blossomer,
> Are you the leaf, the blossom, or the bole?
> O body swayed to music, O brightening glance,
> How can we know the dancer from the dance?
> (Yeats 1982, 245)

The tree and the dancer are images which, in Walter Pater's words,
'aspire to the condition of music', bringing together content and form.
The lines with which the poem ends imply that the tree and the dancer
are equivalent, that they are images only of themselves, and they avoid
extraneous referentiality to the world beyond themselves, which
makes them into ideal images.

In Symons's poems, however, a dancer is not just a poetic image. At
various times, particularly in the *London Nights* volume, she is individ-
ualized. In his most anthologized poem, 'La Mélinite: Moulin Rouge',[10]
a description of the real music hall dancer Jane Avril (1868–1941), the
dancer has a technical mastery of her own art to which the poem pays

tribute in its attempts to recreate it in poetic form, making use of techniques such as anaphora and assonance to supplement rhythm and rhyme to recreate a hypnotic and powerful performance. The poem describes an evening at the Moulin Rouge, where dancers on the public floor both participate in, and observe, a spectacle of dance to a Waltz called 'The Waltz of Roses':

> Down the long hall the dance returning
> Rounds the full circle, rounds
> The perfect rose of lights and sounds
> The rose returning
> Into the circle of its rounds.
>
> Alone, apart, one dancer watches
> Her mirrored, morbid grace;
> Before the mirror, face to face,
> Alone she watches,
> Her morbid, vague, ambiguous grace.
> (Symons 1897, 24)

Avril is presented as having an individuality that is quite specific, and as taking pleasure in her own performance ('she dances for her own delight'), both provoking and evading an erotic response from the viewer. She is as powerful as he is, and is not simply the embodiment of his desires. For Symons, too, the dancer is an aggressively modern figure. Dancers on the stage are lit by electric light: the impressions derived from their performances are pleasurable because of décor, costume and make-up. In 'On the Stage', the poet is fascinated by 'Lights in a multi-coloured mist,/From indigo to amethyst', and with 'wigs, and tights ... and rouge' (Symons 1897, 15). In 'To a Dancer', the dancing woman is presented as inviting an erotic connection across the footlights, with 'her eyes that gleam for me' (5). And although there is often something voyeuristic about these poems, dancers who performed publicly knew they were being watched, and exercised some control over what was seen. So, although Symons's dance poems 'bristle', to use Brake's word, with desire, in the recognition of feminine potency there is potentially a more feminist poetics than the quasi-Victorian purity ideal and will-to-power over the image that is to be found in Yeats's descriptions of femininity. In Symons's poems, the dancer is indeed an object of desire; but she is also a desiring subject. The city is a fertile, not a futile place, in these poems, precisely because it admits of erotic attractions that are not possible elsewhere: and the artifice of the city heightens their effects.

The Yeats that Symons knew was not a city poet. He describes himself in *Autobiographies* as one of a group of poets strongly affected by the writings of Pater: 'we looked consciously to Pater for our philosophy' (Yeats 1955, 303), though he also wonders to himself whether that philosophy, which 'taught us to walk on a rope stretched tightly through serene air', might have been responsible for the tragedy of the tragic generation, since the conditions of modernity were rather unsuitable to the ceremony and reticence of such a philosophy. Arthur Symons famously defined Symbolism in *The Symbolist Movement in Literature* (1899) as aiming: 'To fix the last fine shade, the quintessence of things; to fix it fleetingly; to be a disembodied voice, and yet the voice of a human soul' (Symons 1958, 47). As John Lucas observes about this quotation, 'the cadences are derived from Pater, but the insight is Symons's own. A disembodied voice belongs uniquely to the echoing city streets, to its night cries, to the wanderer or passer-by, for whom utterance does not imply communication or reciprocity. The voice of the human soul echoes back loneliness, isolation' (Lucas 1992, 62). A philosophy that might be liveable in the cloistered colleges of Oxford is not liveable in precisely the same terms in London, or any other modern city. Yeats's poetry – as Eliot's does, though in very different ways – represents a withdrawal from the city. The poetry he wrote whilst he was very close to Symons and Henley bears no echoes of their work. The early collections, beginning with *Crossways* (1889) through to *Responsibilities* (1914) distance themselves from the conditions of modernity; and although the later volumes take a different direction, that distance is maintained. Taking Matthew Arnold at least as seriously as he took Walter Pater, much of Yeats's early work is concerned with forging a literary culture for Ireland, using the mythologies and folktales of his home country as the basis of his poems. In *Autobiographies*, he writes: 'Supreme art is a traditional statement of certain heroic and religious truths, passed on from age to age, modified by individual genius, but never abandoned' (Yeats 1955, 490). Supreme art, in other words, is an Arnoldian 'touchstone', and for a nation like Ireland, struggling to overthrow its imperial history and reassert its own cultural values, such a touchstone is necessary. The Irish heritage also meant that London meant something rather different to Yeats than it did to many of his contemporaries, most of whom were anxious to slough off their provincial manners and mannerisms. For Yeats there was a national pride in 'provincialism', and London is a place of exile, not of homecoming.

Whilst there is clearly a political dimension to the recovery of a culture in danger of being lost because of colonial history – a dimension, for example, that is to the forefront of Lady Wilde's collections of Irish folk-tales – Yeats rather disapproved of party political activism. The return to a magical past in poems such as 'The Stolen Child' (1889) or the Rose poems of 1893 is escapist not activist. The poet seeks to 'sing the ancient ways', but to do so 'no more blinded by man's fate'; he wishes to 'seek alone to hear the strange things said/By God to the bright hearts of those long dead' (Yeats 1982, 35). When, following the Easter Rising of 1916, Yeats had to respond to contemporary events, he did so in a poem which is both a memorial to the Irish martyrs and a statement of why poets should not be involved in politics. The poem 'Easter 1916' (1922) evokes Yeats's personal relationships with some of the rebels, men whom he had met 'at close of day/Coming with vivid faces/From counter or desk/Among grey eighteenth-century houses'. Then there was time to exchange – in a Paterian spirit of ceremonious reticence – 'polite mean-ingless words'. Now that time is gone. The events of rebellions, executions and imprisonments mean that even those to whom he felt a personal antipathy ('this other man I had dreamed/A drunken vainglorious lout') have to be 'numbered' in the song which memorializes their actions. The poem argues that political commitment to a particular cause has a deadening effect on those who participate in it: 'Hearts with one pur-pose alone…seem/Enchanted to a stone'; 'Too long a sacrifice' to an ideal 'Can make a stone of the heart'. The poet's only possible response is a memorializing mythology. The poet's part is:

> To murmur name upon name,
> As a mother names her child
> When sleep at last has come
> On limbs that had run wild …
> We know their dream; enough
> To know they dreamed and are dead …
> I write it out in a verse –
> MacDonagh and MacBride
> And Connolly and Pearse
> Now and in time to be,
> Wherever green is worn,
> Are changed, changed utterly:
> A terrible beauty is born.
> (Yeats 1982, 204–5)

The oxymoron 'terrible beauty', which is the poem's refrain, as well as the failed rhyme of 'verse/Pearse' perhaps express the strain that this detachment entails. Nonetheless, strain or not, splendid isolation is the condition of Yeats's modernist art.

The paradox of Modernism is that it looks backwards at least as much as it looks forward, that it is oriented towards the past at least as much as towards the future. For Yeats, Celtic mythology – derived from an oral tradition, or made by himself in the light of contemporary events – is better than a confrontation with modernity with its 'fumbl[ing] in a greasy till' (120). For Eliot, 'tradition' is the touchstone. In the essay 'Tradition and the Individual Talent' (1919), he argues in a similar vein – though with a different vocabulary to Yeats – that tradition is the necessary element in great art. This does not mean the slavish imitation of previous models, but rather an historical sense achieved by great labour (Eliot 1975, 38). Reading *The Waste Land* or 'Prufrock' makes clear Eliot's allegiance to this position. The London of *The Waste Land* is inhabited by the ghosts of the European literary tradition – Virgil, Dante, Shakespeare – as well as by the ghosts of historical personages who lived in the city in previous centuries – Elizabeth and Leicester amongst the illustrious, Sweeney and Mrs Porter amongst the plebeian. Clock time is a character in the poem, with clocks regulating the flows of crowds over London Bridge, and producing the call of 'Time' in the pub. Wider historical time is also evoked in a constant interplay between then and now. The poem also dramatizes the concept of 'great labour', since reading it for those of us who do not have a classical education is a constant process of referring to notes that gloss the references. The 'usual objection' to this position, to which Eliot alludes in his essay is that it 'requires a ridiculous amount of erudition (pedantry)' (40). He rejects this view, implying that it is not learning as such which makes the difference, but – and Pater's ghost is here too – the artist's sensibility. Eliot immediately retreats from any such implication – in a slightly later essay, 'The Perfect Critic' (1920), he disapproves of Arthur Symons's critical writing, and explicitly connects Symons's impressionistic readings with Pater (51) – moving on instead to discuss the artist's necessary 'continual surrender of himself', 'continual self-sacrifice, a continual extinction of personality', and to discuss impersonality as the ideal condition of the artist.

Pater is not exorcized, however. It was he, after all, in 'The School of Giorgione' who had insisted that criticism needed to pay careful attention to the particular medium of expression, and to pay careful attention to technique over message. Eliot's criticism makes use of this insight, but returns to an Arnoldian concept of community. Instead of asking, 'What is this song or picture, this engaging personality presented in life or in a book to *me*?' (Pater ed. Hill 1980, xix–xx), as Pater had done, Eliot requires that his readers connect the particular to the tradition. 'Prufrock', on the surface at least a dramatic monologue in a tradition developed from Browning, is not an engaging personality. In fact, he may not be a personality at all, for to what extent could Prufrock himself describe, in the language of the poem, the state of mind he is in? He may be conscious of a feeling that his life is wasted and trivial, tortured by the erotic images of women's downy, bejewelled arms, socially uncomfortable and inept; but someone is speaking his lines for him. His personality's inadequacies could not possibly rise to the poetry he allegedly speaks: it is impossible for him to say what he means (Eliot 1963, 16); and indeed it is. Readers do not admire Prufrock – they admire the technique of the poem that bears his name, with its fleeting allusions to Shakespeare and Renaissance drama more generally, Michelangelo, Marvell, the Bible and Hesiod. The personality is placed in the great tradition of European art and literature at the experience of that personality's own expressive individualism.

Yeats, the older man, dealt with his late-nineteenth-century self by self-mockingly mythologizing it and his younger self and by patronizing the memories of the poets he had lived with. He took Symons's key image – the dancer – and turned it into a transcendent image of perfectly synthesized life and art, an image which has many problems for the woman reader in that it de-eroticizes and disempowers the woman in the poem. Eliot dealt with his immediate predecessors by largely disavowing their influence. But, as R. K. R. Thornton has observed: 'Eliot develops both as a poet and a critic on ground prepared by Symons. Prufrock inhabits Symons's London, the "Preludes" are played there, and Eliot's "impersonality" surely develops from Symons's "disembodied voice, yet the voice of a human soul" ' (Thornton 1983, 163). In his Introduction to *Poetry of the Nineties* he even demonstrates verbal and technical echoes between Symons's poetry and Eliot's (Thornton and Thain 1997, xxxix). But there are other echoes too from the earlier period. The cityscape, the different voices, the impressionistic movement through the streets, the sense of a sordid modernity, new kinds of women – and the same kinds of men – are all part of modernism's nineteenth-century inheritance.

Notes

1. See Bergonzi 1980, Thornton and Thain 1997, and Fletcher 1987 for a handful of very different versions of the poetry of this period, and for some rather different defining dates.

2. Sublimation is a Freudian term which signals the ways in which (unacceptable) sexual drives are re-routed into creative, intellectual or other highly valued activities which are more socially appropriate.

3. Poems such as 'Pied Beauty' (Hopkins 1985, 30–1) are precisely about multiplicity resolved in the oneness that is God.

4. In the same volume, Hardy had also included a poem entitled 'Shelley's Skylark', and that poem too is largely pessimistic. The bird might have inspired the poet to 'Ecstatic heights in thought and rhyme', but it ended its days, nonetheless, as 'a little ball of feather and bone' that dropped to its death from the sky (Hardy 1976, 51).

5. It is of course highly likely that the woman remains unreachable for Housman because he did not really want her; his sexuality was male directed so that the unattainable woman is potentially simply a cloak for a desire that cannot be spoken.

6. The mainstream anthologies most commonly used by students such as *The Norton Anthology of English Literature* are very scanty in their treatment of the late nineteenth century generally, and rarely make an effort to show that women were writing poetry at all. Angela Leighton and Margaret Reynolds's *Victorian Women Poets: An Anthology* (1995) makes a valiant attempt to redress that balance, and readers who want to know more about late-Victorian women poets should begin there, and follow the bibliographical details to get more information.

7. This poem can also be found in Leighton and Reynolds 1995, 504.

8. Bluestone is hydrated copper sulphate, used as an emetic.

9. *Nocturne: Blue and Gold* was the title Whistler gave to his image of Old Battersea Bridge; and a number of Whistler's portraits had the title *Harmonies*, with the colour 'grey' as part of the description.

10. *La Mélinite* was the trade name of a brand of explosive used in fireworks in the 1890s. It was one of the soubriquets applied to Jane Avril in the period.

3 The Strange Case of Mr Wilde: or, 1895 and all that

> **earnest** ... *adj.* intent; sincere in intention; serious *esp.* over-serious in disposition; determined or wholehearted, fervent or impassioned; – *n* used in the expression **in earnest** ... *adv* earnestly. – *n* earnestness. – **in all earnestness** most sincerely, urgently; **in earnest** serious, not joking; in a determined or unequivocal way; in reality. [OE *eornost* seriousness; Ger *Ernst*.]

Above is a modern dictionary definition of an important Victorian word – earnest – which sums up the particular kind of moral seriousness associated with Victorianism. When the generation of later Victorian writers wished to mock their immediate predecessors it was earnestness that came under fire. Thus Samuel Butler deliberately names the protagonist of *The Way of All Flesh* Ernest – and shows him failing to live up to the ideals his name conjures up. But the most famous subversive use of the name is Oscar Wilde's play, *The Importance of Being Earnest, A Trivial Comedy for Serious People*, which opened to rave reviews on 14 February 1895. It was Wilde's greatest triumph in the West End, and has continued to be his most popular play ever since. It was also the last success he enjoyed before the guardians of moral earnestness set out to destroy him two months later.

The warnings of what was to come were played out on the opening night when the Marquess of Queensberry, Wilde's implacable enemy and father of his beloved Lord Alfred Douglas, tried to invade the theatre to mount a public insult of the author. When security prevented his entrance, he was forced to satisfy himself by leaving an unusual valentine bouquet of root vegetables as a mark of his disgust. Weeks later, Queensberry would leave a mis-spelled card – 'To Oscar Wilde, Posing Somdomite' – at Wilde's club. Wilde would sue for libel, and lose his case. The evidence brought by Queensberry to support his plea of justification would ultimately lead to Wilde's prosecution under the 1885 Criminal Law Amendment Act, and eventually to his imprisonment with hard labour for two years in May 1895. In the aftermath, Wilde's name would be removed from the West-End theatres where his plays were being performed; the runs of both *Earnest* and *An Ideal Husband* were cancelled despite their success. *The Yellow Book* 'turned grey in a single night' and folded soon afterwards. The conservative press heralded the end of decadence and, according to Yeats's *Autobiographies*, prostitutes danced in the streets to celebrate Wilde's fall.

But before all that happened, the small public that made up the West-End theatre audience had thoroughly enjoyed *The Importance of Being Earnest*. The theatre critic William Archer, writing in *World* magazine was dazzled by it:

> It is delightful to see, it sends wave after wave of laughter curling and foaming around the theatre; but as a text for criticism it is barren and delusive. It is like a mirage oasis in the desert, grateful and comforting to the weary eye, but when you come up close to it, behold! it is intangible, it eludes your grasp. What can a poor critic do with a play which raises no principle, whether of art or of morals, creates its own canons and conventions, and is nothing but an absolutely wilful expression of a witty personality? ... Mr Pater ... has an essay on the tendency of art to verge towards, and merge in, the absolute art – music. He might have found an example in *The Importance of Being Earnest*. (Archer in Beckson 1970, 189–90)

This is highly astute commentary. Archer noted the pleasure of *Earnest*, but also its problems for the conventions that the Victorian critic was used to. The play gives no space for moral commentary, and presents indeed an amoral world where competent lying is presented as the route to romantic success. The enjoyment that audiences felt when they saw the play eluded their assumptions. It does not appear to be a political or moral drama. It eschews the conventional 'problem-play' plotlines that had been at the centre of Wilde's earlier comedies and concentrates on pure farce apparently with no serious intention. It 'tickled' the establishment into laughter wrote George Bernard Shaw, who disapproved of its lack of message (Shaw in Beckson 1970, 195). At the same time, however, *Earnest* is also a potentially highly subversive play, at least in terms of its politics of gender and sexuality. The tragedy that destroyed Wilde a matter of weeks after its premiere has traditionally been taken as a part of the play's meaning: *Earnest* did have a message – though not everyone in the audience could read the code by which the message was transmitted. It speaks in coded language of sexually dissident meanings, and its self-proclaimed triviality is in fact a mask that disguises a sustained assault on dominant views of gender and sexuality. Rather than seeing things steadily and seeing them whole, it is an exercise in impressionistic double vision, and, as Archer's allusion to Pater's 'Giorgione' essay implies, it is a celebration of subjective responses where form dominates content. It has also come retrospectively to stand as the expression of a distinctively homosexual sensibility.

Well, perhaps. More recently a number of critics have expressed their doubts about this view of the play, and of Wilde as the exemplar of *fin-de-siècle* homosexual identity more generally, arguing effectively that such a view of *Earnest* is based on that very dangerous mode of vision provided by hindsight. Neil Bartlett, Alan Sinfield and Joseph Bristow amongst others go to some lengths to undo any simplistic notion that simply because Wilde was 'queer', there must be 'something queer' going on in the plays. 'Many commentators', writes Sinfield, 'assume that queerness, like murder, *will out*, so there must be a gay scenario lurking somewhere in the depths of *The Importance of Being Earnest*' (Sinfield 1994, vi, emphasis in original). He goes on, as Bartlett had done before him, to argue that it is equally plausible to read *Earnest* as a play with a distinctively heterosexual agenda. As Bartlett writes:

> I wonder in what sense of the word was this most famous of homosexuals actually homosexual? He was married. His best and most successful play, *The Importance of Being Earnest*, may be the most precious pearl of English camp, but it celebrates the triumph of marriage over all adversity, brings down the curtain on a trio of engagements, and was deliberately premiered on St. Valentine's Day. What can it tell us in any of its endless revivals, the endless resuscitations of its over-dressed sentiments, except that the work of this man may bear no hint, no trace of his 'true nature', may be a triumphant declaration of the ease with which we distort our own lives. (Bartlett 1989, 34)

The rhetorical questions are rather bitter, and one can imagine why the particular performance of possible gay identity that Wilde chose, which came retrospectively to stand for gay identity *per se*, might not be particularly comfortable or attractive for contemporary gay men. For not only was Wilde married, he lived out his sexual life entirely in a period when same-sex desire was illegal and threatened; he does not make a positive symbol for gay men because his covert self-expression led to martyrdom, not to a happy ending, not even of any kind. Bartlett, however, just as other critics had done before him, wishes to impose an either/or reading on Wilde's life and work. Either he was 'really' gay, or he was not; either the play is a gay play, or it is not. For me, however, part of *Earnest*'s strength lies precisely in its deliberate ambiguity. The play finds a way for the dissident voice to speak – but to speak in such a way that neither the dissident speaker, nor the play's largely straight audience, is threatened by the disclosure of illicit desire. The covert expression is necessary in an era when speaking out and 'coming out' could – and did – lead to imprisonment. As John Stokes has recently observed, it might be better to read *Earnest* not as a 'straight' or gay play, but as a deliberately contradictory and inconsistent drama that swings both ways. Commenting on the 1993 Nicholas Hytner production at the Aldwych in London's West End, where Algy first greeted Jack with a kiss though both appeared to be happily engaged to women at the end, Stokes writes: 'The structure of *The Importance* is paradoxical ... it zig-zags from start to finish. Men who fraternize with men turn out to like some women, and luckily some women turn out to like some men too ... This is a bisexual drama' (Stokes 1996, 184). The play can therefore be read, performed and interpreted as an appeal to a more inclusive, less rigidly defined 'either/or' binarism than is usually associated with Victorian culture. Wilde may not stand as the symbol for all gay men, for all history, but he does stand as a very effective icon of alternative kinds of sexual identities, including gay identities, that it is possible to inhabit at a time when queerness led to queer street. His strategies are historically specific rather than eternal, and they mark an age of transition between Victorian pieties and modernist iconoclasm in their use and abuse of the period's conventions of representation.

From the play's title onwards, what is immediately signalled is that the serious, the important and the earnest are present in the play – but that they are present 'differently' from the ways in which they had traditionally been understood. Earnestness is treated as a language game, a pun on the moral concept and on the name Ernest. And a pun, of course, is a word which depends for its force on the impossibility of deciding which meaning is intended. In this case the serious concept of earnestness, a key marker of what the Victorians understood as proper masculinity which was supposed to signal a quality that marked the 'proper' man, is being turned into a joke. The joke subverts not only Victorian conventions of masculine behaviour, but also Victorian conventions of representation. Names, after all, are extremely important markers in fictions and on the stage. Novelists and playwrights do not usually choose their characters' names at random, but use them to signal, more or less transparently, the qualities of those characters. As Humpty Dumpty observes to Alice in *Through the Looking Glass* (1871), '*my* name means the shape I am – and a good handsome shape it is, too. With a name like [Alice], you might be any shape, almost' (Carroll 1970, 263). And in Wilde's play, Algy observes to Jack, 'You answer to the name of Ernest. You look as if your name was Ernest. You are the most earnest-looking person I ever saw in my life' (Wilde 1994, 361). The straightforward honesty of the name Ernest is, however, being sent up. Both Jack Worthing and Algy Moncrieff appropriate this name which signals honesty in order to deceive. A name that appears to be founded on the concept of truth becomes, in this case, a lie, a forgery, a counterfeit. Appearances are very deceptive.

The name also plays its part in the plot, such as it is. Both Cecily Cardew and Gwendolen Fairfax fall in love with the name. In almost identical words they tell their respective suitors: 'my ideal has always been to love someone with the name of Ernest. There is something in the name that inspires absolute confidence. The moment Algernon first mentioned to me that he had a friend called Ernest, I knew I was destined to love you' (Wilde 1994, 366). This is Gwendolen speaking, but Cecily says much the same thing and even goes so far as to become engaged to be married to a name before she has even met its putative owner. Now, *Earnest* is very much a play of its own time. It is impossible to stage it in modern dress and there have been no attempts to do so in commercial theatre since the 1920s, when it was still just about possible to miss six trains in an hour, when men still wore detachable cuffs, and when very few people had access to a telephone or owned a motorcar. It was also written entirely with the staging conventions – a proscenium arch stage, a more or less naturalistic set – of the 1890s in mind. At the same time, however, it is a curiously modern, almost modern*ist* play, which dramatizes a pre-Saussurean recognition of the absolute separation of the signifier and the signified. In its language games it demonstrates that language itself, the only medium in which truth might be told, distorts rather than mimetically represents the real. 'The truth,' says Algy to Jack with most un-Victorian sentiment, 'is never pure and rarely simple' (362). This is definitely not a world in which one might see clearly, nor tell what one saw in a plain way. Plays on language are essential throughout *Earnest*, and above all, the play makes the claim that language is non-referential and intransitive – that it does not necessarily refer to the world beyond itself, it does not make sense of the world, and nor does it make things happen in that world.

In a remarkably kind review of *The Importance of Being Earnest* (1895) – kind because by the time it was published in *The Free Review* in June 1895, Wilde had been imprisoned and utterly ruined; no one else would write so kindly about him in the aftermath of his trials – the appropriately named Ernest Newman commented on the workings of the play. Newman's description of Wilde's use of language emphasizes a different vision of reality that underlies all his writing, and which undermines the conventional proprieties of the age:

> The function of paradox is really the same as the function of religion – not to be believed; but the Philistine takes the one just as seriously as he takes the other. A paradox is simply the truth of the minority, just as a commonplace is the truth of the majority. The function of paradox is to illumine light places, to explain just those things that everyone under-stands. For example, everyone knows what Art is, and everyone knows what it is to be immoral; but if a thinker says 'Art is immoral', the new synthesis puzzles them, and they either call it a paradox, or they say that the writer is immoral. In reality, he is doing just what they cannot do; he can see round corners, and the other side of things. Nay, he can do more than this; he can give to ordinary things a quality they have not ... We ordinary beings see objects in three dimensions only; a good paradox is a view in the fourth dimension. (Newman in Beckson 1970, 203)

A paradox is a play in language which, like a pun, contains oppositions. As Newman observes, Wilde used paradox in order to break down the habitual and the conventional in thought or received opinion. Wilde had read his Pater, regarded *The Renaissance* as his 'golden book', and knew only too well that 'our failure is to form habits'. On the small scale of individual exchanges in the play, paradox simply functions to provoke laughter; but it often has implications beyond its immediate context. Once the audience can be shaken out of its habits in small things, they might also find themselves shaken out of their habits in larger things as well; if they don't, it does not matter much, for they have had a good laugh in the meantime. The form of the paradox is potentially subversive; but because it is a joke, it also feels unthreaten-ing. Richard Ellmann observes several times of Wilde in his biography that when the writer was faced with contradictory choices, he habitu-ally chose them both, preferring to have his cake and eat it too. The paradox is one symptom of such an attitude.

In *Earnest*, the use of language marks the sophistication of character. All attempts to be sincere (earnestness's po-faced twin) are ruthlessly sent up. Miss Prism and Canon Chasuble are sincerely in love – at *their* age! – which makes them ridiculous straightaway in the topsy-turvy moral universe that Wilde has created. Because of their observation of the conventional pieties of their day, they can only declare their passion in improbable metaphor and tortured periphrases. Their language practices take them as far as possible from the truths they wish to convey to each other about the state of their affections in an extended, though good-natured satire, on 1890s manners. Most other characters in the play, however, are much more linguistically capable. The play is built up of dazzling and artificial conversation in which almost no one says precisely what he or she means. Allusion is made to sensational plots of Victorian melodrama, since the plot centres on a lost child's quest for his origins. Jack plays the role of melodramatic hero when he mistakenly identifies Miss Prism as 'Mother!' and 'forgives' her for the transgression he assumes she has made. But the plot is absolutely unimportant. It is not what is said that matters, but how it is said. And the point behind much of the dialogue is that it is a sustained exercise in avoiding the issue. Opposed to the clarity of realist writing where plot carries message, *Earnest* refuses to have an easily legible message inscribed at the level of event or, indeed, of character.

Indeed, the play refuses to observe the usual rules about character. Wilde's characterization here depends not on individuality, not on people conceived of as unique and distinct, or the predictable products of their milieu. It evades the notion that character is a deep structure that goes right through a person, where action is essence. The characters here exist on the surface only and they are almost undifferentiated from each other. You can very easily mix up the speeches of Cecily and Gwendolen, for example: Gwendolen is just a more sophisticated, citified version of Cecily. The women, for example, both write diaries which, although everything in them is patently fabricated ('one must always have something sensational to read in the train,' observes Gwendolen [398]), they both use as evidence to support their respective claims to their non-existent suitor, Ernest Worthing. Similarly, Jack and Algy are often indistinguishable. The only essential differences between them are that Algy is greedier than Jack and far more successful in satisfying his sensual lusts, though lust is displaced into a harmless desire for cucumber sandwiches and muffins. Importantly both men also lead double lives, leaving behind their rather nebulous social obligations at will in order to seek pleasure. The key difference between them is in the respective locations of their duties and desires: Jack, whose responsibilities are in the country, seeks his pleasure in the town; and Algy, who should be in town, seeks pleasure in the country. Both are what Algy calls – with perhaps a nod towards the euphemistic phrase 'confirmed bachelors' – 'advanced Bunburyists' (362). It is the meaning of this nonsense word, a signifier without a signified (there is no 'real' person in the play called Bunbury), which is crucial to the meaning of the play.

Amateur and commercial productions of the play have tended to assume that the verb to 'Bunbury' simply means 'to seek pleasure', and they do not define the pleasures that the word signals.[1] The word can be read as a mere anodyne piece of fun in an asexual Jeeves-and-Wooster world. This is certainly a tenable reading and the play can be successfully performed as thought it is just a game with some good jokes in it. But the verb is also written with a strong commitment to another kind of reading – a coded message which might, Sinfield notwithstanding, *come out* in performance. Bunbury and buggery share a suggestive assonance.[2] However the word is interpreted, the pleasures sought by Jack and Algy are illicit; the question is of degree. The specific nature of their pleasures is not explicitly written into the play, but there are coded messages available to those 'in the know'. For example, the first act exchange over Jack's lost cigarette case might be seen as a pure plot device which allows Algy to learn of the existence of 'little Cecily' and of Jack's double life. But some members of the original audience would certainly have known of another possible meaning, and would have enjoyed a private joke amongst themselves. The fact that Jack and Algy smoke cigarettes at all, rather than the more manly pipe or cigar, might just have been one indication of a possible effeminacy in their characters. More importantly though, Wilde's intimate circle would have known that the cigarette case was one of his preferred love tokens, the kind of gift he habitually gave to his young male friends and lovers. Indeed, only two months later, cigarette cases inscribed with words of affection would form part of the evidence against Wilde at his trials. No wonder then that Jack is horrified to discover that Algy has read the inscription in his case: 'It is a very ungentlemanly thing to do to read a private cigarette case,' he says (360). His fear is that he has been discovered leading a double life, though ironically what Algy actually discovers is that Jack is far more respectable than he would like to pretend to be. He behaves very well in the country where he adopts 'a very high moral tone on all subjects' (361), so the evidence of the cigarette case ironically proves not criminality but an embarrassing innocence.

Moreover, in the play as Wilde originally wrote it, though this is not the version that is usually performed, there is an extended episode where Jack's double life threatens to catch up with him. Bailiffs arrive to arrest him for debts contracted as Ernest in the city. Financial problems dogged Wilde too in the period immediately around the play's first performances, and he would eventually be bankrupted in the aftermath of the trials. Queer Street, a phrase used in the nineteenth century to describe financial difficulties, was about to become a phrase implying illicit activities of a non-financial kind. This is part of the atmosphere that surrounds Henry Jekyll in Stevenson's *The Strange Case of Dr Jekyll and Mr Hyde* [1885] – and the shift of meaning from financial malpractice to sexual misconduct underlies the atmosphere of that novella, as Showalter has noted (1991, 112). One of the reasons Wilde hit Queer Street in the first meaning of the phrase was that he was being blackmailed for having cruised Queer Street in the second meaning. And certainly some of the audience knew this. The parts of the audience who have access to the code are given a choice about how to interpret these scenes. They can be read 'straight', as simple comedy, or they can be read otherwise: or, faced with the contradiction, we might choose both, and oscillate in pleasurable and un-Victorian undecidability.

As was Wilde's habit throughout his published works, the places in which values are traditionally thought to reside are inverted throughout *Earnest*, in its slight plot, certainly, but also more particularly in its playful use of language. Wilde takes the commonplace and upends it. Consider, for example, Lady Bracknell's quizzing of Jack about his eligibility as a suitor for her daughter. She is glad to hear that he smokes, since 'a man should always have an occupation of some kind'. She is happy that he knows nothing, since 'ignorance is a delicate exotic fruit' and she disapproves of anything that tampers with it (Wilde 1994, 368). This is a joke at the expense of conventional masculinity, where men are supposed to be the 'knowing' ones, and women supposed to be innocent and ignorant before marriage. In Sarah Grand's *The Heavenly Twins*, for instance, Mrs Frayling, one of the heroines' mothers, is appalled by her daughter's pursuit of knowledge, and attributes the failure of her marriage to it. She announces as boast, rather than as a complaint: 'I don't know where she got [her advanced views] ... for I am sure *I* haven't any ... At *her* age I knew *nothing*' (Grand 1992, 103). Lady Bracknell asks traditional questions about income and expectations, but is ironically pleased to discover that his income derives from investments rather than land – despite the fact that land had traditionally been regarded as a more assured basis for financial security. She discovers his extensive property and is only concerned that his house in Belgrave Square is on the unfashionable side of the street. She is pleased that he has no politics, for as Russell Jackson has observed, being a liberal unionist is the 1890s equivalent of a 'don't know'. His family background is only a minor matter until the scene descends into farce with the discovery that Jack appears to have been parented by an item of luggage:

> To be born, or at any rate, bred in a handbag, whether it had handles or not, seems to me to display a contempt for the ordinary decencies of family life that reminds one of the worst excesses of the French Revolution...As for the particular locality in which the handbag was found, a cloakroom at a railway station might serve to conceal a social indiscretion – has probably, indeed, been used for that purpose before now – but it could hardly be regarded as an assured basis for a recognized place in good society...You can hardly imagine that I and Lord Bracknell would dream of allowing our only daughter – a girl brought up with the utmost care – to marry into a cloakroom and form an alliance with a parcel. (Wilde 1994, 369–70)

Apart from the inherent comedy of its hyperbolically inflated rhetoric, for those in the know the remarks about cloakrooms are highly charged. Then, as now, railway stations had something of a reputation, and cloakrooms have a particular resonance as places in which illicit assignations might take place. But the real point here is that Lady Bracknell, representative of moral rectitude and social awareness, does not care that her future son-in-law is an idle, smoking, ignorant layabout so long as he is rich and has better connections than a Gladstone bag. The inquisition about Jack's prospects is an exercise in empty questioning, not a proper attempt to discern moral character. His answers should have disqualified him as an eligible suitor.

Lady Bracknell's questions should, of course, have been asked by Lord Bracknell. It is usually the prospective father-in-law who asks them. But the play as a whole, as well as these particular questions and answers, make it clear that the concept of proper masculinity has no place. It is the women who rule this world, not the men. In a statement that bodes very badly for Jack's future domestic comfort, Gwendolen shows that she is very much her mother's daughter in her easy assertion that in the Bracknell family the conventional gender roles are reversed:

> Outside the family circle, Papa, I am glad to say, is entirely unknown. I think that is quite as it should be. The home seems to me to be the

proper sphere for the man. And certainly, once a man begins to neglect his domestic duties, he becomes painfully effeminate, does he not? And I don't like that. It makes men so very attractive. (Wilde 1994, 397)

The phrase about the 'proper sphere' refers explicitly to the so-called 'separate spheres' debate which had raged from the mid-century onwards. The argument made by conservative writers was that a woman's proper sphere was in the home, whereas a man's field of action was focussed in the public domain. Gwendolen comically reverses the usual placing in this binary with frightening assurance – she will indeed turn out to be a gorgon like her mother.

There are very few attempts in the play to be sincere and honest, and those that occur are treated with contempt. When Cecily and Gwendolen first meet, they agree to call each other by their Christian names, and even to call each other sister. As soon as their disagreement over the non-existent Ernest surfaces, however, as Cecily puts it, they 'cast aside the shallow mask of manners':

> Cecily: When I see a spade, I call it a spade.
> Gwendolen [*satirically*]: I am glad to say that I have never seen a spade. It is obvious to me that our social spheres have been widely different. (Wilde 1994, 399)

For Wilde, the pleasure and the danger of language is that it is slippery because it is not intrinsically linked to the world and things it seeks to describe. Language practice in the above exchange implies that meaning is defined by reception rather than by intention. In *Sexual Dissidence*, Jonathan Dollimore reads this exchange as typical of Wilde's language practices, in which an apparently simple reversal of values has more significance than its jokey tone implies:

> Cecily tries to take over what we might call the high ground of the straightforward as opposed to the low ground of the shallow, the mannered and the duplicitous ... Gwendolen repudiates the implied opposition and kicks Cecily straight back into the domain of class, the 'social sphere'. Never has a spade been so completely 'defamiliarized'. Compare Wilde's use of the same idea in May 1892 when an alderman praised him for calling a spade a spade. Wilde replied: 'I would like to protest against the idea that I have ever called a spade a spade. The man who did so should be condemned to use one.' (Dollimore 1991, 16–17)

Words mean, to put it another way, not according to a Humpty-Dumpty vision of significance, where when one uses a word, 'it mean[s] just what [one] choose[s] it to mean' (Carroll 1970, 269), but according to the definition of the hearer. Intention, which underlies those important concepts of sincerity and earnestness, is no guarantee that the message will be received. Cecily intends one result – to score a verbal point off her opponent – and achieves another. This is a repeated structure of the play: language loses its intended meaning between utterance and reception. The characters find themselves speaking therefore in intransitive and non-referential words.

Only Jack really takes language seriously: well, he would, wouldn't he, given that his name is 'really' Ernest. When Algy tells him not to eat the cucumber sandwiches, Jack does not eat the cucumber sand-wiches. Language thus acts transitively on Jack in that it makes him do, or not do, particular things. Part of the comedy arises precisely from the fact that he is incapable of seeing that there is no intrinsic rela-tionship between signifier and signified – for when Jack tells Algy not to eat the muffins, Algy ignores him. Similarly, when Jack turns up at his country house in a simulated performance of mourning for his fictional dead brother Ernest, only Miss Prism and Canon Chasuble – the play's fools – take him seriously, and read the semiotics of his performance as he *intends* that they should. It is a mark of her superior intelligence that Cecily takes one look at his mourning clothes and refuses to connect signifier with signified. (She is, of course, right to distrust the performance – but she is not to know that; this is her usual behaviour and it contrasts with the behaviour of fools and dupes.) So, just after Jack has repeated his lies about his brother having died most shockingly in Paris to the Canon and the governess, Cecily walks into the scene and comments:

> Uncle Jack!... what horrid clothes you have got on! Do go and change them... What's the matter, Uncle Jack? You look as if you had toothache, and I have got such a surprise for you. Who do you think is in the dining room? Your brother!... He arrived about half an hour ago. (Wilde 1994, 382–3)

Cecily may have been partly cast as the play's ingénue, but she knows what her uncle will never know – that appearances and reality seldom match up. He acts sorrow, and looks like he has toothache; his costume is not read by her except as a sartorial disaster.

Another example is Cecily and Gwendolen's tea when the two women are in a suppressed fury with each other over their claims to Ernest. They cannot relieve their feelings in a slanging match because of the inhibiting presence of the servants, a detail which emphasizes the extent to which upper-class life must have always been a performance based in the repression of real feelings. In the tea-table exchange Gwendolen is caught out being naïve, and connecting language with action as though there might be a relationship between the word and the world. She gives Cecily very strict – and very snobbish – instructions about the serving of her tea, which Cecily proceeds to ignore in their every detail, rendering Gwendolen's language intransitive: she might as well have been speaking to herself. She shows her fury in her loss of self-control and her direct contradiction of her favourable 'first impressions' of Cecily:

> You have filled my tea with lumps of sugar, and though I asked most distinctly for bread and butter, you have given me cake. I am known for the gentleness of my disposition, and the extraordinary sweetness of my nature, but I warn you, Miss Cardew, you may go too far … From the moment I saw you, I distrusted you. I felt that you were false and deceitful. I am never deceived in such matters. My first impressions of people are invariably right. (Wilde 1994, 400)

The absurdity of the assertion that Gwendolen could possibly have a reputation for sweet nature is just one of the comic elements in this speech. Its real force is in its multiple instances of the misuse of language and its dramatization of the Structuralist truth that language will not live up to its promise to make sense of the world. Gwendolen notes that instructions have not been obeyed; and she directly contradicts herself in her attack on Cecily's moral character. In subverting the very medium through which truth is supposed to be expressed, it opens up the possibility that civilized society is based on lies. Or worse: it suggests that lies and truths are category errors – there is no such thing as either of them. If this were a less funny play, it would feel nihilistic. What matters, as Algy knows, is that language is 'perfectly phrased', not that it tells anything substantial.

Jack never discovers this. He is an unsophisticated user of language who never fully understands its inherent potential for deception. When he is caught out by the two girls in the lie of his brother's existence, he says:

> It is very painful for me to be forced to speak the truth. It is the first time in my life that I have been reduced to such a painful position, and I am really quite inexperienced in doing anything of the kind. However, I will tell you quite frankly, that I have no brother Ernest. I have no brother at

all. I have never had a brother in my life, and I certainly have not the smallest intention of ever having one in the future... Not even of any kind. (Wilde 1994, 402)

The comic reversal of man admitting the pain caused by telling the truth is funny in itself. But though Jack intends to tell the truth here, the truth is rarely pure and never simple; it is certainly not an absolute value and its meaning alters as the plot moves on. Jack Worthing, indeed, has no brother, not even of any kind; but when Jack becomes Ernest Moncrieff, he does have a brother – of sorts – and at the end of the play he rediscovers him in the person of Algy, and confronts the 'terrible thing for a man to find out... that all his life he has been speaking nothing but the truth' (418). Only, he had no intention of doing so. On the contrary, he intended to deceive, to lie and to separate the signifier from the signified. It is a moot point whether, this being the case, he has ever in fact told the truth at all, since by any traditional definition of truthfulness intention would be as important as performance. Truth ought to be a function of sincerity and earnestness rather than of accident and coincidence. This oscillation between value systems, between trivial and serious, between convention and outrage is a function of Wilde's deliberate construction of double vision in the service of evading totalizing and limiting views of the word and the world, and of the people who live in it.

Doubles and double vision

> I want them to write on my tombstone: ... 'Here lie the two Oscar Wildes: socialite and sodomite, Thames and Liffey, Jekyll and Hyde, aristocrat and underdog.' (Eagleton 1989, 64)

Others, I am not the first as the above quotation suggests, have drawn a parallel between Oscar Wilde and Robert Louis Stevenson's *The Strange Case of Dr Jekyll and Mr Hyde*. Indeed, Stevenson's proto-Freudian tale of a double life, where civilization is a very thin veneer covering savage and primitive instincts, has traditionally been taken as the keynote of high culture at large in the late nineteenth century. In *Sexual Anarchy*, Elaine Showalter observes that the homosexual man of the *fin de siècle* (necessarily closeted because his sexual preference had been criminalized) 'may have read the book as a signing to the male community' (Showalter 1991, 115). The outwardly respectable life lived by Henry Jekyll, with its dark shadow of illegal activities including murder, are explicitly identified in the novella with Queer Street. Stevenson's story can very easily be made to stand as an allegory of the fate of 'deviant' men.

It is not, however, simply a question of the figure of outlawed desire. In his biography of W. B. Yeats, significantly subtitled *The Man and the Masks*, Richard Ellmann argues that 'the implication of the esthetes' conception of the artistic personality is that a man is really two men' (Ellmann 1979, 75), and he lists multiple examples of the figure of the double in late-nineteenth-century writing – including in his list both Wilde's *The Picture of Dorian Gray* (1891) and Stevenson's *Strange Case* as classic instances of an 'atmosphere of doubling and splitting of the self' (77). Yeats, in his *Autobiographies*, himself wondered whether the nineties represented 'an age of transition', or an era torn by the pursuit of antithesis (Yeats 1955, 304), both of which comments could be interpreted as the effects of doubling. An age of transition, after all, is an age which looks in two directions – towards the future as well as towards the past; and the feeling of antithesis is the articulation of a double vision.

In his dialogue essay 'The Decay of Lying', which originally appeared in *The Nineteenth Century* in January 1889, Wilde twice makes reference to Stevenson's story, and does so in a way that suggests that double vision is the condition that the story provokes. On the first occasion, Vivian (Wilde's mouthpiece in the dialogue) comments that even Stevenson, 'that delightful master of delicate and fanciful prose, is tainted with' the modern vice of realism; 'the transformation of Dr Jekyll reads dangerously like an experiment out of the *Lancet*' (Wilde 1994, 1074). On the second, Vivian tells an anecdote in the service of his argument that life imitates art, not the other way around, which is why we need lies, for lies are what great art consists of. His story is about a friend of his named Hyde who had unwittingly replicated Edward Hyde's act of brutality in trampling a child, had been pursued by an angry crowd, found sanctuary in a doctor's surgery, paid off the crowd, and then discovered as he left when the danger had passed that 'the name on the brass door-plate of the surgery … was "Jekyll". At least it should have been' (1084). In its context, the anecdote is certainly not supposed to be taken as true, and that throwaway line that the name '*should* have been' Jekyll advertises that fact. All the same, the anecdote does have a tendency to feel like evidence. The eyewitness who speaks about what he saw, or what he knows to have happened from a friend of a friend, vouches for his good faith in the very act of speaking to his peers. There is a spurious but nonetheless compulsive authority to anecdote. The two references to Stevenson's story – one of which is disparaging about Stevenson's aesthetics, the other of which is nonetheless prepared to make use of a despised novella in the pursuit of an argument – are not quite consistent. But then, as Vivian has already commented: 'Who wants to be consistent? The dullard and the doctrinaire, the tedious people who carry out their principles to the bitter end of action, the *reductio ad absurdam* of practice' (1072). Here is a man who does not believe that art should make you behave differently – literature itself is constructed as intransitive. Consistency would require a single coherent vision as its prerequisite. Wilde, however, is the writer of complex double visions in which contradictory opinions are simultaneously voiced. *The Importance of Being Earnest* is merely the most famous example of this tendency in his work. Wilde, of course, did not know that it would be his last major work. It appears retrospectively as the apotheosis of his double visions, though had its author not been tried and imprisoned for being a Hyde in disguise as a respectable Jekyll, there would probably have been other examples. The point about *Earnest*, as about almost all of Wilde's writings is that he is both Jekyll *and* Hyde, not Jekyll *or* Hyde.

His two most famous essays which set out the 'principles' of aesthetic criticism, 'The Decay of Lying' and 'The Critic as Artist' (originally published in *The Nineteenth Century* in July and September 1890) dramatize doubling. They are both couched as dialogues between an older aesthete and a younger man who is shocked (or who pretends to be shocked) at the implications of his interlocutor's arguments. The dialogue form had very particular advantages for Wilde. Firstly, it is an ancient pedagogic tool, deriving from the fourth century BC Socratic dialogues of Plato, where instead of *telling* his pupils what to think, Socrates discussed philosophical issues in conversations with them. In the course of their talk, by the asking of well-placed questions, Socrates would *lead* his followers to his own favoured conclusions: it is not for nothing that word *education* is derived from the Latin verb *ducere* meaning 'to lead'. The Ancient Greek pedigree of this teaching method lent intellectual and academic respectability to those who used it. At the same time, though, Wilde recognized an erotic charge at the heart of the pupil/teacher exchange (seduction shares the Latin root of education, and pedagogy and pederasty might sometimes be linked terms). Intimate conversations might at once be spaces of intellectual intercourse – but exchanges between like minds might also be a form of flirtation leading to an entirely different kind of intercourse. Finally, the dialogues both present what mainstream culture would have regarded as rather outrageous views. But the views expounded can be disavowed by Wilde himself; they are the characters' views, not the author's. Wilde was not above contradicting himself in more straight-forwardly presented essays, writing in 'The Truth of Masks' (1885, orig-inally published in *The Nineteenth Century* as 'Shakespeare and Stage Costume') an essay about archaeological accuracy in the representa-tion of Shakespeare's plays:

> Not that I agree with everything I have said in this essay. There is much with which I entirely disagree. The essay simply represents an artistic standpoint, and in aesthetic criticism, attitude is everything. For in art there is no such thing as a universal truth. A Truth in art is that whose contradictory is also true. (Wilde 1994, 1173)

The dialogue form simply allows him to dramatize this position through the very form of the essays.

'The Decay of Lying' begins with Cyril's invitation to Vivian to come outside to smoke cigarettes and enjoy nature on a perfectly lovely afternoon. Vivian's response is that no cultivated person can enjoy nature at all: nature is uncomfortable, full of insects and inartistic, an assault on the entire Romantic tradition of nature-worship that had descended to the Victorians through the worship of William Wordsworth's poetics and aesthetics. He then goes on to read his essay on lying – an essay about the failure of realism as an artistic movement – to Vivian for the next several pages, and over some hours. But ironically, from his original refusal to go out and smoke cigarettes amongst the glories of nature, the piece ends with Vivian inviting Cyril to do just what he had refused to do before: 'now let us go out onto the terrace, where "droops the milk-white peacock like a ghost", while the evening star "washes the dusk with silver". At twilight, nature becomes a wonderfully suggestive effect, and is not without its loveliness, though perhaps its chief use is to illustrate quotations from the poets. Come! We have talked long enough' (Wilde 1994, 1092). Discussion leads to a kind of seduction, and a glorious inconsistency in action and argu-ment. This essay, along with 'The Critic as Artist', stands as a rehearsal for Lord Henry Wooton's seduction of Dorian Gray.

The erotic basis of 'The Critic as Artist' is even more self-evident. The two speakers are Gilbert and – significantly – Ernest, who will be defeated in argument by his friend. The dialogue develops and subverts Arnold's arguments about the necessity of criticism for fine art to have any existence in a framework Wilde derived from Pater.

Gilbert suggests that a creative artist is his own greatest critic since the artistic process necessarily demands the rejection of unsuitable forms, and it is the critic inside the artist who knows what to select and what to reject. He claims further that the critic who is not an artist as such has the same, if not greater, importance for art as a whole. The agonized Ernest, named for common sense and straightforwardness, asks Gilbert if he is really suggesting that criticism is a creative art. Of course it is, says Gilbert: 'Why should it not be? It works with materials and put them into a form that is at once new and delightful. What more can one say of poetry?' (1125). Form, not content is what matters: 'In every sphere of life, form is the beginning of things ... Forms are the food of faith ... The Creeds are believed, not because they are rational, but because they are repeated. Yes: form is everything' (1148–9). This is a scandalous thing to say. The creeds, the central statements of Christian belief, are powerful not because they are logical or rational, but because they have a repetitive structure, and because they are oft-repeated. Our response to them is an emotional response to their form, not a logical response to their content – they are habits, and as such, they are failures. In *Sexual Dissidence*, Jonathan Dollimore argues that Wilde inverts and subsequently deconstructs what he calls the 'depth models' of our society's beliefs about action and character. Dollimore constructs a list of binary oppositions including surface versus depth, lying versus truth, and style/artifice versus authenticity (Dollimore 1991, 15) in which the second term of each opposition is the one most usually valorized. Wilde upends these binaries, and in doing so undermines the binary structure of either/or, replacing it with and/both. In Gilbert's argument, the depth model of religious faith, for example – a model to do with sincerity, truth, authenticity and even earnestness – is radically destabilized, and faith is reduced to an aesthetic response.

At the end of the dialogue, Ernest is not convinced, but that does not matter. Gilbert has attained a very different end than conviction. The two men have stayed up all night talking about outrageous things – like lovers, perhaps. They stay up, and watch the sunrise at the end of the dialogue, when manly young men with economically productive jobs and beautiful wives should be in bed. Rationality has little to do with the seductive potency of powerful conversation, nor with its potentially demoralizing and subversive effects over nineteenth-century norms of masculinity.

The dialogue form is simply the explicit statement of something that Wilde consistently did in all his essays, whether couched as dialogues or not. Borrowing a manner from Matthew Arnold, and an ethical framework from Walter Pater, an essay such as 'Pen, Pencil and Poison: A Study in Green' (1889, first published in *The Fortnightly Review*) is also an exercise in rhetorical seduction. Arnold's published essays are filled with a disguised rhetoric that is very close to conversation as opposed to oratory. In writing oratorical prose, the writer thinks of himself as dominating his audience from a platform. In writing conversational prose, he presents himself as being on a level with his audience. Whereas the orator speaks to an audience made up of the many, the conversationalist presents himself as addressing me or you much more personally. The conversational writer assumes a manner that says: 'All reasonable people, like you and me, will of course agree with me.' It is a kind of manipulation through flattery and it makes contentious arguments more problematic to combat: the audience would not wish to appear either unreasonable or rude. These elements can be seen in Arnold's style: the interjections that begin sentences ('Well!', 'So', and so on), the slang and homely imagery, the combination of suave gentlemanly interlocutor and outrageous anecdotalist are the constructions of a persuasive authorial personality. As Pater had done before him, Wilde adapts and adopts Arnold's authority for very different purposes.

'Pen, Pencil and Poison' is a text that raises the question of genre, amongst other things. What kind of essay is it supposed to be? Moreover, it is also about forgery, which is a kind of lying – and it values forgery – in a period when authenticity and sincerity were both supposed to be the markers of the moral character of masculinity. The function of genre is that it signals a horizon of expectation to the reader, gives clues about how to read and interpret what is presented. The first readers of 'Pen, Pencil and Poison' in *The Fortnightly Review*, would have read it in the expectation that it was a literary essay, presenting an argument on rational grounds, addressed to an audience of gentlemanly (and perhaps ladylike) readers who would be expected to share the presuppositions of the author. Straightaway, however, the subject of this essay, Thomas Griffiths Wainewright, distorts the assumptions underlying the form of the polite essay. We are told in the first paragraph that Wainewright was not only a 'poet and a painter, an art-critic, an antiquarian, and a writer of prose, an amateur of beautiful things and dilettante of things delightful, but [he was] also a forger of no mean or ordinary capabilities, and as subtle and secret a poisoner, almost without rival in this or any age' (1093). The first part of the sentence is a nod in the direction of the polite essay memoir;

the second part is an absolute deflation of that tradition. The two parts of the sentence do not belong together. There is a dramatic inconsistency in the values signalled by the writing. The satire is not entirely aimed at the reader, though the reader becomes implicated by it in that rhetorical gesture that presumes the reader's agreement. But this is also a serious threat to the essay genre. The form in which the text is apparently written asks its readers to accept that forgery and poisoning are equivalent arts to writing and painting. The very concept of Art as a touchstone value is threatened in this juxtaposition. In precisely the urbane language that lends authority to the literary essay, Wilde unpicks its assumptions. Describing Wainewright's childhood for example, Wilde writes:

> the little child seems to have been brought up by his grandfather, and, on the death of the latter in 1803, by his uncle George Edward Griffiths, whom he subsequently poisoned. His boyhood was passed at Linden House, Turnham Green, one of those many Georgian mansions that have unfortunately disappeared before the inroads of the suburban builder, and to its lovely gardens and well-timbered park, he owed that simple and impassioned love of nature which never left him through his life, and which made him particularly susceptible to the influences of Wordsworth's poetry. He went to school at Charles Burney's academy at Hammersmith. Mr Burney ... seems to have been a man of a good deal of culture, and in after years, Mr. Wainewright spoke of him with much affection ... as an admirable teacher who, while he valued the intellectual side of education, did not forget the importance of early moral training. It was under Mr Burney that he first developed his talent as an artist, and Mr. Hazlitt tells us that a drawing-book which he used at school is still extant, and displays great talent and natural feeling. Indeed, painting was the first art that fascinated him. It was not till much later than he sought to find expression by pen or poison. (Wilde 1994, 1093–4)

I've quoted at length but the means by which the effects of this piece are achieved have to do with accumulated inappropriate juxtapositions rather than simple small examples. Much of the quotation is made up of entirely conventional observations of the kind one would usually expect to find in the world of the polite essay. A social background is built up for Wainewright. Details such as addresses, dates, the name of his school and his schoolmaster imply sober informative discourse. Remove just the final sentence, and the clause that informs us that he later poisoned his uncle, and Wainewright is being presented in an entirely proper way. The bulk of convention, however, is nothing against the pinpricks of those asides about his later career, which utterly deflate everything else, and give it all a new context and meaning.

To a Victorian audience, bred upon the realist narratives of cause and effect, Wainewright's early training – his good schooling, his pleasant surroundings in his Uncle's home – should have led inexorably to a good moral life. The nostalgic mention of that Georgian house with its resonances of light, airy, healthy rooms, set in wooded parkland, should have exposed the little child to all the morally beneficent effects of nature, made explicit in the naming of Wordsworth, *the* poet of nature as moral good, are all signals that everything should have gone well. This good beginning should have led to a good subsequent life. That Mr Burney the schoolmaster emphasized morality ought also to have been significant in the final formation of Wainewright's character. But in this context, all these things, and the conventions they stand for, are debunked in the casual reiteration that Wainewright was a forger and a poisoner.

In other words, in Wilde's double vision, a polite conversational tone is appropriated for outrageous effect. Social comedy and farce morph into disguised political commentaries; genre is used *and* undermined. Masks are real faces; performances are indistinguishable from essences. Readers have to look *both* ways.

1895: or, looking both ways?

For many reasons, 1895 is a key year in the British literary history. It marked the endings of a number of eras. Not only did it see Wilde's disgrace and the destruction of the British decadent movement, such as it was, it also has many other claims to be read as the 'real' end of Victorian literature. The year saw the last gasp of the three-volume novel, as Mary Elizabeth Braddon, doyenne of mid-century sensation fiction, abandoned it. The circulating libraries lost their hold on the marketplace and went into a steady and fatal decline as the prices of books came down to the reach of the ordinary middle classes, if not quite to levels that ordinary people more generally could afford. Thomas Hardy gave up writing fiction after the hostile reception to the publication of *Jude the Obscure* in 1895 in which a different kind of sexual anarchy was played out, and which also made very timely reference to contemporary theories of degeneration in its portrayal of the suicide of Father Time. For, as well as endings, the year saw new beginnings in both literature and cultural writing more generally. Max Nordau's *Degeneration* was translated and published in its first English edition during the maelstrom of Wilde's trials. H. G. Wells published *The Time Machine*, and helped to initiate a new genre; on the other hand, Marie Corelli published *The Sorrows of Satan* and George MacDonald published *Lilith: A Romance*, both allegories in their different ways of exemplarily Victorian morality. Conrad's first fiction, *Almayer's Folly*, was published in 1895, as a precursor to Modernism, appearing alongside Arthur Symons's proto-modernist poems, *London Nights*, which came out – with very bad timing – just as the Wilde scandal hit the press. Grant Allen's potboiler, *The Woman Who Did*, rode the quest of a wave of interest in the elusive figure of the New Woman in 1895. Röntgen discovered x-rays; the Lumière brothers pioneered the cinematograph. Freud ventured into print with Fliess on the subject of hysteria. What does this partial list tell us? That any age of transition is marked by both beginnings and endings – 1895 had its own particular version of double vision, looking both backwards and forwards.

Wilde stands neatly as a transitional figure precisely because he also looked backwards towards the conventions of the past, which he had internalized to an amazing degree, and forwards, away from them; *because* he had internalized them he could see their limitations. He was not averse to making use of the new things for his own purposes. In one of the letters he wrote from prison, petitioning the Home Secretary that his sentence be commuted, he showed just how *au courant* he was with contemporary thinking:

> ... such offences are forms of sexual madness and are recognised as such not merely by modern pathological science but by much modern legislation, notably in France, Austria, and Italy, where the laws affecting these misdemeanours have been repealed, on the grounds that they are diseases to be cured by the physician, rather than crimes to be punished by a judge. In the works of eminent men of science such as Lombroso and Nordau ... this is especially insisted on with reference to the intimate connection between madness and the literary and artistic temperament. (Wilde ed. Hart-Davis 1979, 142)

It is a sign of desperation on Wilde's part that he hoped his words would have some effect – that they would behave transitively and buy him his freedom, just as the judge's sentence had acted transitively to perform that sentence upon him. There was to be no early release. But it is also a sign of his modernity that he tried to make this argument at all.

We can read what happened to Wilde as the last gasp of Victorian morality having its revenge on its prodigal son. More plausibly, however, we can read his tragic ending as a symptom of the continuing grasp that Victorian morality had on British culture in the years that followed. In 1913, the young Beverley Nichols was caught by his father reading *The Picture of Dorian Gray*. This discovery provoked an extraordinary display of paternal violence:

> In an ecstasy of incoherent rage, his father proceeded to spit repeatedly on the pages until his chin was covered with saliva; then he lifted the book to his mouth and dismembered it with his teeth. When his innocent son persisted in demanding what it was that Oscar Wilde had done, he received an answer written on a scrap of paper: *Illum crimen horribile... quod non nominandem est.* (qtd in Lilly 1993, 28)

Although the outward hysteria died down with time, as Neil Bartlett has observed, by 1948, one could read Wilde as 'a literary classic, albeit one for whom it would have been suspect to show an excessive enthusiasm' (Bartlett 1989, 33). No spitting, perhaps, but the attitudes of 1948, whatever the calendar said, were not so very different from those of 1895 or 1913. Not until 1968 would the law under which Wilde was convicted be repealed. It is a grim irony that a playwright who tried to make a virtue out having it both ways has also come to stand for continuing double visions. Double vision can be subversive, playful, a game: it can also represent two-faced hypocrisy. I think we know which Wilde 'intended'; but his message was not always received.

Notes

1. John Stokes, however, has shown in his book *Oscar Wilde: Myths Miracles and Imitations*, that at least one recent production did begin by bringing a homoerotic subtext to the fore in the opening scene. In Nicholas Hytner's 1993 production of the play at the Aldwych theatre already alluded to, Jack and Algy greeted each other on first meeting with a kiss. See Stokes 1996, 166–7.
2. Similarly, as Patricia Flanegan Behrendt and Timothy D'Arch Smith have both observed, there is a further pun on the name 'Ernest', which sounds very close to *uraniste*, a coterie term for same-sex desire in the 1890s. See Flanegan Beherendt 1991 and D'Arch Smith 1970.

4 Masculine Romance, Cultural Capital and Crisis

One of the key ways of defining what has come to be known as literary modernism is as an epistemological crisis. At its simplest, epistemology refers to the knowledge of the world that can be gained through written language. For the *avant-garde* writers of the early twentieth century, who often made it their business to reconstruct their immediate forebears as hopelessly naïve, the idea that language – written or spoken – can articulate anything substantial about the nature of reality, was old-fashioned and simplistic. Modernism, on this basis, can certainly be partially understood as a loss of faith in the expressive adequacy of the word. Examples of this crisis abound in what we have come to call modernist fiction – in the works of Virginia Woolf, James Joyce, E. M. Forster, D. H. Lawrence and Joseph Conrad. The labyrinthine complexities of Henry James's late prose (in texts such as *The Turn of the Screw*, 1898 for example) are, in the authorized version of literary history, its immediate precursor; and the equally complex writings of Pater are the ghost at the modernist feast.

In *The Good Soldier* (1915), for instance, Ford Madox Ford repeatedly dramatizes through the narrative of John Dowell, the extent to which words fail in their expressive purpose. Thus Dowell, describing the four points of view that made up his marriage to Florence, and the marriage of his friends, the Ashburnams, is virtually incapable of making any statement whatsoever about what actually happened, and about what it meant. He begins by describing the friendship between the two couples as an extremely sedate and civilized dance:

> Our intimacy was like a minuet...we could all go, all four together, without a signal from any one of us, always to the music of the Kur orchestra, always in the temperate sunshine, or if it rained, in discreet shelters. No indeed, it can't be gone. You can't kill a minuet de la cour...No, by God it is false! It wasn't a minuet that we stepped; it was a prison – a prison full of screaming hysterics, tied down so that they

might not outsound the rolling of our carriage wheels as we went along
the shaded avenues of the Taunus Wald. (Ford 1995, 11–12)

The fascination of *The Good Soldier* is that every positive statement
('our intimacy was like a minuet') is undermined, sooner or later, by a
counter statement ('it wasn't a minuet; it was a prison … full of scream-
ing hysterics'). Dowell and his friends were 'always in the temperate
sunshine' – always, that is, except when it rained. This pattern is
repeated throughout the text, so that at the end, neither reader nor
narrator has much sense of what 'really' happened. Moreover, Dowell
has no proper sense of perspective or scale. His similes routinely
compare unlike with unlike, often with grotesque exaggeration. Just
before the passage quoted above, he has commented: 'Someone has
said that the death of a mouse from cancer is the whole sack of Rome
by the Goths, and I swear to you that the breaking-up of our little four-
square coterie was such another unthinkable event' (11). What is being
compared to what in this statement? A mouse dying of cancer, quite
apart from its improbability is surely in no sense comparable to the
Sack of Rome despite the spurious authority lent to the comparison by
the phrase 'someone has said'; and the sadness of a series of unhappy
relationships can be compared to neither. What, then, if anything, has
Dowell said?

At the end of novels like *The Good Soldier*, Forster's *Passage to India*,
Conrad's *Heart of Darkness*, Woolf's *To the Lighthouse*, one cannot be
sure about the events of the narrative. These are fictions that get part
of their effect by the fact that you cannot paraphrase them, that you
cannot quite say what they were about – at least in the conventional
terms in which novels are discussed by lay readers – in terms of their
plots. Such fictions are a world away from the Arnoldian ideal of seeing the world steadily, and seeing it whole, and the confusions come
from each novelists' presiding sense of the incapacity of language to
tell the world in a plain way.

It might perhaps seem perverse to seek the same kind of crisis about
the potency of language in the writings that I am going to call, following Elaine Showalter, masculine romances (1991, 80), though they
have had other names.[1] The articulation of epistemological crisis was
resolutely not the avowed intention of writers such as Robert Louis
Stevenson, H. Rider Haggard, Arthur Conan Doyle, Bram Stoker or
Richard Marsh. Indeed, in published statements about the nature of
what they were doing, there is consistently a rather 'gung-ho' attitude
to language and the purpose of literature: it is taken for granted that

language *can and does* express the world, and that the function of the novelist is simply to entertain his readers with a relatively comfortable version of reality in which, despite the monsters that inhabit it, the good – provided they are middle class – will indeed end happily, and the bad will get their just deserts. Thus the novelist Andrew Lang, friend and champion of Stevenson and Haggard, in his 1887 article 'Realism and Romance', written for the *Contemporary Review*, protested against realism's insistent concentration on 'the Unpleasant Real in character ... I think that the Realists, while they certainly show us the truth, are the fondest of showing that aspect of it which is really the less common as well as the less desirable' (101). Lang argues implicitly for a common-sense attitude to and in fiction. And he connects this attitude to gentlemanly virtues. Too much information about the private desires of men and especially of women 'makes [him] feel uncomfortable in the reading, makes [him] feel intrusive and unmanly' (102). He claims to like all kinds of books, but prefers 'boys' books' – tales of adventure which eschew the feminine world of home, and which scarcely even represent women as characters at all.

Elsewhere, at much the same time and in similar vein, Robert Louis Stevenson was arguing in print (with Henry James and Walter Besant) about the nature of good fiction. Good fiction, in the end, is what Stevenson likes, what he has an appetite for. In 'A Gossip on Romance' (1882), he centres his discussion on a metaphor of consumption, making it clear that reading is, for him, a sensual pleasure at least as much as an intellectual one. There is certainly no anxiety about language, except inasmuch as language is more or less able to produce the effect of pleasure:

> In anything fit to be called by the name of reading, the process itself should be absorbing and voluptuous; we should gloat over a book ... Eloquence and thought, character and conversation, were but obstacles to brush aside [in boyhood reading] as we dug blithely after a certain sort of incident, like a pig for truffles. ... I liked a story to begin with an old wayside inn where, 'towards the close of the year 17—, several gentleman in three-cocked hats were playing bowls' ... Give me a highway man and I was full to brim ... a highway man was my favourite dish ... One and all ... read story-books in childhood, not for eloquence or character or thought, but for some quality of the brute incident. (Stevenson 1999, 52–3)

Any writing that drew attention to its own status was writing which detracted from uncomplicated pleasure. In Stevenson's metaphors, an appetite for fiction is like a physical appetite for meat. Stories might be 'nourished with the realities of life' (56); but realism and fine writing were far less important than the kinds of striking incidents that could leave readers 'rapt clean out of ourselves' (52). Imagined worlds matter more than the real world in this critique. Thus when Stevenson later responded to Henry James's strictures on adventure fiction, in which James had complained that such writing left no room for critical thought, Stevenson argued that the point of pleasurable reading was precisely that it permitted, even encouraged, the suspension of the critical faculties: 'The luxury to most of us, is to lay by our judgement, to be submerged in the tale as by a billow, and only to awake, and begin to distinguish and find fault when the tale is over' (86). He accuses James of never having been a child, the point presumably being that the childlike sense of wonder is far more fun than any adult critical theorizing:

> if he has never been on a quest for buried treasure, it can be demonstrated that he has never been a child. There never was a child ... but has hunted gold, and been a pirate, and a military commander, and a bandit of the mountains; but has fought, and suffered shipwreck and prison, and imbrued his little hands in gore, and gallantly retrieved the lost battle, and triumphantly protected innocence and beauty. (Stevenson 1991, 86)

Well, actually, I believe I was a child once, and I never did quite these things; but then, when I was a child, I was a little girl. This is a highly gendered description of a supposedly generic child. These are *boys'* own adventures, played out by little boys, and read about in fictions written for them. In defending romance against the novel of character and incident, of eloquence and thought – the Realist novel – Lang and Stevenson are defending a masculine dream of or a masculine aspiration towards the exercise of power and certainty in one's own actions.

The suggestion that I want to make here is that the late-nineteenth-century vogue for masculine romance comes from two conflicting sources. On the one hand, as Elaine Showalter, Joseph Bristow, Patrick Brantlinger and others have argued, it is an assertion of manliness. 'What did it mean to write for boys?' asks Showalter; 'Little boys who read will become big boys who rule, and adventure fiction is thus important training,' she answers (80). The masculine romances in which little boys like Stevenson immersed themselves had the important moral function of teaching those same little boys to become the conquerors and administrators of the British Empire. But the problem of masculine romance is summed up in that phrase 'conquerors *and* administrators'. To what extent can the virtues of the warlike and adventurous soldier be seen as the virtues of the civilizing civil servant? Prudence, innocence and decency are not the skills required for conquest but those required to reign over the conquered lands, to consolidate them into an empire, to turn savages into civilized beings through good example.

In Stevenson's description of romance, the emphasis is on pleasure, not on responsibility. These are books in which you can lose yourself to simple, uncritical joys. But if such books are focused on the pleasure of adventure, to what extent are they primers for the administration of empire? Losing yourself in pleasure means that you risk becoming a lotus-eater – one who 'will return no more' to more weighty responsibilities. Or, alternatively, it means that you risk 'going native'. As Patrick Brantlinger observes: 'In early Victorian literature, the numerous offspring of Robinson Crusoe...hold out manfully against the cannibals ... [but] late Victorian literature is filled with backsliders, like Conrad's Kurtz, who become white savages' (39). You either fight against the forces of savagery with sword and gun; or you administrate the savages with railway technology, Christian education and the law; or – you become savage yourself.

My basic definition of masculine romance includes the following assumptions about the mode of address and the implied audiences of the fictions. Rider Haggard has the narrator of *King Solomon's Mines* (1885) Allan Quatermain dedicate his account of quests into Africa to 'all the big and little boys who read it' (Haggard 1989). In a similar vein, the dedication to *Allan Quatermain* (1887), written in Haggard's own voice, reads:

> I inscribe this book of adventure to my son ... in the hope that in days to come he, and many other boys whom I shall never know, may in the acts and thoughts of Allan Quatermain and his companions herein recorded, find something to help him and them to reach to what, with Sir Henry Curtis [hero of the novel], I hold to be the highest rank whereto we can attain – the state and dignity of English gentlemen. (Haggard 1994)

These quotations point out explicitly what remains implicit in other versions; masculine romances are fictions written by men for a male audience and have as part of their aim the will to teach English boys to become English gentlemen – although women obviously can and do read them, they are not quite for women or little girls. This also means that the content of the stories must evade the most usual content of domestic fictions, the stories of love and marriage that were the main-stay of the circulating libraries. Stephen Heath has noted the almost complete absence of women from Stevenson's *Strange Case* (Heath 1996, 64ff); one could make the same point about *Treasure Island* (1883), inspiration for Haggard's *King Solomon's Mines*. Sex has been displaced from the centre of the narrative.[2] Even *Dracula*, which has some notably sexualized content, turns sex into something despicable because only the vampire 'does it', and it is therefore monstrous, not desirable. And although Mina plays a major role in the novel, she is only able to do so because she has a man's brain in her woman's body.

Masculine romances avoid sexual romance because they are pro-foundly interested in the making of proper masculinity, in the figure of the gentleman. Part of what defines gentlemanliness is the repres-sion of unsuitable desires, and particularly the suppression of sexual appetite. Their content therefore focuses on adventure and action, whether this be imperial adventure in exotic locations, or a more domestically inclined quest to root out monstrosity, criminality or other aberrations at home. The ideal of the gentleman – the late-Victorian standard of proper masculinity – is essential to their conception, but that ideal is always problematic. Thus although Allan Quatermain may occasionally doubt his right to that title, his doubts in fact are sup-posed to point out gentlemanliness in his behaviour and attitudes: 'am I a gentleman?' he asks in the first chapter of *King Solomon's Mines*:

> What is a gentleman? I don't quite know, and yet I have had to do with niggers – no, I'll scratch that word 'niggers' out, for I don't like it. I've known natives who *are*, and … I've known mean whites … who *aint* … I was born a gentleman, though I've been nothing but a poor travelling trader and hunter all my life. Whether I have remained so I know not … Heaven knows I've tried. I've killed many men in my time, but I have never slain wantonly or stained my hand in innocent blood, only in self-defence … I have never stolen, though I once cheated a Kafir out of a herd of cattle. But then he had done me a dirty turn, and it has troubled me ever since into the bargain. (Haggard 1989, 9–10)

Modern readers will certainly have some trouble with the racism – whether scratched out or not – of Quatermain's discourse. But the orig-inal readers were meant to see a touching lack of arrogance in his uncertainty about his status, whether social and economic, or moral and ethical, in laying claim to the title of gentleman. Like any figure involved in empire, he has done violence but not for pleasure since unmotivated violence is savage or primitive. He has been involved in morally dubious transactions, but his conscience has troubled him, marking him as civilized. His gentlemanliness is an ambiguous status, something he was born with and therefore it is intrinsic, but also and something he can acquire, keep or lose through the standards of his behaviour, which means it is rather differently defined. One of the functions of masculine romance is to dispel that ambiguity with moral certainty, and it will usually do this by producing an ending that appears to uphold the standard. The process by which the ending is reached, however, has a shocking tendency to unravel its own ideological workings.

The fictions I am about to discuss, then, are texts which – often unconsciously – represent masculinity in crisis, for if ambiguity haunts the concept of the gentleman, no matter how much it is shored up in fictions which support its status, the very fact that it needs to be shored up points out that the concept of gentlemanliness is insecure. What I want to suggest is that the existential or ontological crisis of proper masculinity in these texts is expressed as an epistemological crisis in their form. They are all novels which, to some extent, replicate what Christopher Craft, writing on *Dracula* has called 'a predictable, if variable, triple rhythm. Each of these texts invites or admits a monster, then entertains and is entertained by monstrosity for some extended duration, until in its closing pages it expels or repudiates the monster and all the disruption he/she/it/ brings' (Craft 1999, 93–4). Or, at least, that is the 'cover story', the immediately accessible format of these books. My suggestion is that no matter what is going on on the surface, where beetles are killed by the modern technological disaster of a train crash, where vampires are staked out and staked to death, where double personalities are unified into single corpses, where criminals get caught because crime mustn't pay, and where the monstrous regiment of foreign women is disciplined to death, something of the horror each monster represents survives. Its survival is guaranteed by the ways the stories are told in which readers and writers are denied clear vision, and the explicit messages of masculine romances about full-blooded manliness are thereby subverted.

The Gothic and obscure vision

Part of the fundamental décor of the Gothic genre is obscurity of vision. One cannot see clearly the monsters that threaten to leap out of dark corners of dusty rooms, or the sublime landscapes of foreign lands, or the foggy labyrinth of the modern city. Indeed, if you could see them clearly, they would not frighten you. When Sigmund Freud described the literary figure of the Uncanny in psychological terms in his 1919 essay, his whole discussion took place in the realms of ambiguity, in that space where you cannot quite *tell what you saw*. Freud sought to develop this insight in relation to his own particular philosophical and psychological position. Nonetheless, the key terms of that description, uncertainty caused by obscured vision, and the inability to 'clear up' that uncertainty have significant bearing on the functioning of uncanny effects in gothic fictions of the late nineteenth century.

In multiple instances in fictions of the late-Victorian period, what you see – at least as an ordinary observer – is not what you get. The quasi-realist world of the Sherlock Holmes stories, for example, is filled with uncanny effects, often produced by the 'hero' Holmes himself, as he repeatedly makes his clients 'start' with amazement (being made to jump is one of the symptoms of the Uncanny) because he has *seen* with an almost preternatural clarity signs and clues that are invisible to other observers. Holmes sees more, and sees more clearly, than anyone else, and Dr Watson, the reader's substitute in the text, is incapable of reproducing his effects, though he is able to tell what Holmes has seen 'in a clear way'. Thus in 'The Adventure of Empty House', the story in which Holmes returns from the dead – itself an uncanny activity, which makes Watson jump when he realizes – before Holmes's return, Dr Watson has tried to replicate the processes used by Holmes to solve a 'locked room' murder. 'All day, as I drove upon my round,' Watson says, 'I turned over the case in my mind, and found no explanation which appeared to me to be adequate' (Doyle 1981, 483). Neither Watson nor his reader can see so clearly as the remarkable detective.

More usually, though, the effect of the uncanny is produced by the impossibility of deciding quite what it is that has been seen. The figure who feels the uncanny effect is more like Dr Watson than Mr Holmes. In Stevenson's *The Strange Case of Dr Jekyll and Mr Hyde* (1886) for example, when Mr Utterson first meets Hyde he finds himself in a state of 'mental perplexity':

> The problem that he was … debating was one of a class that is rarely solved. Mr Hyde was pale and dwarfish; he gave an impression of deformity without any nameable malformation, he had a displeasing smile, he had borne himself to the lawyer with a sort of murderous admixture

of timidity and boldness, and he spoke with a husky whispering and somewhat broken voice, – all these were points against him; but not all of these together could explain the hitherto unknown disgust, loathing and fear with which Mr Utterson regarded him. 'There must be something else,' said the perplexed gentleman. 'There *is* something more, if I could find a name for it...the man seems hardly human!' (Stevenson 1979, 40)

Stevenson's narrator clearly distinguishes between what can be *seen* in Mr Hyde's physical bearing and how it makes the viewer *feel*. Hyde might not be pretty to look at but the feeling he produces is much more significant than mere appearance and manners should produce. It is precisely the feeling of the uncanny that is evoked here because vision does not lead to full interpretation. In addition Hyde is also a creature in human form who does not seem to be quite human to the eyes of those who see him, emphasizing his uncanny status.

In the Introduction, I described Pater's creative evocation of Leonardo's Mona Lisa as a text that has ambiguous effects, in part because of a context that points to moral confusion. That confusion, I also suggested, comes from the fact that Pater's text relies on the subjective feelings of the viewer, rather than on an intellectual or objective response to the object that is seen. The masculine gothic romances of the late nineteenth century are perhaps the last place where one would expect to find any evidence of Paterian influence, and I don't suppose that many of their writers had actually read him: H. Rider Haggard scarcely reads like a man who had much time for Aestheticism, and in his Preface to *King Solomon's Mines* he quite deliberately eschews such values, constructing his narrator as a man proud of his 'blunt way of writing' and of the absence of 'grand literary flights and flourishes' in his discourse (Haggard 1989, 6). But in *She* (1886), though the narrator is similarly blunt and forthright (he's an academic – no time for flights and flourishes), the description of Ayesha when she unveils to Holly is remarkable for its similarities to Pater's *La Gioconda* as well as for its foreshadowing of the Freudian concept of the Uncanny.

> ...all of a sudden the long, corpse-like wrappings fell from her to the ground, and my eyes travelled up her form...How am I to describe it? I cannot – I simply cannot! The man does not live whose pen could convey a sense of what I saw...Though the face before me was that of a young woman of certainly not more than thirty years, in perfect health, and the first flush of ripened beauty, yet it had stamped upon it a look of unutterable experience, and of deep acquaintance with grief and passion.

> Not even the lovely smile that crept about the dimples of her mouth could hide this shadow of sin and sorrow. It shone even in the light of the glorious eyes, it was present in the air of majesty, and it seemed to say: 'Behold me, lovely as no woman was or is, undying and half-divine; memory haunts me from age to age, and passion leads me by the hand – evil I have done, and with sorrow have I made acquaintance from age to age, and from age to age evil I shall do, and sorrow shall I know till my redemption comes.' (Haggard 2001, 159)

Ayesha is a beautiful woman, but she is scarcely human. Her clothes and veils resemble the wrappings of a corpse; her form defies description, becoming virtually unspeakable. And the reason that she is so threatening is that she cannot be seen clearly (Holly is blinded by this vision of troubling beauty), and what can be seen cannot be described in a clear way. She is made up of contradictions – a young woman, but with centuries of experience, divine, but also devilish: she refuses definition, just as the Mona Lisa had done for Pater.

In a very different book, Richard Marsh's *The Beetle* (1897), it is the gender ambiguity of Pater's passage that comes to the fore. I have argued elsewhere that when the viewer cannot tell the sex of the person viewed, the effect is uncanny, and potentially even horrific (Robbins 2000, 182–6). That effect is exacerbated when the viewer cannot be even sure of the species of what he observes. The tramp, Robert Holt, who comes across the Beetle in the novel's first pages cannot at first see what the creature that dogs him is because the room is dark. When a light is struck, having been dazzled, Holt comments: 'I did see something; and what I did see I had rather have left unseen' (Marsh 1994, 13).

> I could not at once decide if it was a man or a woman. Indeed at first I doubted if it was anything human. But, afterwards, I knew it to be a man – for this reason ... that it was impossible such a creature could be feminine ... only his head was visible. ... His age I could not guess; such a look of age I had never imagined. Had he asserted that he had been living through the ages, I should have been forced to admit that, at least, he looked it. And yet I felt that it was quite within the range of possibility that he was no older than myself. (Marsh 1994, 13–14)

A pattern begins to emerge from these descriptions of monsters, a pattern to do with seeing only obscurely and speaking haltingly about what one has seen. Monsters are ambiguous partly because of their etymology: a monster is that which is shown (from the Latin *monstrare*, to show), but which ought not to have been shown.[3] Monsters there-fore stand for unveiled mysteries. As such they are somehow blasphe-mous figures; the unveiling of a mystery is conceived as an outrage or an obscenity. So much for seeing the world clearly, and for telling what one has seen in a clear way. Monsters are also timeless; they live for centuries (this is also true of Dracula), and as such they are outside a human time frame that would make them more easily understood. All this means that monsters are fundamentally ambiguous. Ayesha is beautiful but also evil – and the viewer obscurely understands that she is both, despite the fact that all his training leads him to the view that beauty and goodness should go together. The beetle is disgusting, but also compelling; he has hypnotic qualities that fascinate and compel the viewer to act according to his wishes. Both have human character-istics, but neither is fully human. They cannot be taken in at a glance and it is virtually impossible to describe them and their effects.

Degeneration: the context of late-nineteenth-century monstrosity

Alongside whatever fundamental concepts make monsters monstrous, it is also true that each generation creates monstrosity anew. What we fear is dependent on the context in which we live. The particular mon-sters of the late-nineteenth-century gothic tradition function as the articulation of a particular set of fears specific to that period, the fear of degeneration.

Degeneration is a concept deriving from Darwin's theories of evolu-tion. In *The Origin of Species* (1859) the fundamental hypothesis was that the current state of species on the planet was the result of minute and gradual changes in previous species, changes that had taken place over millions of years. (Here we must recall that monsters are timeless at least in the sense that they exist outside the framework of ordinary human existence.) The effects of evolutionary thought were immensely far-reaching. There was a massive effect on conventional religious belief; and in addition, on biological science which now dis-placed man from the centre of the universe and began to view human-ity as just another species like all the rest. The idea of evolution and its implications for man produced two distinct responses amongst biolo-gists and other scientists. On the one hand, it was understood as positive: man had evolved from primeval slime, to land creatures, to primates, to the fundamentally brilliant creature he had become by the nineteenth century. In other words, evolution could be understood as a story of progress, in which the gradual changes represented a nearer approach to human perfection. But of course, the nineteenth century was not always quite so pleased with itself. When some thinkers looked around them at the world they inhabited, they could not agree that their period represented a move towards perfection: urbanization, industrialization, and their corollary of mass poverty did not look ideal. More pessimistic thinkers argued therefore that evolution did not necessarily mean that everyone was improving biologically (and thence socially). Indeed, evolution also showed that some species simply died out, that, as Tennyson had put it in *In Memoriam* (1850), nature was 'careless of the type', and was simply an amoral force, 'red in tooth and claw', indifferent to the fate of whole subgroups of biology. And if, as Darwin's writings clearly pointed out, humanity was just another biological species, like any other, it was perfectly possible that humanity, too, could become extinct: thus, evolution could be understood not necessarily as a structure of progress, but as one of decline. The idea of evolution as something that might produce regression was first fully articulated by the scientist Edwin Ray Lankester, in a book entitled *Degeneration: A Chapter in Darwinism* (1880). And it was an idea that immediately took very serious hold.

This is the conceptual framework in which Wells's scientific romances take place. *The Island of Dr Moreau* in which a mad scientist speeds up the process of evolution in his vivisectionist experiments that turn animals into human beings is one consideration of the dark side of progress, a test case of what evolutionary science could mean. *The Time Machine* (1895) is another. In the novel, the unnamed Time Traveller gets onto a contraption that bears a strange resemblance to a bicycle, and travels forward in time to the year 8002701. At first, he finds it hard to interpret what he finds there; it appears to be an Edenic world, inhabited by gentle – though also tiny – creatures who feed on fruit and appear to do no work. He wonders to himself if he has stumbled on a golden age, but is also a little disappointed by the appearance of the people who surround him, who may be gentle but who also seem intellectually enfeebled. These people are called the Eloi and the Time Traveller describes them thus:

> a little group of perhaps eight or ten … exquisite creatures were about me. One of them addressed me. … Then I felt other soft little tentacles on my back and shoulders. They wanted to make sure that I was real.

There was nothing in this at all alarming. Indeed, there was something in these pretty little people that inspired confidence – a graceful gentleness, a certain childlike ease. And besides, they looked so frail that I could fancy myself flinging the whole dozen of them about like nine-pins. ... looking more nearly into their features, I saw some further peculiarities in their Dresden-china type of prettiness. Their hair, which was uniformly curly, came to a sharp end at the neck and cheek; there was not the faintest suggestion of it on the face, and their ears were singularly minute. The mouths were small, with bright red, rather thin lips, and the little chins ran to a point. The eyes were large and mild; and – this may seem egotism on my part – I fancied even then that there was certain lack of the interest I might have expected in them. (Wells 1993d, 24–5)

The Time Traveller observes here the process of evolution in action. The Eloi are clearly human, but they are gentler, more childlike, and more ethereal than the people of the present. They look pretty unreal to him – like dolls rather than people, and thus their effect partakes of the uncanny. At first he sees them as ideal, as the result of thousands of years of evolution, which has got rid of unnecessary biological attributes (small ears, very little hair), and has produced a race of spectacularly beautiful people. As he gets to know them a little better however, he begins to understand that what he is seeing is not an ideal world, but a world of horror. The Eloi are not the lords of perfected evolution, but its victims. Even before he discovers the true horror of the situation, he comments to himself: 'It seemed to me that I had happened upon humanity on the wane. The ruddy sunset set me thinking of the sunset of mankind' (31). He soon discovers that they are childlike in more ways than one, and in particular, they are afraid of the dark. This is no unreasonable or superstitious fear. They are scared of the dark because at night, a second evolutionary branch of the human race comes into its own.

The Traveller has noticed, as he scans the landscape, that there are massive ventilation shafts bored into the countryside. The shafts service an underground community of other human beings, named the Morlocks. The Morlocks are ugly, powerful and violent, and the Time Traveller feels an instant antipathy for them. They live in the underground world of caverns they have excavated, and – as the Traveller eventually discovers – they feed on the Eloi, whom they treat pretty much as cattle are treated by agriculture. In a description of a Morlock, encountered accidentally by the traveller as he explores a dark building (the Morlocks are afraid of the light, and do not go abroad in daylight),

Wells makes the reverse side of evolutionary progress abundantly clear:

> Suddenly I halted spellbound. A pair of eyes, luminous by reflection against the daylight without, was watching me out of the darkness. ... At once the eyes darted sideways, and something white ran past me. I turned with my heart in my mouth, and saw a queer little ape-like figure, its head held down in a peculiar manner, running across the sun-lit space behind me ... My impression of it is, of course, imperfect; but I knew it was a dull white, and had strange large, greyish-red eyes; also that there was flaxen hair on it head and down its back. But, as I say, it went too fast for me to see distinctly. I cannot even say whether it ran on all-fours, or only with its forearms held very low. ... It made me shudder. It was so like a human spider! (Wells 1993d, 46–7)

This creature has all the appearances of being an evolutionary throw-back. It is human, but the animal origins of humanity are clearly visible – it has eyes adapted like an owl's or a cat's, to see in the dark; it has more hair than people today have; it moves very fast, like an animal, and it's impossible to tell whether it is bipedal, or four legged. It is like an ape, and like a spider. It is not like a human being at all – especially in the fact that it has no gender. The Eloi are all very effeminate, but it is still possible – just – to distinguish between male and female. With the Morlocks, this essential characteristic of humanity (essential because Freud told us that sex is the first question we always ask and answer about a person) is missing. What is clearly at stake in *The Time Machine* is the fear that evolutionary science predicts not progress, but decline.

At much the same time as evolution was being debated, in France, Germany and Italy in particular, other scientists were trying to apply Darwinian ideas to already existing human populations, both in their own countries, and in their empires. They called their study anthropology – the study of mankind. Today anthropology is a more or less respectable academic study but its origins are very unsavoury. Evolution told us that man was a biological specimen, just like any other biological specimen, subject to the same evolutionary laws. In order to understand human biological development – and to prevent man's degeneration into possible extinction – the continental scientists attempted to study mankind just as they would study cattle or fruit flies. They set out to measure the physical characteristics of different groups and races, and to test the mental capacity of their specimen groups in order to come to some kind of conclusion about whether degeneration was already happening, to discover how it might be stopped if it was, and to ensure that degenerative evolution was arrested and returned to a progressive model. Once the data was gathered, it seemed simply to be a question of managing human populations in much the same way as farmers manage their animal stock: to breed only from the intelligent and healthy, and to prevent the damaged, the stupid, and the different from breeding at all. In this way, the concept of degeneration becomes related to the concept of eugenics, a word deriving from the Greek for 'well born, of good stock', meaning the genetic improvement of a race (especially the human race) by judicious mating and helping the better stock to prevail.

The problems with this 'science' are self-evident. The most obvious question is: who is to decide, and on what criteria, what human 'fitness' consists of? The continental scientists concentrated their attention on what they perceived as subgroups within their own societies: they wrote about criminals, about the insane, the mentally handicapped, and those suffering from inherited diseases (especially sexually transmitted diseases such as syphilis). The scientists assumed that they themselves were 'normal', and measured their subgroups against their own white, middle-class, masculine, educated, intelligent and physically healthy selves. (They did not study themselves, nor did they really question their own presumption of normality.) Two names in particular crop up again and again. One is Bénédicte-Auguste Morel (1809–73), whose particular interest was in insanity. He wrote books such as: *Clinical Studies: The Theory and Practice of Treating Mental Illness* (1852); *A Description of Mental, Physical and Moral Degeneration in the Human Species* (1857); and *On the Development of Various Kinds of Degeneration, or, New Elements of Morbidity in Anthropology* (1864). Perhaps the more significant name is that of Cesare Lombroso (1835–1909), an Italian doctor, who wrote huge numbers of books about degeneration and criminality, including: *The Delinquent: Studies in Anthropology, Legal Medicine and the Discipline of Imprisonment* (1876); *Criminal Man* (1895); *Crime: Its Causes and Remedies* (1911) and *The Delinquent Woman, The Prostitute and the Normal Woman* (1893), a truly fascinating title in the assumptions made via its juxtapositions. Lombroso in particular used the relatively new technology of photography as part of his technique of measuring fitness. He collected hundreds of case histories of convicted criminals, of the criminally insane, and of the mentally disabled, and photographed his specimens in order to build a composite picture of the criminal face, hoping to make a science of knowing the mind's construction by observing its physiognomy. The case studies included the crimes of which his subjects had been convicted; but as well as observing what he saw as physical evidence of criminality, he also speculated on a typical parentage for a criminal, a typical socio-economic background, and on repeated patterns of alcoholism and sexually transmitted disease. His intention was to make it possible to breed criminality out of the social system. In other words, Lombroso set out to make a *science* out of knowing the mind's construction by the face.

And then, in 1895, the first English translation of Max Nordau's *Degeneration* (1893) was published, applying these ideas to the concept of culture. Culture, a word used to describe the intellectual and artistic products of a society is a dangerous word as I noted in Chapter 2, because it is based in an organic or biological metaphor. We may not think that books have much to do with biology, but culture literally means 'growth' as in a bacterial culture, or as the ghosts of its earlier meanings in terms like horticulture, viticulture or agriculture all suggest (see Williams 1976, 87–93). Nordau's argument was based on the premise that literary and artistic cultures of a nation state were much like the biological characteristics of a particular race. If one could gauge the biological health of a group of people by measuring its physical characteristics, one could equally gauge the cultural health of a nation state by measuring the standards of its cultural products. Nordau particularly disapproved of decadent and symbolist art as an assault on standards of common sense. He argued that Impressionism in the visual arts was usually the result of 'the visual derangements' of degenerate artists who could not see clearly because they had inherited bad biology (Nordau 1993, 27). But he also found the symptoms of cultural decline in the popular taste for sensational fictions – ghost stories, tales of criminality and insanity, and exotic adventure: 'The book that would be fashionable must, above all, be obscure … Ghost-stories are very popular, but they must come in scientific disguise, as hypnotism, telepathy, somnambulism. … So are esoteric novels in which the author hints that he could say a deal about magic, kabbala, fakirism, astrology and other white and black arts, if he only chose' (Nordau 1993, 13–14). The use of fiction to stimulate new sensations, and the use of the arts to satisfy virtually animal appetites, was a clear and obvious marker of cultural degeneracy. Nordau might have been peddling nonsense, but it was highly influential nonsense.

These ideas were circulating in a Western Europe obsessed with its own position of power and dominance in the world, figured in the scramble of Western powers for colonial/imperial territories which was exemplified in the 1884 Berlin Conference on the division of Africa. In addition to looking at the subclasses of western societies, therefore, there was what we can now identify as a profoundly racist and sexist tendency in the methods of the so-called scientists of degeneration. It was in their interests, in the context of imperial expansion, to say that men like themselves represented the highpoint of evolution – that is, that white, Western European men were the apotheosis of evolutionary development. Degenerate types within western cultures (criminals, mad people, those with mental and physical disabilities, and women generally) were therefore 'found' to share the characteristics of the so-called lesser races, the subject peoples of colonial expansionism. In particular, western scientists argued that Black Africans, the Polynesian peoples of the Pacific islands, and the Aborigines of Australia, were the least developed subspecies of humanity. Within that basic racist framework, sexism was at work too. A white woman was always registered as a superior being to a black man, but she was always inferior to a white man. In the hierarchy of genetic development implied by criminal anthropology and degenerative discourses, the white man was at the top of the developmental pyramid; followed at a suitable distance – ten paces perhaps? – by the white woman; Western Europeans regarded themselves as more advanced than Eastern Europeans, who were seen as tainted by their association with degenerate Slavs and Semites. Northern Europeans felt themselves superior to Southern Europeans, who were tainted by their close racial proximity to the Arabs of North Africa. Asians from the Indian subcontinent, the Japanese and Chinese, all had higher places in the hierarchy than Black Africans and Polynesians. The lowest form of humanity that was recognized *as* humanity in this completely unscientific and entirely racist schema, was the Hottentot woman, a native of South Africa. (See Arata 1996, Brantlinger 1988, Greenslade 1994, and Pick 1989.)

No matter how revolting these ideas seem to be, they had enormous popular currency in the 1880s and 1890s and beyond, amongst almost all reasonably educated white, middle-class Europeans. The evidence resides in the fact that these views are perpetuated quite openly, without embarrassment, with no sense of their absurdity, in the popular fictions of the age. They were so widespread, indeed, that they are openly produced with the assumption that all readers will recognize them. Thus Cesare Lombroso is explicitly name-checked in *Dracula* (Stoker 1993, 439). And in Conan Doyle's 'The Empty House', Holmes comments on the villain Colonel Moran:

> There are some trees, Watson, which grow to a certain height, and then suddenly develop some unsightly eccentricity. You will see it often with

humans. I have a theory that the individual represents in his development the whole procession of his ancestors, and that such a sudden turn
to evil stands for some strong influence which came into the line of his
pedigree. The person becomes, as it were, the epitome of the history of
his own family. (Conan Doyle 1981, 494)

Monsters such as the Beetle, or Ayesha or Dracula represent in a single
person the evolutionary process that Holmes posits here, because they
have survived through the generations. Holmes by extension, in many
ways, represents the epitome of the degeneration theorist, for like
them, he is primarily concerned with reading a symptomatology onto
the bodies and faces of those he meets. Mostly he is concerned with
issues such as what a man or woman does for a living; but their heredity underlies his judgement, and it is no accident that in the cases of
men and women preyed upon by their families, stepfathers proliferate
as the villains (in 'The Adventure of the Speckled Band' [1892] for
example) so that the victimized heroes and heroines are not tainted by
ties to bad blood. Holmes is the supreme realist because he can see
symptoms of criminality and bad behaviour so clearly. His clear vision
dispels the nightmare. Sadly for the rest of us it is seldom so obvious.

Telling clearly ...? The eyewitness and cultural capital

If the Gothic is associated with complex vision, it is also associated
with complex telling. Key formative texts such as Mary Shelley's
Frankenstein (1818) make great play of the layering of narrative, deny-
ing the reader the implied security of a single authoritative point of
view. In *Frankenstein*, where the Monster gets to speak in his own
behalf, we find ourselves sympathizing with him despite the facts that
he murders a child, is responsible for the hanging of an innocent
woman, and that he strangles Frankenstein's bride on her wedding
night. The reader is denied clear vision and a secure perspective from
which to judge in part because the story is not being told in a clear way.

The proliferation of complex narrative forms in the masculine gothic
romances of the late nineteenth century is, of course, part of the traditional formation of the gothic mode, just as much as obscure vision is.
It is the way in which the reader is offered the opportunity to share vic-
ariously in the confusions of the protagonists. A narrating character
who only has a partial view of events cannot, by definition, see clearly;
and if he cannot see, then he cannot tell clearly either. In fictions of this
kind, the point of view shifts. In Stevenson's *Strange Case*, for example,

we begin with what looks like an authoritative and realistically inclined third-person omniscient narrative. The voice that begins to tell the story sets out to give the impression that he (it is certainly a masculine voice, though it is never explicitly identified as such) is a realist narrator, speaking anecdotally but truthfully to a coterie audience of like-minded men in much the manner that Wilde addresses his essay audiences (see Chapter 3). The introduction to Mr Utterson the lawyer is an introduction to a man we are supposed to approve of, in part because we are supposed to be like him. Utterson is the strong, silent type (Stevenson 1979, 29). But if the reader is softened up by a narrative focalized through Utterson's eyes to sympathize and identify with such men, what happens to the reader's view of the world described when the narrative is handed over to Henry Jekyll? Jekyll is not after all so dissimilar in outward appearance to Utterson. If Utterson enjoys the theatre and fine wine, but prefers to mortify his tastes for such things, Jekyll similarly tells us: 'the worst of my faults was a certain impatient gaiety of disposition … [but I had] a certain imperious desire to carry my head high, and wear a more than commonly grave countenance' (81) – precisely what Utterson also does. The repression of desires does not, Freud shows us, make the desires go away. It is not just that Jekyll and Hyde are brothers under the skin; there is also a family resemblance between Utterson and Jekyll and thence Hyde; and a further resemblance is therefore hinted at between the implied reader and the characters.

In other such texts, the implied audience for the fiction is written into the fiction itself. Utterson is in part one such figure; he is a lawyer and he reads the accounts of Dr Lanyon and of the scientist Henry Jekyll as part of his professional duty to the two dead men. The Time Traveller's story is likewise told to a representative sample of middle-class men who are not given names but social functions denoting the class to which they belong – the hegemonic middle class. Amongst them are a Psychologist, a Provincial Mayor, a Medical Man and an Editor, all men who are necessarily well-educated and part of the social status quo. Conrad's Marlow tells his story of darkness in deepest Africa to a Director of Companies, a Lawyer and an Accountant, men, it must be inferred, who are not given to fanciful notions or to the easy suspension of disbelief. *Doctor* Watson witnesses and tells Sherlock Holmes's adventures. Allan Quatermain might be a bit of a rough diamond, but he shares his adventures with a retired ship's captain, John Good, and with an English squire, Sir Henry Curtis. Horace Holly who encounters the horrors of *She* is a university professor.

And the band of brothers who track down Dracula include a doctor, a lawyer, an American (with a laconic, sceptical attitude) and an English aristocrat. Van Helsing for good measure is both a doctor and a lawyer, as well as having God on his side in his profound knowledge of both theology and mythology.

All of which suggests that for this kind of fiction to have effect at all, the witness has to be a credible witness, even if he scarcely saw anything at all. He has to be an *eyewitness* who, in the implied statement, 'I was there, this happened to me', states the fantastic as if it were a fact. In law, the eyewitness account is compelling evidence, and so too with fiction. But it is particularly important that the eyewitness be a man[4] of undoubted integrity, a man who has a share in what E. J. Hobsbawm has called the 'collective recognition signs' of middle-class status, signs which include 'a combination of income and education', professional status, and, in England especially received pronunciation (Hobsbawm 1987, 181). The proliferation of professional men in these fictions, where a profession is defined by the taking of an oath which promises high standards of morality and probity, is highly significant in the creation of that impression of integrity and truthfulness. Witnesses in these fictions are men who inhabit what Pierre Bourdieu has called the structures of 'cultural capital' (see Womack in Wolfreys 2002, 296). They are intrinsically trustworthy because of their class and professional status.

Indeed, considerable lengths are gone to in many cases to establish authenticity not just in terms of the eyewitness's credibility, but also in terms of the process of documentation. The most striking example is *Dracula* to which I shall turn in a moment. But one finds elements of the construction of verisimilitude via cultural capital in a great many of the masculine romances. Richard Marsh's under-read *The Beetle* for example presents itself as a series of first person accounts of different people's encounters with the monster. The first section is told by Robert Holt, now a tramp, but formerly a clerk down on his luck; the second part by Sydney Atherton, a scientist and inventor; the third by Marjorie Lindon, daughter of an aristocrat and fiancée of a British MP; and the denouement comes in the 'Casebook of the Hon. Augustus Champnell, Confidential Agent' (Marsh 1994, 189). In their different ways, each of these characters is invested with significant cultural capital deriving either from professional status or from high birth. (We must presume that Champnell, who glories in the title 'the Honourable' must have both.) We read in good faith, expecting to hear the whole story. But at the centre of the novel there is a massive ellipsis.

Marjorie Lindon's narrative breaks off when she is left in the Beetle's London lair, observing what she thinks is a pile of rugs that turns out to be inhabited by the beetle him/it/self. We know that the Beetle hypnotizes her, dresses her in male clothing and shaves her head because her own clothes and, chillingly, her hair are found in the house by the men in pursuit of the Beetle. The rest of what the Beetle does to her remains unspoken; she appears not to remember it, and the narrative she wrote in the months after her abduction breaks off and adds no more information – which of course adds a frisson of suggestion that what happened was literally and figuratively 'unspeakable'. In addition, the last page of the novel informs us that the narrative of Robert Holt was in fact 'compiled from the statements which Holt made to Atherton, and to Miss Lindon...when a much-stained, shattered derelict he lay at her father's house' (277). In other words, Holt's narrative is merely hearsay evidence, and his cultural capital, never the strongest in the first place has been seriously dented by our last view of him as a shattered derelict. And the most authoritative of the narrators, the professional witness Champnell who has 'unimpeachable authority' (276) for the authenticity of the story, has to admit at the end that he has no idea what the Beetle was, no idea what really happened, and that he is an eyewitness who never even saw the monster.

The procedure of Haggard's fictions is slightly different. The whole of the narrative of *King Solomon's Mines* is given over to honest Allan Quatermain, who has to be viewed as a reliable witness, because if one is going to describe the fantastic and the weird, the witness has to be credible. His bluffness and anxiety over his ability to write the story are all part of the process of guaranteeing his truthfulness. At the same time, however, Haggard does not allow us simply to rely on Quatermain's intrinsic honesty. He gives the novel an editor who intervenes briefly at rare intervals, sometimes to correct the under-educated Quatermain's errors, sometimes to add information of a kind that Quatermain simply could not know. In either case, the editor functions as a support system for the narrative, as a properly cultured reader who sees connections that the writer has missed, and who upholds the narrator's view because he never directly contradicts him. *She* has a much more elaborate, quasi-academic paraphernalia, as is appropriate to the narrative of a man (Horace Holly) who is a distinguished academic. Haggard had a 'facsimile' of the Sherd of Amenartas – the evidence of Leo Vincey's lineage – fabricated as part of the framework of the text. It was reproduced in the original edition of the novel to aid the impression of authenticity, and to make the fiction read like a travel narrative or a learned treatise. Horace Holly's narrative is framed by an 'Editor's' Introduction; and this editor also intervenes in the narrative providing footnotes that translate unknown phrases, that supplement the story with supporting quotations from the classics (thereby pointing out the editor's cultural capital), and which correct Holly's occasional factual scholarly errors: thus when Holly describes the Sherd of Amenartas as a cartouche, the editor steps in to say: 'The cartouche...cannot have been that of Kallikrates as Mr Holly suggests. Kallikrates was a priest and not entitled to a cartouche which was the prerogative of Egyptian royalty' (Haggard 2001, 44). But the editor's role is not to undermine Holly's story or to question his authority. Indeed, he buys into it pretty fully, commenting on the scarab that 'proves' Vincey's heritage, 'I have little doubt that but that it played some part in the tragic story of the Princess Amenartas and her lover Kallikrates, the forsworn priest of Isis' (161). The erudition he displays elsewhere is a kind of guarantee that his feeling about the authenticity of the scarab is guarantee of the authenticity of the rest of the story. The Holmes-inspired reader, however, must proceed with caution.

Dracula: (cultural) capital and (epistemological) crisis

Near the beginning of *Dracula*, Lucy Westenra and Mina Murray, on holiday in Whitby, make a habit of sitting in the churchyard which overlooks the cliffs, chatting with the local 'characters'. Mina's journal carefully records her conversations with an elderly man named Mr Swales who she meets there. On the first day, he tells her that newspapers are 'full of fool-talk' and lies (Stoker 1993, 87). On the second occasion he raises doubts about the truthfulness of the tombstones with which they are surrounded. He begins with a sceptic's dismissal of all kinds of myths and legends as merely a plot by the hegemonic class (represented in his discussion by parsons) to keep ordinary folk scared, pliable and obedient, before moving on to say with shocking directness that the vast majority of the stones in the churchyard have lies inscribed upon them. In many cases, the lies are about the whereabouts of the bodies reputed to be in the graves they mark: the stones might say 'Here lies the body' or 'Sacred to the memory', 'an' yet in nigh half of 'em there bean't no bodies at all' (Stoker 1993, 88), for in a seaport, many of the bodies were lost at sea. The old man is having fun with Mina, but there is a serious point about his shock that there is no proper relationship between the words on the stones and the bodies that they commemorate. For him, it is a scandal because the tomb-stone is part of the evidence that the recording angel will make use of on the Day of Judgement: 'it'll be a quare scowderment at the Day of Judgement,' he says in a local dialect that proves his lower-class and therefore comic status, 'when they come tumblin' up here in their deathsarks, all jouped together an' tryin' to drag their tombsteans with them *to prove how good they was*' (88–9, my emphasis). The suicide, George Canon, will make Gabriel 'keckle' with laughter when he 'comes pantin' up the grees with the tombstean balanced on his hump, and asks it to be took as evidence!' (91). The structures of cultural cap-ital mean that readers are not encouraged to take the old man very seriously. He is working class, very elderly and clearly ill-educated, and, despite his stated scepticism, he believes very literally in the Angel Gabriel, all of which point to his having no significant status as a reliable witness. But the novel as a whole will vindicate his suspicions about lying words and the fakery of written evidence. He knows, before Saussure, that there is no relationship between sign and referent, and before the adventure even begins he throws doubt on Mina's statement of good faith that she will do her best to remember everything he has said, and 'put it down' (88).[5]

The old man speaks a kind of post-structuralist truth about language, *avant la lettre*, one might say, and it is a truth profoundly threatening to the men who go in pursuit of the vampire. One of the markers of their professional status is the keeping of records. So, Jonathan Harker, as Stephen Arata has noted, keeps his journal in the same way that a pro-fessional travel writer or ethnographer would do as he journeys across Eastern Europe (Arata 1995, 131). As he is beset by horrors in Dracula's castle, he comments to himself in that diary, 'Let me be prosaic so far as facts can be; it will help me to bear up, and imagination must not run riot with me' (Stoker 1993, 37). In other words, he writes precisely to keep himself rational and objective. His wife keeps her shorthand diary to practise her secretarial skills so that she will be able to help her hus-band in his legal practice after they are married. The meetings of the 'Crew of Light' are conducted in a highly business-like way, with Mina as secretary recording the minutes. In the case of the doctors and lawyers amongst them, such records are the stuff of their professional life, and they have an immense status – a legal status, indeed – as evidence. As Van Helsing says to Seward in his broken English:

> You were always a careful student, and your casebook was ever more full
> than the rest … I trust that good habit have not fail. Remember, my

friend, that knowledge is stronger than memory, and we should not trust the weaker. Even if you have not kept the good practice, let me tell you that this case of our dear miss [Lucy] is one that may be ... of such interest to us ... Taken then good note of it. Nothing is too small. I counsel you, put down in record even your doubts and surmises. (Stoker 1993, 157)

This is advice that Holmes might have given too. The reading of the situation depends on the minute gathering of the evidence, just as it would for the detective. And the novel comments repeatedly and explicitly on the importance of ordering events, placing them in logical and chronological sequences in order to see the patterns the events make: Mina argues that 'dates are everything, and I think that if we get all our material ready, and have every item put in chronological order, we shall have done much' (288). Harker continues the collation process so that very early in the pursuit proceedings, the collected materials will be able to 'show a whole connected narrative' (289). As Elisabeth Bronfen has suggested, the dangers that threaten Dracula's antagonists, including the danger that they might even go mad, are 'soothed by accurate documentation' (Bronfen 1999, 64). And the novel as a whole is prefaced with a statement about the perfect reliability of those records:

> How these papers have been placed in sequence will be made manifest in the reading of them. All needless matters have been eliminated, so that [the] history ... may stand forth as simple fact. There is throughout no statement of past things wherein memory may err, for all the records chosen are exactly contemporary, given from the standpoints and within the range of knowledge of those who made them. (Stoker 1993, 6)

That is a problematic statement, though. Van Helsing on the one hand advises Seward that no detail is too small to record; yet the preface writer tells us that needless matters have been eliminated. An editing process, in other words, has taken place. Indeed, in the very act of reading the novel, we know that this must be true, for when Mina transcribes Seward's diary she does so with the express purpose of suppressing the exclamations of personal agony he made as he watched Lucy fade away: no one, Mina says, must hear those exclamations spoken again (286). Moreover, we know that no one ever writes exactly contemporaneously with the events that they set out to describe. There is necessarily some delay; and memory as well as the occasional necessity to suppress emotions both play tricks on the accuracy of the record. All the same, Dracula himself recognizes the power in those recorded words; on the night of his worst attack on Mina, he destroys the manuscript copies of the testimony and the wax cylinders of Seward's phonograph. In one sense, this does not matter. Mina, efficient secretary as ever, has made three copies of all the documents. But it does mean that at the end of the novel, Jonathan Harker has to comment on what remains as evidence of their adventure after their return: 'We were struck with the fact that in all the mass of material of which the record is composed, there is hardly one authentic document; nothing but a mass of type-writing ... We could hardly ask anyone, even did we wish to, to accept these as proofs of so wild a story' (486). The last words are given to Van Helsing who declares that proofs are not necessary – the only believer they need is Mina and Jonathan's son who 'will one day know what a brave and gallant woman his mother is'. The rationality and logic that were central to Dracula's defeat are displaced into sentiment and clichéd emotion in that final statement.

Of course, the rationality to which the adventurers lay claim through their professional masculine status has already been profoundly assaulted. Before they can track Dracula and defeat him, they have to suspend their scientific, objective and legalistic views of the world; the prerequisite for defeating the monster is that they have to *believe* in him – and belief of this kind depends absolutely on the undoing of the rational training which is the basis of their cultural capital. Much of the early part of the novel is taken up with the process of convincing Seward, Morris and Lord Arthur that such things as 'the grims an' signs an' warnin's' identified as nonsense even by the old man in the churchyard actually exist (88); they are sceptical at first but are taught by Van Helsing of the necessity to 'believe in things that you cannot' (249). Indeed, the Dutchman points out the inadequacy of science alone to provide an explanatory framework that would render Lucy Westenra's death comprehensible:

> You are a clever man, friend John; you reason well, and your wit is bold; but you are too prejudiced ... Do you not think that there are things which you cannot understand, and yet which are; that some people see things that others cannot? ... it is the fault of our science that it wants to explain all; and if it explain not, then it says there is nothing to explain. (Stoker 1993, 246)

And although logic, science and technology all play their part in the pursuit, they are clearly not the only weapons in the armoury of the band of brothers. Thus, Mina's remarkable way with train timetables and typewriters, with phonographs and shorthand, and her understanding of the modern science of degeneration theory in her references to Lombroso and Nordau facilitate the victory. At the same time, though, the superstitious paraphernalia of garlic and crosses, the consecrated host and significance of twilight and dawn are the primitive context of the process as well. As Jennifer Wicke has recently argued, the effects of *Dracula* are partly to do with the clash of extreme modernity (trains, telegraphs, phonographs and typewriters) with an atavistic and primitive past: '*Dracula*, draped in all its feudalism and medieval gore, is textually completely au courant,' writes Wicke (Wicke 2002, 579). And indeed it is; but the medieval gore is profoundly important because it unsettles the security of a world in which train timetables stand as a marker of organization and logic.

Why, then, describe this as a crisis in masculinity? It was certainly not Stoker's intention that we should read his novel as exemplifying the threats that assaulted the figure of the gentleman: his motivation, like Stevenson's, was to provide an audience with fun and fear in a safely fictional form, and the novel's ending surely validates the powers of the gentlemen (and one lady) who defeated the primitive forces of vampirism. As I've already suggested, however, the final words of the novel rather undermine that view in the sense that they mark a return to sentiment and emotion over rationality and logic, as well as describing an editorial process that has destroyed all the original evidence for the events the novel describes. Thus the novel unwittingly raises through its whole length the self same epistemological questions raised by *The Good Soldier* in its circular statements and withdrawals: What can we know about the world if the (written) evidence is tainted and scarcely counts as evidence at all? The narrative of *Dracula* is sustained only by 'good faith', by the credulity of the reader in the written record. We are asked to be complicit in our duping, and to believe in the process that the world is indeed an ordered space.

Alongside darkness and ambiguity, one of the traditional elements of the gothic genre in British incarnations is Catholicism, that religion of superstition and fundamental foreignness. One of the key weapons that Van Helsing brings to bear against Dracula is the consecrated host, that holy symbol of the uncanny which is the body of Christ in an unrecognizable form. Catholicism also makes great play of the symbol of the cross, to the extent that non-Catholics often regard the Catholic emphasis on the symbol as a form of idolatry. As Jonathan Harker travels into Eastern Europe, a peasant woman he meets along the way gives him a crucifix to wear as a protection against the evil eye. He takes it from her under protest, merely to be polite, as befits an English gentleman; but as the events in Dracula's lair unfold, he comments in his diary:

> Bless that good, good woman who hung the crucifix round my neck! for it is a comfort and a strength to me whenever I touch it. It is odd that a thing which I have been taught to regard with disfavour and as idolatrous should be in a time of loneliness and trouble be of help. Is it that there is something in the essence of the thing itself, or that it is a medium, a tangible help, in conveying memories of sympathy and comfort? Some time … I must examine this matter and try to make up my mind about it. (Stoker 1993, 41)

The rational western gentleman is a peasant underneath his civilized clothes, it is suggested (and since Dracula borrows Jonathan's clothes to go marauding, the two figures begin to appear almost interchangeable). He may cloak his credulity with an aspiration to examine the matter further, but in the meantime he will clutch at the crucifix as a comfort despite his training. What the many such examples in the novel imply is that there is a clear sense in which Jonathan and his co-conspirators have been 'un-manned' by their confrontation with the supernatural. They are forced to act emotionally, instinctively, and eventually, violently, to defeat the monster. The men with the sedentary professions of doctor and lawyer are turned into adventurers and men of violence: Telemachus becomes Ulysses, administrator becomes warlord, in a move that civilized values must clearly see as retrogressive, atavistic or even degenerate. This is not gentlemanly at all. Stephen Arata has argued that most of the masculine romances of the late nineteenth century, and *Dracula* in particular, are instances describing the fear of 'reverse colonization'. Such fictions, he suggests, are responses to 'cultural guilt. In the marauding, invasive Other, British culture sees its own imperial practices mirrored back in monstrous forms. Stoker's Count Dracula and Haggard's Ayesha frighten not least because their characteristic actions – appropriation and exploitation – uncannily reproduce those of the colonizing Englishman' (Arata 1996, 108). That seems to me to be quite right. The fear of 'going native' is very much the same as the fear that the native might actually be like 'us', the implied readers of the fictions.

These fictions in general, then, – and *Dracula* in particular – also produce their creepy effects because they force the recognition that self and other are not so very different. The crafty use of superstitions against the object of superstition is a regular feature of such fictions. In *King Solomon's Mines*, for example, much hilarity (!) is caused by the fact that Captain Good is first seen by the natives without his trousers, face half-shaved and with his false teeth out: he appears to them as a monster, and uses their fear of his monstrosity against them. Similarly, Curtis, Good and Quatermain describe their gun technology as powerful 'magic' to scare off the Kukuanas. The Roman Catholic props of *Dracula* are another such instance. To fight the monster, one must become a little (or a lot) like him (or her). But what Conrad's Marlow calls 'the idea', or ideal, behind colonial expansion, is that the Western gentleman, highpoint of evolution and messenger of enlightenment, is bringing benefit to those he attacks and whose land he appropriates. But it is not a pretty thing when you look into it because close examination and clear vision produce the self-evident message that 'we' are just like 'them'. Finally, then, the complex narrative structures of masculine romance serve the purpose of obscuring the real story of adventure: western men can be savages too.

The good ended happily ...?

I began this chapter with a brief discussion of *The Good Soldier*. I began there because despite the manifest differences between the spirit in which Ford's novel was conceived and written, and the spirit of the adventure story, something of the flavour of masculine romance survives in the later novel, albeit in extremely attenuated form. In part this is down to the very title: a novel called *The Good Soldier* might well sound to the unwary reader like an adventure fiction. A similar disappointment must have awaited unwary readers of Conrad's *The Secret Agent* (1907). Moreover, Edward Ashburnham whom the title describes, in other contexts and at other times, could very easily have been the hero of a masculine romance. John Dowell has no idea what Ashburnham's attraction is – he has not got the 'seeing eye', he says of himself (Ford 1995, 16–17). But he is drawn to Edward all the same by his own construction of him as the very type of the English gentleman, whose profession is 'full of the big words, courage, loyalty, honour, constancy' (25), which are, of course, the words of masculine romance. For Dowell, he is also the representative of solid English virtues: 'the fine soldier, the excellent landlord, the extraordinarily kind, careful and industrious magistrate, the upright, honest, fair-dealing, fair-thinking, public character' (66). To Dowell it scarcely matters that Ashburnham is none of these things in reality, that he is 'really' a philanderer who has behaved despicably with other people's wives and has even been subjected to blackmail and a court case for kissing an unwilling girl in a train: in other words, it is not unreasonable to see Edward Ashburnham as a monster. Dowell, however, wants Edward to be a hero of the old-fashioned and straightforward kind, commenting at the end of the novel:

> I can't conceal from myself that I loved Edward Ashburnham ... If I had the courage and the virility and possibly also the physique of Edward Ashburnham I should ... have done what he did. He seems to me like a large elder brother who took me out on several excursions and did many dashing things whilst I just watched him robbing the orchards, from a distance. (Ford 1995, 161)

That confession is one of the reasons that *The Good Soldier* partakes of a very different genre from the one that it appears to belong to. Comradeship, love, admiration and emulation between men are what marked masculine romance; and the stories of such romances are told by fathers to sons (Quatermain addresses his son; the *Dracula* narrative is for young Quincey Harker), and by surrogate brothers to their younger siblings as moral exemplars. These words are the expression of the 'idea' that Conrad's Marlow fetishizes as the idol that imperial conquerors bow down before. Dowell turns to Ashburnham for those things in his own life despite the fact that the Englishman in no way deserves his praise. Ashburnham has occasionally behaved like a hero in the more traditional senses of the word to the irritation of his wife: 'One of their bitterest quarrels came after he had, for the second time, in the Red Sea, jumped overboard from the troopship and rescued a private soldier' (113); but there is a strong hint that his heroism is simply a form of suicidal mania undertaken to escape from Leonora. And this is one of the reasons why masculine romances eschew sexual romance and the marriage plot.[6] No man, wrote Madame Cornuel, 'is a hero to his valet' and heroism is probably a difficult virtue for a wife to live with as well. Domesticity and intimacy expose all kinds of failings that the public man is able to disguise.

Dowell of course is nothing like the supposed hero of an adventure. He describes himself in terms that emphasize his effeminacy rather than his proper masculinity. He is a cuckolded husband whose role in life has been confined to that of a 'nurse attendant' (151), first to his wife, and then to Nancy Rufford. Ashburnham confides in him at various moments during the novel, not because he is strong and manly, but because he 'appeared to be like a woman or a solicitor' (158), inherently trustworthy and utterly unjudgemental. Nor is he a reliable narrator, commenting repeatedly that he never did see clearly, and lamenting the fact that he cannot tell what happened clearly either. 'I don't know. I leave it to you,' he writes on many occasions. At the end of his story, Dowell is left with a moral vacuum with no way of navigating the rights and wrongs of what happened – he's not always sure he knows what happened, and doesn't know how to judge it. All he does know is that the conventions he is used to judge by are no longer appropriate:

> Well, that is the end of the story. And, when I come to look at it, I see that it is a happy ending with wedding bells and all. The villains – for obviously Edward and the girl were villains – have been punished by suicide and madness. The heroine – the perfectly normal, virtuous and slightly deceitful heroine – has become the happy wife of a perfectly normal, virtuous and slightly deceitful husband … A happy ending, that is what it works out at. (Ford 1995, 160)

Not only is this not the end of the story (Dowell typically has forgotten to tell us the story of Ashburnham's suicide and has to come back to it), but it is manifestly not a happy ending except in the sense that Miss Prism might have thought so. The mad child who believes in an omnipotent deity, and the suicidal 'good' soldier who believes in nothing, are not fit subjects for poetic justice. But for once, Dowell writes with self-conscious as opposed to unwitting irony in his summation of the story. The ending has not brought about the desired consummation of meting out just rewards and punishments.

Similarly, there is a significant degree of ambiguity in the masculine romance's ending. A surface story tells of the defeat of evil and of a simple black and white morality where white men triumph – with their superior civilized virtues of comradeship, love, admiration and emulation between men, and their superior technologies – over the forces of darkness, often with dark skins, with their attendant savagery and superstitions. But because the heroes have been implicated in savagery and superstition in the process of bringing about victory, neither reader nor character can be entirely reassured that they are really good, nor that the ending is really happy. In Christopher Craft's terms, entertaining a monster – and being entertained by one – will usually end up in the repudiation and defeat of the monster, and a return to the status quo. But one has also been forced to partake of that monstrosity, and ambivalence survives beyond the ending.

Notes

1. Patrick Brantlinger calls them examples of Imperial Gothic (1988, 227–8); they could also be called adventure stories or yarns, and imperial fictions.
2. Actually, of course, *King Solomon's Mines* is an extremely sexualized book. The very landscape, figured in the map which the adventurers follow, is a skewed representation of a headless naked female torso. And Quatermain does make an exception for the native girl Foulata, who falls in love with Captain Good, but who conveniently dies happy, knowing that miscegenation must be avoided, and that dark skinned girls cannot marry men with beautiful white legs. Nonetheless, the sex is displaced; it is there but not central, and the pre-adolescent reader would certainly be able to read Haggard's novel and keep his/her innocence intact.
3. In the Catholic Church, for example, a monstrance is an object used to 'show' the consecrated host – but for most of the time, the host remains resolutely hidden, veiled in mystery.
4. In this pre-feminist age of the 1880s and 1890s, such figures had to be men. Professional status was largely denied to women (except in very exceptional cases in medicine) because women could not take degrees that qualified them to work in the law, in finance, in education or business. Similarly, in courts of law in Britain, women could not participate in the jury system. Jury members were chosen from amongst wealthy householders, ratepayers and *voters*. Those who judged the truth of an account in a court of law were therefore necessarily men.
5. She will later comment that she has always wanted to be an interviewer for the papers. One of Jonathan's friends has told her that memory is the trick in such work – you 'must be able to put down exactly almost every word spoken, even if you had to refine some of it afterwards' [235]: 'exactly almost' does not inspire confidence that the verbatim account is other than a fabrication.
6. Dr Watson gets married and Sherlock Holmes mocks him for it. Luckily the wife dies, conveniently offstage at a very early point in the Holmes canon, and feminine domesticity is expelled from the stories thereafter. There is an awful lot of casual misogyny in Conan Doyle's stories. As Holmes comments in *The Sign of Four* (1890), 'women are never to be entirely trusted – not even the best of them' (Conan Doyle 1981, 129).

5 New Women for Old: Politics and Fictional Forms in New Woman Writing

Defining the New Woman

Who or what the New Woman of the 1880s and 1890s was very much depended on who was defining her. The term itself is often said to have originated in an article, 'A New Aspect of the Woman Question' in the *North American Review* for 1894, coined by the New Woman novelist Sarah Grand, who chose – of course – to define the term positively to 'refer to a type of well-educated, middle-class woman who was openly critical of the traditional roles established for women, especially marriage and motherhood, and who was influenced by the feminist movement to speak out in favour of equal education for women and equal purity for men and women' (Senf 1992, xiii).[1] The positive definition of the New Woman, then, insists on her intelligence and her intellectual capacities being equal to those of her male middle-class contemporaries. The New Woman is not, in this reading at least, a working-class woman. In Grand's particular version of the phenomenon, she is also defined as being superior to her fellow men at least in terms of her moral and sexual purity. Save for the latter – though it is a very important exception – Olive Schreiner's Lyndall is a New Woman before the phrase existed, as we shall see.

Such a positive gloss, however, was not a consistent feature of the New Woman's representation in the conservative press. More typical is a cartoon from *Punch* on 26 September 1891 in which, beneath a heading that reads 'The Sterner Sex', two women dressed mannishly in straight skirts and severe blouses discuss their clothes.

> 'Hello Gerty! You've got Fred's hat on, and his cover coat!'
> 'Yes. Don't you like it?'

'Well – it makes you look like a young man, you know, and that's so effeminate!'

The cartoon is 'just' a joke – but only just. It articulates a whole matrix of negative assumptions about what happens when middle-class women stop being sweetly feminine and compliant. If they do not become like Lyndall, neurotic and ailing, then they become disgustingly masculine. They are shown as having abdicated their femininity in their adoption of a particular style of dress. Other cartoons in *Punch* and elsewhere, as Ann Heilmann has very thoroughly and brilliantly demonstrated (Heilmann 2000, 3–47), develop these themes. The New Woman is associated with books – since intellect and attractiveness do not mix in 'nice' women; with cigarettes – the adoption of a masculine habit to go with her masculine attire; with bicycles, which assert independence from such old-fashioned notions as chaperonage; and rational dress – you cannot ride a bicycle in a corset; with work outside the home; with neurosis; with ugliness and ridicule – for women who cannot get a man (and what sensible woman would work for her living, or make other women her friends if she had the choice of relying on men economically and emotionally?) are self-evidently laughable, so the papers say.

Throughout the Victorian period the Woman Question had been a significant cultural phenomenon, with debates of various kinds raging in the pages of newspapers and journals. The argument was extremely polarized. On the one hand some women – and some sympathetic men – were in favour of social change leading to the emancipation of women. On the other, hostile forces in the press hurled journalistic vitriol at the rebels, naming feminist campaigners as Revolting Women, Wild Women, the Shrieking Sisterhood, as harridans and hags, and drawing on the mid-century's ideologies of femininity to link woman with nature and woman with the home as the centre of all that was pure and decent. One of the most important and sustained of these attacks is the campaign over two decades (from the late 1860s to the early 1890s) of Eliza Lynn Linton (1822–98), conservative novelist and journalist, waged in the pages of *The Saturday Review* and *The Nineteenth Century*. Beginning in the 1860s with a series of articles entitled 'The Girl of the Period' and continuing into the 1890s with 'The Wild Women' series, Linton voiced conservative disapproval of all attempts by women to widen their sphere of action. Her weapons were nostalgia and ridicule, and in particular, she argued by implication that women who sought emancipation in the social arena were probably not 'nice' in the sexual arena. 'Time was,' she wrote in 1868, 'when the ... phrase "a fair young English girl", meant the ideal of woman-hood ... a creature generous, capable, modest' (Linton in Hamilton 1995, 172). This English girl was obviously better in every way than continental European women; she had 'innate purity', and was happy to act, when married, as her husband's companion, 'but never his rival'. This paragon's virtues were related to her Englishness, to her purity, modesty, generosity and self-abnegation, all of which made her apt for servicing the home in her roles as wife and mother. At the time of writing, however, Linton identifies that these virtues of a Golden Age are beginning to pass away with the evolution of a new kind of woman, whom she christens the 'Girl of the Period'. This girl is defined by the outrages she commits against the cherished values of the past. She dyes her hair, paints her face, regards the pursuit of 'fun' as the most important element in life, disregards her parents and the advice of authority figures generally, dresses like a courtesan, and lacks all Christian feeling, especially in relation to those tenets of Christianity that regard self-denial and the care of others as paramount.

But the real problem with this girl is not that she is outrageous, but that she is unmarriageable – or at least, that is what Linton's anonymous narrator wishes to say:[2]

> The marvel, in the present fashion of life among women is, how it holds its ground in spite of the disapprobation of men ... the girl of the period does not please men ... All men whose opinion is worth having prefer the simple and genuine girl of the past, with her tender little ways and pretty bashful modesties, to this loud and rampant modernization, with her false red hair and painted skin, talking slang as glibly as a man, and by preference leading the conversation to doubtful subjects ... though men laugh with her they do not respect her, though they flirt with her they do not marry her ... all we can do is wait patiently until ... our women come back again to the old English ideal ... the most beautiful, the most modest, the most essentially womanly in the world. (Linton in Hamilton 1995, 175–6)

It would be a long wait, not least because in her attempt to portray the new type of woman as hideous and inappropriate, Linton actually makes her seem quite attractive (I know which I would rather be given the choice between someone who has 'fun' and someone who is merely modest and compliant). At work in this discourse is a kind of schizophrenia. The girl of the period is at once unattractive to men – the men won't marry her; but she is clearly also very attractive to the men who laugh with her, flirt with her and – heaven forbid! – talk slang with her.[3] It is just possible, after all, that the 'Girl of the Period' does not wish to marry, but that is an inadmissible possibility in Linton's rhetoric. Schreiner's Lyndall has some very scathing things to say about marriage to Em, who stands precisely as the modest girl whose 'idea of love was only service' (Schreiner 1995, 180).[4] Lyndall is contemptuous of that ideal of love, saying of marriage: 'I am not in so great a hurry to put my neck beneath any man's foot; and I do not greatly admire the crying of babies' (184). Conservative commentators could not believe that this might be true of any proper woman since the ideology in which they were participating had no space for the women who did not marry or mother children. They returned over and over again to the same arguments: the New Woman was not a proper woman – she was unnatural or even artificial, as Linton's strictures on her dyed hair and make-up imply; and she would never be able to find a husband, thereby reinforcing the idea that women who question the status quo are necessarily unattractive.

The argument that a woman's career should be her marriage, however, was threatened by more than middle-class women's dissatisfaction with the limitations it placed on them. It had been clear for many years that there were large numbers of women who simply could not marry, not because they were not feminine or pretty enough, but because there were around half a million more women than men in Britain. (The proportions varied somewhat, but from the 1861 census onwards, it was increasingly clear that marriage could not be the career path for all nice women.) Unless there was to be a new fashion for polygamy the Woman Question, stated ironically by Frances Power Cobbe in *Fraser's Magazine* in 1862 as 'What Shall We Do With Our Old Maids?', required another answer. If that answer partially implied the training of middle-class women[5] for the world of professional work commensurate with their class status, it also implied the rewriting of the ideology of the Separate Spheres in which a woman's place was the home, and a man's was the world of work and public affairs. As Rhoda Nunn remarks, in George Gissing's *The Odd Women* (1893), as she describes the project of her training school for middle-class women who need to earn their own living:

> [My aim is] to make women hard-hearted … do you know that there are half a million more women than men in this happy country of ours? … So many *odd* women – no making a pair with them. The pessimists call them useless, lost, futile lives. I, naturally – being one of

them myself – take another view. I look upon them as a great reserve. When one woman vanishes into matrimony, the reserve offers a substitute for the world's work. True, they are not all trained yet – far from it. I want to help in that – to train the reserve. (Gissing 1980, 37)

It required a rethink about the nature of female education; if women needed to work, they needed to be educated for work; if women showed intellectual capacity by competing for Higher Education places, it also implied that there should be no real bars to women entering the professions and the civil service rather than sticking with the nurturing professions of nursing and teaching that had traditionally been open to them. Rhoda Nunn's declaration that women needed to become hard-hearted implied a more worldly and individualistic approach to feminine existence. It meant refusing the models of femininity that depended on self-sacrificial behaviour and non-assertion of personal rights. Her militaristic language – unmarried women are a reserve army – would certainly have been viewed as unwomanly, but the arguments she makes are based on the real issues raised by a changing social demographic. Broadly speaking, it is these issues – alongside reforms to marriage laws surrounding women's property and divorce – that made up the political backdrop of the New Woman fiction written by women.

Fiction identified as New Woman fiction was, however, also written by men. From the notorious pen of Grant Allen, whose *The Woman Who Did* was published in 1895, to the marginally more measured responses of George Gissing (*The Odd Women*, 1893) and Thomas Hardy (*Jude the Obscure*), to the ironic distance of H. G. Wells (*Ann Veronica*, 1909), the baffled incomprehension of Arnold Bennett (*Hilda Lessways*, 1911), the amused tolerance of E. M. Forster (*Howards End*, 1910), and D. H. Lawrence's sturdy disapproval (*Sons and Lovers*, 1913 and *The Rainbow*, 1915), women who wanted more than convention usually permitted them filled the pages of turn-of-the-century fiction. The key difference between the male writers who exploited the fashion for the New Woman, and the female writers who had a serious political commitment to her aspirations, was sexuality. Sarah Grand spoke for many feminists when she argued in novels such as *The Heavenly Twins* (1893) and *The Beth Book* (1897), and in her journal articles, that women were 'naturally' purer than men. She occupied a higher moral ground that would permit her to mount an argument, based ironically in Ruskinian notions of feminine purity, that women had to protect both men and themselves from men's baser lusts. It was a calculated act of self-publicity which was also an assault on that higher ground, that led Grant Allen, no friend to feminists, deliberately to create Herminia Barton as the woman *who did* engage in sex outside marriage. This was an offence to the pure ideals of womanhood of both conservative and radical writers which assured the maximum impact for Allen's very slight text. The heroine self-consciously embarks on a love affair without the benefit of clergy, gives birth to an illegitimate daughter, has her lover die intestate, and is left virtually destitute. Although she manages to bring up the child and supports herself and her daughter through her own labour, at the end of the novel, her daughter rejects her mother's principles primarily because they debar her from a conventional marriage to an eligible young man of good family. Herminia, broken-hearted, commits suicide like a latter-day Madame Bovary, and this reader for one is left extremely confused about what the point of the narrative might have been.

Of the male novelists listed above, only Allen was explicitly riding the crest of the popular wave of interest in feminist fiction, even if he did so for his own purposes. Hardy famously and dishonestly, in the Preface to the 1912 Wessex edition, denied that *Jude the Obscure* had been written with that vogue in mind, noting bemusedly that it was a German reviewer who had pointed out the novel's connection to the New Woman novel: 'an experienced reviewer ... informed the writer that Sue Bridehead was the first delineation in fiction of the woman who was coming into notice in her thousands every year – the woman of the feminist movement – the slight, pale "bachelor" girl – the intellectualized, emancipated bundle of nerves that modern conditions were producing' (Hardy 1998b, 468). It is a neat touch that he had to be 'informed' about what he had been doing for as both John Goode and Gail Cunningham have noted, there is a very clear resemblance between certain episodes involving transvestism and getting wet, as well as jumping out of windows, in Grand's *The Heavenly Twins* (which Grand had sent to Hardy) and *Jude* (Cunningham 1978, 111; Goode 1988, 158). Of the others, only Wells explicitly makes mention of the New Woman phenomenon in *Ann Veronica*, where the heroine's father puts down his daughter's uppitiness to her reading: 'It's these damned novels. All the torrent of misleading, spurious stuff that pours from the press. These sham ideals and advanced notions, Women who Dids, and all that kind of thing' (Wells 1993e, 19). But each of these writers in turn shows women of 'advanced' ideas – intellectual ambition and in most cases, the pursuit of a career – having sexual intercourse outside marriage as if this is the natural result of female ambition.[6] One has to be suspicious that this is much closer to masculine fantasy than to feminist aspiration in an era still deeply committed to female purity, and for very good reasons – before reliable contraception, sexual emancipation for women was much more likely to be a masculine dream than a feminine one.

It is probably true that purity does not sell so well as sex, at least in our generation, and the social purity arguments mounted by novelists like Sarah Grand have a slight tendency to seem laughable to post-1960s readers. But, as Ann Heilmann perceptively argues, we should not read the apparent 'frigidity' (the negative word for 'purity') of New Woman fiction, in which there is often an ongoing attack on male sexuality and an 'absence of fulfilling personal relationships [as] ... a reflection of the writers' sexual repression' (Heilmann 2000, 87). Nor should we simply assume that the 'just say no' message of Grand's novels articulates her simplistic internalization of her society's norms. That is to read through post-sexual liberation eyes. There is a value to purity both for a feminist argument more generally, and in terms of an alternative aesthetics of the novel.

Olive Schreiner

In the Preface to the second edition of *The Story of an African Farm* (1883), Olive Schreiner, sheltering under her aggressively masculine pen name Ralph Iron, had a number of observations to make about her novel and its reception. She observed that her book had been well received despite the unfamiliar territory that was its backdrop. Nonetheless, she appeared nettled by two apparent misreadings of her text. In the first, some people had commented that the two strangers who appear out of nowhere at the farm must really be the same person, appearing once and 'leaving behind him no more substantial trace than a mere book', and reappearing 'to fill some more important part than that of the mere stimulator of thought'. Readers who thought this, Schreiner suggests, were imposing the realist convention of patterning on the design of the text, and such patterning had not been her intention at all:

> Human life may be painted according to two methods. There is the stage method. According to that each character is duly marshalled at first, and ticketed; we know with an immutable certainty that at the right crises each one will reappear and act his part, and, when the curtain falls, all will stand before it bowing. There is a sense of satisfaction

in this, and of completeness. But there is another method – the
method of the life we all lead. Here nothing can be prophesied. There is
a strange coming and going of feet. Men appear, act and re-act upon
each other, and pass away. When the crisis comes the man who would
fit it does not return. When the curtain falls no one is ready...The
canons of criticism that bear upon the one cut cruelly upon the other.
(Schreiner 1995, 29)

Presumably *The Story of an African Farm* is best read as belonging to
the second, more randomized, less patterned mode. The novel, she
fears, has been misjudged by a set of criteria that belong to a different
kind of fiction writing. Schreiner's second point in defence of her novel
is related, but different. A 'kind critic' had suggested that 'he would
better have liked the little book if it had been a history of wild adventure, of… "encounters with ravening lions and hair-breadth escapes" '
(29–30). In other words, the kind critic would have preferred her to
have written a masculine romance, since that is how Africa had most
usually appeared to British readers in the imperialist fictions of the
period; fidelity to that genre would have made a lot more sense to such
readers because it would have provided a set of ready-made criteria
against which to judge it. Schreiner is scathing about this view, arguing
that most romance fiction is produced by people who have never been
to Africa. They misrepresent the reality of Africa, seeing it merely as a
place for romance, not as a place where humdrum lives are lived out in
all their mediocre tedium. If realist patterning was not Schreiner's aim,
neither was romantic falsification.

This Preface, though brief, is an interesting starting point for any
investigation in the phenomenon of so-called New Woman writing
at the end of the nineteenth century because it demonstrates the extent
to which New Woman writers had to create the audience for whom they
wrote and to mould a taste for their own politicized fictions. Moreover,
some of the objections that 'Ralph Iron' identified to her work have
dogged New Woman fiction more generally in the intervening century.
Such writing has been castigated for sacrificing aesthetic values to political polemic; it has been dismissed as inartistic: 'the New Woman novelists were little concerned with artistic perfection,' writes Peter Keating
(1989, 187–8). The novels therefore are of interest merely to the histo-
rian of obscure corners of literature. The passionate expression of deeply
felt personal wrongs, especially since most New Woman writers could
not imagine realistic solutions to those problems, rendered the fiction
repetitive and narrow. Even some of those critics who have set out to

recuperate the New Woman writers of the late nineteenth century (Stubbs 1979, Showalter 1978, Cunningham 1978, for example) for a wider readership have been highly dubious about the quality of what they were reading, and have struggled in vain to reconcile their taste for the aesthetics of the high Modernist novel with the politics of an overtly polemical mode of writing. They want to claim value for novels by Sarah Grand, Ménie Muriel Dowie, Mona Caird and 'Iota'. But the kind of value that they claim is often that of historical curiosity opposed to artistic value.

The novel to which Schreiner's Preface stands as a partial introduction, although extremely popular when it was first published, must also have appeared as a strange hybrid form to circulating library readers whose fiction was more usually produced to a known formula, and it continues to seem a very strange book. That formula – the code of feminine fiction, as opposed to that of masculine romance discussed in the previous chapter – is bound up in the intricacies of the marriage plot. Masculine romance, as we have seen, depends on a public stage, on the assertion of an often-brutal kind of heroism, on action and adventure; in contrast feminine romance traditionally focuses on the private sphere of the home, and on the understated – but well understood – desires of individual female characters. As Jane Eldridge Miller observes: 'Marriage had been essential to the novel, both as a subject and as a structuring principle from its inception: marriage served as a paradigm of social integration and stability within the narrative, while the desire for marriage provided narrative impetus and the achievement of marriage offered a means of resolution' (Miller 1994, 44). She goes on to suggest that there is an intimate connection between new ideas about marriage arising in the late nineteenth century, including its reform, and sometimes even its outright rejection, ideas which arose from the new articulation of the aspiration for women's emancipation, including education, the right to paid work outside the home for middle-class women, and freedom of movement, and new forms in the novel. If the traditional novel – whether highbrow or popular – had focussed on marriage, and used it as a central narrative structure, in a new context where ideas about marriage had changed, then the very form of the novel needed to change as well. Miller identifies the formal shift in fiction as an Edwardian rather than as a late-Victorian New Woman phenomenon (45). But there is nonetheless something to say about Schreiner's novel as an early exemplar of an aesthetic shift taken up at least as much in the service of a political message as in the interests of experimentation with the novel form for its own sake.

The Story of an African Farm is generically mixed, and it operates its considerable force via an explicit commitment to formal innovation; it performs a sustained act of defamiliarization on its readers, which is why neither critics attached to realism, nor those attached to romantic adventure, whether masculine or feminine in tone, could make much sense of it. The relative absence of Schreiner's novel from academic syllabuses until very recently tells us much about the ways in which the academy has made assumptions about the relative value of male- and female-authored novels of protest. In addition, critics schooled in the allegedly apolitical versions of aesthetic modernism cannot see the connection between Schreiner's chosen forms in her fiction and modernist poetics, because a narrow definition of Modernism demands the expurgation of explicitly political writing. If Modernism is largely defined as experimentation *for its own sake*, a rewriting for the early twentieth century of the aestheticist code of 'Art for art's sake', then it cannot encompass the highly politicized writings of the New Woman writers, which used experimentation as part of a commitment to political goals.

There are reasons why it is important to *make* the connection between Modernism and the experiments of its Victorian and Edwardian forebears. Modernism is, after all, a highly valued term and it is given enormous prestige by the academy. As such, it seems to me that there are political reasons for insisting on the connections between Modernist forms and some of the New Woman writers, not least because it would permit some of that value to be claimed for feminist fictions. Sally Ledger has observed that we must be careful in making that connection, since much New Woman writing – much of it in the form of essays, plays, poems, and avowedly realist fictions – had no real commitment to aesthetic experimentation at all (Ledger 1997, 181), and that is a warning to take seriously. But New Woman fiction particularly does demonstrate the limitations of realism for representing alternative realities, and alternative outcomes for female characters to live through, and for readers to aspire to. When Woolf argued that 'Georgian' writers needed new tools to represent the new conditions of modernity – that failure was to form habits by continuing to represent reality using the old methods – her argument clearly holds just as true for Olive Schreiner (or for George Egerton) as it does for herself and her own contemporaries. It even holds partially true for those who continued to use the 'old' methods, as Sarah Grand did. The perceived failure of marriage, in life as well as in fiction, is just one of those new conditions requiring a new mode of writing if it was to be appropriately represented.

Despite these potential difficulties in making sense of *African Farm*'s fragmented form and alien story, however, for a generation of politicized women readers Schreiner's story meant a great deal. In her *Memories of a Friendship*, Mary Brown (to whom the novel is dedicated) wrote:

> I asked a Lancashire working woman what she thought of *Story of an African Farm* and a strange expression came over her face as she said, 'I read parts of it over and over'. 'What parts?' I asked, and her reply was 'About yon poor lass [Lyndall]', and with a far off look in her eye, added, 'I think there is hundreds of women what feels like that but can't speak it, but she could speak what we feel.' (Mrs John Brown 1923, qtd in Flint 1993, 244)

One of the striking elements about this anecdote is the emphasis on *parts* of the novel, rather than on the novel as a whole: for one working-class reader at least, the judgement of a book's quality is not to do with some predetermined standard of aesthetic coherence and unity, and she did not demand a novel that presented things steadily and whole. She has re-read those *parts* 'over and over' because she identifies a shared experience of oppressed femininity in Lyndall's story. As such the novel should certainly be read as a call to arms to overthrow those conditions. And, indeed, throughout the text, Lyndall is extremely articulate in her diagnosis of feminine powerlessness and its causes, describing with contempt female education and the limited aspirations to which her society demands she acquiesce. There is a *part* of *African Farm* which is a demand for action in the cause of emancipatory politics, in which accurate diagnosis of social ills (seeing clearly) is articulated very forcibly (told in a plain way). At the same time, though, the Lancashire woman also identifies Lyndall as 'yon poor lass': Lyndall's insights and intelligence about the current make-up of society do not enable her to *change* her world, and she dies at the end of the novel just like any other 'fallen woman' in Victorian fiction, from the curse of female sexuality in the form of a disease associated with the birth of her bastard child. She has managed to say what 'we feel' – to say what is wrong with the world; but she has not been able either to imagine or enact an alternative world, and dies defeated. As Lyndall herself comments, having described the story of Napoleon Bonaparte, which she conceives as having ended 'badly' in exile and defeat, 'It is a terrible, hateful ending... and the worst is, it is true. I have noticed ... that it is only the made-up stories that end nicely; the true ones all end so' (Schreiner 1995, 48). Lyndall admires Napoleon, but her sense that his story ends disastrously foreshadows what will also happen to her, despite her own rather less grandiose heroism; those who dare to aspire to something better will be defeated. There is, in other words, also a part of *African Farm* that is absolutely mired in a realist tradition of conventional narratives (fallen women die) and a realistic assessment of what happens when gifted women cannot live out their visions. It points out what the limitations of realism must be for anyone committed to an alternative political and social reality.

Schreiner's text blends genres in ways that, had the novel not also been a political text, would certainly have been retrospectively understood as heralding some of the experiments of Modernism in its aesthetics of displacement and fragmentation. The remarks in the Preface about the 'second' way of writing fiction, after all, are not so dissimilar from Virginia Woolf's proscriptions in her essays 'Modern Fiction' and 'Mr Bennett and Mrs Brown'. *African Farm* is a novel that looks in many directions. It is an English novel (the main female characters, Lyndall and Em, are English speaking settlers in South Africa as is Gregory Rose whose surname signals at once his feminization and his Englishness). It is also regarded as the first real example of a home-grown South African fiction. As such, it 'writes back' to the heart of Empire in England, yet also writes self-consciously about the specificity of a colonial experience which most certainly was not made up entirely of adventures with lions, cruel queens, battles with the natives and the pursuit of fabulous treasure. For Schreiner, Africa is at once a real place where people really live out very ordinary lives, and a fantasy landscape, marked by its geographical distance from the norms of the imperial power. It is as a place where a distance from the social norms commensurate with that geographical distance from power can be achieved, or at least imagined.

The representative of empire, of the white settler class in its masculine form, is Gregory Rose. His is a very attenuated masculinity. He is offered the love of Em, who wants nothing better than to serve him, offering him the chance to assert the conventional masculine values of ownership and mastery pretty much on a plate. Instead, he tries to earn Lyndall's love, which requires of him an absolutely abasing servitude, so selfless, indeed, that at the end of the novel his very gender identity has virtually dissolved as he shaves off his beard and dresses as a woman to nurse the dying heroine. This 'new mannism' is profoundly unrewarding. Lyndall, a masochistic Victorian heroine for all her intelligence, tells the nameless stranger who is her lover and who fathers her child when he asks her why she loved him: 'Because you are strong. You are the first man I ever was afraid of' (Schreiner 1995, 238). She is momentarily prepared to marry Gregory Rose because she is not afraid of him, and she identifies him as a man who has forgotten how to rule. She will not marry the stranger who could 'master' her – there will be no 'love, honour and *obey*' ending in conventional marriage even though Lyndall begins the novel with aspirations that are remarkably similar to those of the conventional heroine, where she wishes for pretty clothes and a wider social circle. In the end, nor does she marry the man who does not demand her obedience either.

The Preface argues that *African Farm* is a novel that focuses on grey reality (which is not quite the same thing as realism), and which will eschew colourful adventures. The first part of the novel is a largely realist account of what it was like to grow up on an isolated African farmstead without culture, books or education to stimulate the imagination. Tant'Sannie, the Boer woman who is Em's stepmother and Lyndall's step-aunt, signifies the gross reality and sterility of that existence. The novel's first page evokes the intense romance of an African moonlit night where the quality of the light on the landscape is alien to English readers, but also compellingly beautiful. Almost immediately, however, that romance is dispelled by our vision of Tant'Sannie asleep, dreaming bad dreams of 'the sheep's trotters she had eaten for supper that night. She dreamed that one stuck fast in her throat, and she rolled her huge form from side to side and snorted horribly' (Schreiner 1995, 36). Tant'Sannie's gross bulk is deliberately created to squash the romance out of the place.

Overlying that realism of presentation, there are elements of both brutality and farce on the one hand, and moments of lyricism interspersed with outspoken polemic on the other. The novel, in its allegiance to competing and contradictory genres, evades the authoritative inescapable narrative voice of realism which implies that there is only one reality, only one way of seeing the world. Schreiner's text creates the 'other sides' by combining realist technique with alien landscape; by offering swift transitions from one point of view to another; by juxtaposing passages of lyrical description, such as the one with which the novel opens, with Tant'Sannie's gross materialism; by allowing Lyndall to give voice to overtly political views; and by inserting into the novel allegorical visions, such as the story of the hunter, spoken by a stranger who arrives at the farm. The generic confusion undermines the idea of any single authoritative version of reality. The different versions compete, but none has, as it were, the last word.

As such, therefore, this is a political novel whose 'message' is hard to discern. It is clear that Schreiner had an explicitly feminist agenda – the most articulate passages in the novel are those where Lyndall describes the limitations of femininity. At the same time, however, it does not tell its readers what to think in anything approaching a clear way. If women readers empathized with Lyndall who could speak what they felt, they still could not take her as a positive role model – just look what happens to her. In the contrasts between the two little girls on the farm, the complexities of a feminist response to conformist femininity are played out, dramatized for a period in which there was no authorized version of how to be a woman who could think and act in her own behalf. No version of femininity is shown as positive, for if the intellectual woman ends up anorexic and dead, the domestic woman is merely fat and complacent. A key example takes place after Bonaparte Blenkins has beaten Waldo and locked him into the fuel store. The two girls respond to this act of gross injustice according to different codes: Em weeps as befits the helplessness of proper femininity and Lyndall acts, as a 'proper feminist' should. Em is passive in the face of adversity, and accepts the authority of adults, even when those adults have patently forfeited the right to obedience; she uses the feminine wiles of tears and entreaty to cajole her stepmother and the bastard surrogate father to behave better, and can think of nothing else to do when those attempts fail. Lyndall, on the other hand, believes in direct action. Whilst the rest of the house seethes, she appears to play the part of domesticated femininity, sewing calmly as Em weeps and the adults enjoy their power. But in an emblem of her rejection of that passive role, and of the proper femininity it symbolizes, she screws up her sewing as she screws up her courage, and directly enacts the redressing of justice, taking the key from the adults and releasing Waldo from his imprisonment. This act of defiance goes unchecked because in the childlike world of the farm, where even the adults are partially children, they dare not punish this insurrection. On the other hand – and this is part of the text's honest representation of confusion – Lyndall's action is self-abnegatory; she does it for Waldo, not for herself, and resumes a version of proper femininity in her childish attempt to comfort him with a kiss.

Lyndall's move away from the false Eden of the farm is a move into sexual experience. Finally, it is her biology that lets her down, since when she returns to the farm for the last time, she is pregnant – though this is referred to only very obliquely. One of the areas of knowledge she has gained is sexual knowledge, a most improper knowledge for the conventionally feminine woman. Having suffered a sexual 'fall' as well as her other disillusionments, Lyndall is forced by circumstance and loss of will to become a caricature of femininity. She maintains the interest of her unnamed lover through feminine capriciousness, holding him fascinated by apparent indifference: 'you love me because you cannot bear to be resisted,' she tells him. 'You resolved to have me because I seemed unattainable' (238). And as Gilbert and Gubar have argued, she ends as a parody of the limitations of femininity, not as a feminist icon:

> Disease, weakness, confinement, paralysis, thwarted ambition: these are the fate of the female parasite that Lyndall first outlines and then typifies as she travels alone … across the Free State of the Transvaal, to give birth to a baby that dies. Later, haunted by her dead baby, lying on a couch, wasting away, unable to eat, and furnished with a lapdog, a mirror, and a wardrobe full of lovely dresses, she is an image of the 'curse' of femininity. (Gilbert and Gubar 1989, 51)

At the end of the novel, readers do not generally think that Lyndall's death 'serves her right'; they feel that she has been martyred. In that final image she is not merely a stereotypical fallen woman ending badly, but also a dramatic indictment of the conditions that produced her 'fall' and death. She stands as the embodiment of the central problem of feminist-inflected New Woman writing in that her ambition is thwarted because neither heroine nor author can imagine an alternative happier ending in the current state of society. Only in fantasy could she be happier because 'true' stories always end badly. Realism with its commitment to reality lets Lyndall down just as badly as reality lets down real women.

Sarah Grand: seeing things purely

When Thomas Hardy published *Tess of the D'Urbervilles* in 1891, he subtitled it *A Pure Woman*. The reviews he received were mixed: some, like Clementina Black writing in the *Illustrated London News* (9 January 1892), praised his moral courage in articulating the 'perception that a woman's moral worth is measurable not by any one deed, but by the whole aim and tendency of her life and nature', and heralded him as 'one of [a] brave and clear-sighted minority' (Black in Cox 1970, 187). Others, notably Margaret Oliphant in *Blackwood's Magazine* and Mowbray Morris in the *Quarterly Review*, were much less convinced, and read the subtitle as a deliberate provocation. Morris commented that reading Tess as a pure woman 'entails something of a strain upon the English language … It is indisputably open to Mr. Hardy to call his heroine a pure woman; but he has no less certainly offered many inducements to his readers to refuse her the name' (Morris in Cox 1970, 215). And Mrs Oliphant for one could not believe in Tess's purity:

> That she should have been taken advantage of, and dragged into degradation by mingled force and kindness, is possible; but not that pure-minded and spotless, yet already alarmed and set on her guard as she had been, she should have trusted herself at midnight with the unscrupulous young master who was pursuing her, and whose inhabits she was full informed of … (Oliphant in Cox 1970, 206)

That beggars belief, as far as the reviewer is concerned.

Hardy, of course, had chosen his title very deliberately as a critique of the discourse of 'purity' that surrounded nineteenth-century femininity. Purity, to borrow a phrase, should not mean simply being a woman 'who *didn't*' in the argument that *Tess* presents. But in that choice he was not only attacking conservative forces, but was also mounting an attack on contemporary nineteenth-century feminist theory. For 'purity' was a word held dear not only by those conservators of tradition who wished to keep women in the domestic sphere of the home, but also by those who sought a wider role for women on a more public stage. The word had become embattled because of its adoption by the feminist campaigners against the Contagious Diseases Acts of 1864, 1866 and 1869, a series of legislative attempts to regulate prostitution, at first in garrison towns where large numbers of soldiers were gathered, later in the population at large. The Acts were provoked by the fear that the British Army and Navy were susceptible to the ravages of venereal diseases because individual service men habitually consorted with diseased women. They required women suspected of prostitution in garrison towns to undergo forcible medical examinations for the presence of sexually transmitted diseases, and to undergo treatment in 'Lock' hospitals (effectively prisons masquerading as hospitals) if disease was found to be present. The fact that there was no effective treatment for such diseases was not felt as a bar to locking up working-class women for the protection of the virility of soldiers and sailors. The whole system of regulation was based on serial injustices. There was no proper regulation of the process by which a woman might be accused of prostitution – it might simply be on the say so of a jilted boyfriend, or a malicious neighbour. The authorities simply had to say that they suspected immorality, and had no duty to prove their suspicions before moving in to incarcerate their suspects. Moreover, men who consorted with prostitutes were not examined or treated at all: sexual disease was perceived as a problem with women, and the 'solution' was played out entirely on women's bodies. As Josephine Butler (1828–1906) wrote in 1869: 'By this Law a crime has been *created* in order that it may be severely punished; but observe, that has been ruled to be a crime in women which is not considered to be a crime in men. There are profligate men who are spreading disease everywhere, but the law does not take effect on *these*' (Butler in Jump 1999, 166). If men were diseased, that was just the prostitute's bad luck. This system of examination and incarceration was one of the most dramatic instances of a sexual double standard being enacted by the law. It enraged many respectable women who perhaps would never have become involved in political agitation, especially on a sexual subject, but for their outrage that sexual licence for men was being given a kind of legal status, and that the whole of social basis of sexual morality was laid at the door of women.[7]

Josephine Butler was one of the key campaigners against the acts, mobilizing a discourse that twinned sisterhood (prostitutes were the less fortunate sisters of the middle-class campaigners) with purity (a demand for equal standards of sexual propriety for men and for women). In her appeal against prostitution she argued that the women – rich or poor, pure or impure – were not the only people to be considered in regulating sexuality, and that one could not protect 'pure' women merely by inspecting 'impure' ones. 'It is curious,' she wrote, that conservative male writers and politicians ignore 'the existence of that intermediate class, who convey the contagion from [the prostitute] to [the pure woman of the middle class family]. Certain persons resent, as if it were an indelicacy, any allusion to that most important link, the adulterous husbands and fathers who are dispensing disease and death in their families' (Butler in Jump 1999, 167). If the men abstained, the problem would go away. It took over twenty years for the Contagious Diseases Acts to be repealed in 1886. But the battle left an ongoing commitment amongst many late-Victorian feminists to redressing the balance of the sexual double standard where a woman who *did* became known as a whore, where a man who *did* remained socially acceptable. Hardy's novel, which presents Tess Durbeyfield as a 'pure' woman inserted itself into this discourse in a highly uncomfortable way. On the one hand, the novel clearly stakes a claim for equality between men and women in sexual matters; the reader is supposed to be shocked when Angel Clare admits his own prior sexual misconduct, 'when, tossed about by doubts and difficulties, he went to London and plunged into eight-and-forty hours' dissipation with a stranger' (Hardy 1998a, 225), but refuses to see that Tess's case is precisely similar to his own.[8] When asked for his forgiveness, he declares; 'Forgiveness does not apply to the case. You were one person; now you are another ... the woman I have been loving is not you' (228–9). At the same time, however, whilst making a feminist argument, in using that phrase *A Pure Woman* Hardy fatally undermines the feminists' language practices, using their words to very different ends. Tess might be a pure woman in the sense that she represents the very essence of femininity – at least for a certain brand of masculine fantasy in the 1890s; but she is not 'pure' in the ways that word was most often used. Hardy's subversion of feminist vocabulary might well have been undertaken with the best of intentions, and with a far more radical sexual agenda than was usual in the Victorian novel, but it did not serve the arguments or preferences of his feminist contemporaries at all well.

New Woman novelist Sarah Grand (pseudonym of Frances McFall, 1854–1943) would not have been sympathetic to Hardy's view. In her massive tomes on the woman question, *The Heavenly Twins* (1893) and *The Beth Book* (1897), she harks back to the Social Purity campaigners' use of the word 'purity' to represent a standard of sexual propriety that is supposed to be seen as the responsibility of both sexes. *The Heavenly Twins* is a morality tale in three-volume form, concerning three women. Purity looms very large in the plot and is explicitly the novel's moral message. The first of the three women, Evadne Frayling, undertakes a course of self-education. She reads widely in whatever interests her, including medical textbooks which discuss sexual diseases. She then falls in love with an apparently eligible man, Major Colquhoun, troped as conspicuously manly (for which, read sexually attractive) by virtue of his profession in the forces. But since the Contagious Diseases Acts were aimed at the protection of profligate soldiers, we should also be suspicious about his career and the kind of life it may have led him to. Sure enough, after the ceremony, but before the wedding breakfast, Evadne receives a letter from an anonymous woman, offering information about her husband's sexual past. The discovery that he has not been 'pure' revolts her, and she runs away, refusing to live with her husband on the usual terms, and only agreeing to a *mariage blanc* in order to avoid scandal. But, as Sally Ledger observes, there is a real cost attached to this act of self-preservation. Evadne might not die of syphilis, but she has to repress her desires for her eligible husband 'and the desire she feels for [him] is made manifest' (Ledger 1997, 114). Even an intelligent woman like Evadne is susceptible to the idea of being in love, and of having a home of her own. Grand 'quotes' a 'professor' describing the emotion she feels when she consents to become Colquhoun's wife thus:

> 'All excitements run to love in women of a certain – let us not say age, but youth … An electrical current passing though a coil of wire makes a magnet of a bar of iron lying within it, but not touching it. So a woman is turned into a love-magnet by a tingling current of life around running round her … ' This passage indicates exactly the point at which Evadne had now arrived. (Grand 1992, 52)

It is not, then, that women do not feel desire (though Grand tends also to emphasize that the desire is bound up with the vocation of maternity); but that desire cannot be safely admitted in a world of inequitable sexual arrangements. Evadne refuses to condone her husband's former misconduct, and she complains bitterly to her father that he should not have condoned impropriety in her husband of a sort that he would never condone in a wife. Evadne has to repress her natural feelings to preserve her life, a repression does lasting damage to her mental health.

Evadne is proven right by the parallel story of Edith Beale to have been quite right to insist on her principles, and to have been lucky to have educated herself to understand the implications of her husband's former amorous career. Edith, the daughter of a Bishop, is appallingly innocent and ignorant. If Evadne deliberately educates herself, Edith prays: 'Dear Lord … keep me from all knowledge of unholy things' (157). When she becomes engaged to marry one of Colquhoun's fellow officers, Evadne warns her not to go through with the ceremony, but Edith cannot be warned because she has no inkling of what Evadne is hinting at. She marries Mosley Menteith, a syphilitic rake who passes his disease on to his unsuspecting wife and to their child. Edith dies a raving lunatic; the child is mentally and physically defective, but lingers on as a reproach to Edith's parents for keeping her in such appalling innocence.

The third story is that of Angelica Hamilton Wells, one of the heavenly twins of the title – her brother, Theodore, known as Diavolo, is the other. The figure of male and female twins is placed at the service of an argument about the ways in which intellectual equality is stifled by social inequity. Angelica is by far the brighter and more energetic of the twins, but has no outlet for her talents. Whilst a career in the army is planned for her brother, her whole life is to be narrowed down to marriage. This infantilizes her – her husband is many years her senior, and she calls him, very uncomfortably, 'Daddy'. With nothing to do, no outlet for her energy and intellect, she remains a child, causing mischief, and only when that mischief leads indirectly to the death of the Tenor at Morningquest Cathedral does she rein herself in and start to think in a more mature way, deciding that her life must be lived as a service for others. Service is, for Grand and other social purity writers, a feminine ideal. Angelica comes to a kind of maturity by writing political speeches for her elderly asexual husband. Meanwhile, Evadne has been widowed, and at the end of the novel marries a second husband who is clearly much more suitable than her first. But there is no happy ending projected beyond the novel's end in an epilogue. The life of repression she led with George Colquhoun has marked her permanently as a hysteric, prone to suicidal impulses, and unable to resist them despite the supposedly redemptive and restorative powers of motherhood. She survives only because her second husband, a doctor, watches over her. Her existence is reduced to shadows; in the sequel, *The Beth Book*, she is an invalid, alluded to, but never actually appearing on the scene of the second book because she is too sick to participate in social gatherings.

This rather bald summary tends to emphasize what subsequent generations of readers have found to be wrong with the New Woman fiction. Art is sacrificed for message; the plots are repetitive; men are melodramatic villains, right down to the twirling of their hyper-virile moustaches and the women are helpless virgins who, despite a certain amount of education, are unable to evade the marriage plots that society has written for them; character is reduced to function; conversation is made up of set-piece rhetoric; like the sequel, *The Beth Book*, this is a novel written to a pattern. Fair comment, so far as it goes. One could, of course, make a similar argument about *Tess*, as, indeed, one early reviewer did. Mrs Oliphant objected that the characters in Hardy's novel were lifted directly from the types of the ballad tradition, with Alec a seducer in the mould of Mr B. in Richardson's *Pamela* (1742) (Oliphant in Cox 1970, 212). But Hardy of course is a 'great' novelist, so that has not mattered much to posterity. When Hardy descended to melodrama and sensationalism, the 1890s reviewers disapproved and associated him with the despised Naturalist tradition of Emile Zola, but subsequent generations rehabilitated him and praised his unwillingness to compromise with the fictional conventions of his day. Grand did the same things, and did them more blatantly and with far less self-conscious artistry, it has to be admitted; and she ended up being forgotten for most of the twentieth century. As Sally Ledger has noted, *Tess* was the best-selling novel of 1892 and *The Heavenly Twins* the best-seller of 1893, but interceding history has treated the two writers very differently, and this is not all down to the fact that Hardy was the greater talent. Moreover, Hardy cannot quite be understood in his own context without a reading of Grand. His own refusal to admit the influence of New Woman writing is not a reason why we should take him at his word.

George Egerton and impurity

In the period running up to and in the aftermath of the Wilde trials in April and May 1895, numerous articles about the 'tendencies' of modern literature appeared in the British press – most of which were highly unflattering to the experimental forms and dubious moral content that the writers discerned in contemporary literary production. In the unlikely pages of John Lane's *The Yellow Book*, a radical publication which deliberately courted a shady reputation with its yellow covers (which reminded readers of the covers of naughty French novels) and its provocative illustrations by Aubrey Beardsley, Arthur Waugh argued that there must be more reticence in literature. Though frankness and outspokenness are national virtues, there are limits, he argued: 'there never was a truly wise man yet but tempered his natural freedom of speech by an acquired habit of reticence' (Waugh 1894, 203). What is true for life is all the more true for literature: 'It is unmanly, it is effeminate, it is inartistic to gloat over pleasure, to revel in immoderation, to become passion's slave; and literature demands as much calmness of judgment, as much reticence, as life itself' (210). In the same year, Thomas Bradfield discoursed upon 'A Dominant Note of Some Recent Fiction' in *The Westminster Review*, identifying that 'note' as unbridled sexuality. Bradfield was nostalgic for an older morality in fiction, and feared that the tendency, particularly amongst recent women writers, to discuss sexual issues in relation to the Woman Question was leading English literature into Decadence. He singled out Grand's *The Heavenly Twins* and a slim collection of short stories by George Egerton, entitled *Keynotes* (1893), which, like *The Yellow Book*, was also published by John Lane and also designed by Aubrey Beardsley, as particularly appalling examples of that modern tendency.

> When, some fifteen or twenty years ago, it was apparent that even the strong meat of Miss Braddon's early style[9] ... was not sufficiently gratifying

> for the sated taste, something new and more highly seasoned was soon forthcoming. As one result, there sprang into fashion, a class of story, with the central pivot of its interest bound up with the passion of two young, ardent, attractive beings, in the chains of whose rapturous inter-course one indispensable link was however wanting to render it fair and honourable. It was not that adultery or illicit intercourse between men and women was any new feature in fiction; but the exceptionally attrac-tive manner in which these were draped gave this new presentation a subtly insidious character. (Bradfield 1894, 537–8)

The missing element, of course, is marriage; and the attractive manner of presentation refers to the fact that adultery was not necessarily pun-ished in plot outcomes in some of the fiction and drama of the period. Bradfield's rhetoric strongly suggests that he finds that there is some-thing unsavoury – even gamy – about the new kinds of writing.

The Wilde trials led to these vague expressions of dislike becoming much more strongly written. In June 1895, a few weeks after Wilde had been sent to jail, Hugh E. M. Stutfield spluttered in print that the whole of modern literature was fundamentally 'Tommyrotics', meaning both that it was rubbish that scarcely required to be attacked (tommyrot), and that it was based on an overemphasis on eroticized content and neurotic tone – which demanded that right-thinking critics would attack it after all. Stutfield was horrified by the influence of 'neurotic and repulsive fiction' he saw in print all around him:

> Its hysterical origin shows itself chiefly in the morbid spirit of analysis. Judging from their works, the authors must be vivified notes of interro-gation. Their characters are so dreadfully introspective. When they are not talking of psychology, they are discussing physiology … They are oppressed by the sense that everything is an enigma, that they them-selves are 'playthings of the inexplicable'; or else they try to 'compass the whole physiological gamut of their being' – whatever that might be. I am quoting from Miss George Egerton's 'Discords', a fair type of English neurotic fiction. (Stutfield in Ledger and Luckhurst 2000, 122)

Discords, Egerton's second volume for John Lane's publishing house, had been published in 1894. In even this very small selection of Stutfield's discussion it is easy to discern the distaste for any kind of writing that does not hold true to the older values represented by Arnold and Ruskin. Introspective characters cannot possibly be seen steadily and whole; characters who do nothing but ask questions can-not possibly be 'told' in a plain way. The attempt to express anything of the mystery of existence is deflated in that common-sense remark 'whatever that might be', which implies that the writer has distorted the proper use of the English language for no good expressive purpose.

George Egerton was the pen name of Mary Chavelita Dunne (1859–1945), who took her pen name from the husband she married after a spell as another man's mistress, and who was – as that detail implies – no stranger to scandal in her private life. In the late 1880s, she had eloped with one Henry Higginson, a highly unreliable man. He had married Mrs Melville Whyte bigamously, and when he decamped with Miss Dunne to Norway in 1887, he took some of his 'wife's' money with him. Higginson died there, probably of alcoholism, in 1889, having made Dunne's life very difficult indeed in the two years they spent together. On the other hand, her Norwegian sojourn had furnished Chavelita Dunne with a knowledge of Scandinavian languages and literature that would stand her in good stead in later life (she would translate the works of Knut Hamsun), and a series of adventures that were to become the content of her most famous fictions. If Sarah Grand exalted femininity, regarding it as necessarily purer and more ideal than masculinity, Miss Dunne was perhaps more realistic, debunking the idealized view of women as if in recognition that a pedestal is a very narrow place to stand. Elsewhere in her writings, she disapproves of sentiment as a trap, calling it bitterly in 'A Cross Line' 'that crowning disability of my sex' (Egerton 1983, 27); she regards conventional religion as an intellectual fetter that leads to double standards, and understands that hypocrisy might well be the condition of femininity in an era of sexual inequality where men create their ideal image of women, refusing to see them as they are. Meditating on female desire in the same story, the heroine thinks to herself:

> But it is there, sure enough, and each woman is conscious of it ... and each woman in God's wide world will deny it, and each woman will help another to conceal it – for the woman who tells the truth and is not a liar about these things is untrue to her sex and abhorrent to man, for he has fashioned a model on imaginary lines, and has said, 'so I would have you,' and every woman is an unconscious liar, for so man loves her. (Egerton 1983, 22–3)

Egerton refuses to buy into the discourse of feminine purity that other feminists had claimed as their own special grounds for argument; and she refuses – both personally and professionally – to pretend. For as she wrote many years later, describing her characteristic themes in *Keynotes*:

> I realised that in literature, everything had been done better by man than woman could hope to emulate. There was only one small plot left

> for her to tell: the *terra incognita* of herself, as she knew herself to be, not
> as man liked to imagine her – in a word to give herself away, as man had
> given himself away in his writing. (Egerton in Gawsworth 1932, 58)

Focusing on female desire gives her a new subject for literary practice.
The new subject in turn demands a new kind of writing.

The form in which Egerton produced her most important work is the
short story. In many ways, despite the extremely long history of tales
and fabliaux, the short story is the modernist form *par excellence*. In
the publishing explosion of the late nineteenth century, there was a
ready market for short fiction. In publications such as *The Strand* and
The Picadilly, amongst serious articles about the events of the period,
readers also found the Sherlock Holmes stories of Arthur Conan Doyle,
tales which told of criminality at the heart of Empire. But stories
like Doyle's in the popular magazines operated largely on realist
assumptions – the detective story, with its neat lines of cause and effect,
problem and solution, is a key exemplar of realist patterning, of narratives which make sense of the world. Egerton's stories, on the other
hand, deal sometimes with realistic – even naturalistic – situations, but
they eschew realist technique and prefigure the modernist aesthetics
of the short story form. They were published before Chekhov's short
fiction was translated into English by Constance Garnett in 1910, but
they share some of his preoccupations with interior monologue rather
than external situation as the key motivation to the story. In turn, they
also foreshadow something of the flavour of Joyce's *Dubliners*, and of
Katherine Mansfield's and of Jean Rhys's fictions. They are fragments
that give flavours of a state of mind, rather than stories that operate
according to the rules established by Edgar Allan Poe, in which the
short story or tale is defined by a single significant incident, and by the
accumulation of meaning in the narrative's 'twist' in the tale's ending.
What's striking about the stories is their elliptical technique. In the
opening of 'A Cross Line', more information is missing than present:

> The rather flat notes of a man's voice float out into the clear air, singing
> the refrain of a popular music-hall ditty. There is something incongru-
> ous between the melody and the surroundings. It seems profane, indel-
> icate, to bring this slangy, vulgar tune, and with it the mental picture
> of footlight flare and fantastic dance into the lovely freshness of this
> perfect spring day.
>
> A woman sitting on a felled tree turns her head to meet its coming,
> and an expression flits across her face in which disgust and humorous
> appreciation are subtly blended. Her mind is nothing if not picturesque;

her busy brain, with all its capabilities choked by a thousand vagrant fancies, is always producing pictures and finding associations between the most unlikely objects. (Egerton 1983, 1)

In this opening, as in others, the reader is dislocated by the fact that s/he does not know where or when the story is taking place. There is no solidity of specification, and the story will not provide it as it unfolds. Moreover, it is written unusually in the continuous present tense rather than the perfect tense with which realism habitually constructed its sense of the perspective that leads to judgement. We are invited to intimacy with the figures of whom we read, but it is not an intimacy based on the accumulation of detail. We are not told simple things such as the names of the story's agents. We never actually find out whether the relationship between the man who sings and the woman who listens is a sexual one. The narrative is evasive and elliptical.

Following on from that passage, it is also instructive to note how much of the stories of *Keynotes* and *Discords* are couched in dialogue rather than in impersonal third-person narrative. The reader has to intuit what is going on by reading between the lines of the dialogue, rather than having easy access to what is meant by their conversation from the intervention of an omniscient narrator. No seeing things steadily and whole here. The 'what' of the plot in 'A Cross Line' is relegated in favour of the 'how' of its expression, and modern readers will have some difficulty in following the conversations because of the specialist vocabulary of fly-fishing with which it is peppered, and because of the use of 1890s slang, which has dated in the meantime. That the subject is the possibility of adultery is disguised by the story's refusal to speak clearly. The cross line of the title implies incomprehension as in that most up-to-date modes of communication, the telephone, where crossed lines rendered conversation incomprehensible. In the context of the heroine's preference for fly-fishing, it is also an evocation of tangled fishing lines which come to stand for emotional entanglements amidst a healthy physical life. Dénouement, it is as well to recall, is the French for untying or disentangling, and traditionally, it is narrative time that performs the Gordian miracle of sorting out textual loose ends. At the end of 'A Cross Line' however, time does not tell in the usual way. The heroine discovers that she is pregnant; but she has already made the decision to stay with her husband, despite his emotional density, having already told her lover (if that is what he is) that his moment with her is over (Egerton 1983, 30). Maternity returns her to the conventional path, but not for the conventional reasons.

The heroine is excited – in a frankly sensual way – about the discovery of the life quickening inside her. There is a self-sufficiency in her enjoyment of the sensations of pregnancy, and perhaps it is the first time that such emotions had been expressed in fiction from the point of view of the woman herself.

Before pregnancy, of course, there is sex. Not for George Egerton the virtually virgin births that Sarah Grand's heroines submit to. As De Vere White comments, 'for the first time in English the heroine admits to sexual feeling' (De Vere White 1958, 10). 'A Cross Line' contains a remarkably frank evocation of sexual foreplay, where the married couple in conversation are shown physically teasing each other, with bites on the ears, fierce kisses, nuzzling, eroticized attacks and counterattacks that lead inevitably to bed:

> He looks so utterly at sea that she has to laugh again, and, kneeling up, shuts his eyes with kisses, and bites his chin and shakes it like a terrier between a terrier in her strong little teeth … Catching her wrists, he … drops her on to the rug. Then, perhaps the subtle magnetism that is in her affects him, for he stoops, snatches her up and carries her up and down … His eyes dilate and his colour deepens as he crushes her soft little body to him and carries her off to her room. (Egerton 1983, 17–18)

The sexual attraction and desire is mutual, not one-sided: sex is not just about satisfying male lust, as in the purity discourse, but is also about fulfilling female needs. And, in the most remarkable passage of the story, the heroine daydreams a remarkable masturbatory fantasy.

> … a great longing fills her soul to sail off somewhere … away from the daily need of dinner-getting and the recurring Monday with its washing; life with its tame duties and virtuous monotony. She fancies herself in Arabia on the back of a swift steed. Flashing eyes set in dark faces surround her, and she can see the clouds of sand swirl, and feel the swing under her of his rushing stride. Her thoughts shape themselves into a wild song, a song to her steed of flowing mane and satin skin; an uncouth rhythmical jingle with a feverish beat; a song to the untamed spirit that dwells in her. (Egerton 1983, 18–19)

The fantasy continues with the heroine as Salome, dancing in flimsy clothes before a large audience, provoking desire, but also feeling it:

> She can see herself with parted lips and panting, rounded breasts, and a dancing devil in each glowing eye, sway voluptuously to the wild music that rises, now slow, now fast, now deliriously wild, seductive, intoxicating,

with a note of human passion in its strain. She can feel the answering shiver of feeling that quivers up to he from the dense audience...she stands with outstretched arms and passion-filled eyes, poised on one slender foot, asking a supreme note to finish her dream of motion. (Egerton 1983, 20)

Sexuality is the secret of her power, she decides – 'the keynote of woman's witchcraft and woman's strength' (22). If all women admitted their desires, it would bring about a revolution, the story seems to imply, because it would require a rethink about what femininity really meant.

On the other hand, in current conditions, that sexuality might also be seen as the source of her weakness. As Ann Heilmann has argued, Egerton's fictions are perhaps really apolitical, and appeal above all to a male readership rather than to the specifically feminist project of the New Woman proper.

By exposing domestic and sexual violence ('Virgin Soil', 'Gone Under' and 'Wedlock', all in *Discords*) *and* exploring female sexuality ('A Cross Line'...), she seems to position herself both in the centre [of feminist politics] (violence against women) and at the margins (women's sexual pleasure) of the genre, yet her celebration of the 'eternally feminine' principle replicated rather than challenged patriarchal thinking about women. (Heilmann 2000, 45)

'Egerton's sexual fantasies proved considerably less challenging than the feminists' demands,' she concludes (46). It is an interesting reversal that recent critics have begun to argue, in contrast to earlier critiques, that far from the politics disabling the art, the art of some New Woman writers is not political enough. It is true enough that the heroine of 'A Cross Line' is not only strong and sexually independent but that she is also nervous, subject to psychosomatic illnesses and hysteria. She is caught between two worlds. Her dreams are feminist visions because they articulate and celebrate female complexity. But her responses to her own particular life problems are more conventionally feminine. She returns to her husband despite his incomprehension of her. His attraction is presumably based on his sense that he feels she is a companion as a man might be a companion, as well as a sexual equal – he loves the 'beast' in her. There is, nonetheless, something rather tame in the woman's compliance in the stereotype of maternity as redemption. (In another story, 'The Spell of the White Elf', a modern woman, a professor, wishes the narrator a white elf – a small child – of her own (89) as the best way to be fully human. That narrator takes her advice, and marries her childhood sweetheart on the strength of the advice.) At the same time, however, Egerton is remarkable for her insistence on self-fulfilment first. The sad characters who populate the two volumes of stories are those who do not achieve sexual happiness, especially when they do so out of mistaken ideas about propriety or convention. Success is relative, but in Egerton's writing it is always based on some element of sexual fulfilment for the woman, and that is a remarkably new way of looking at it even if motherhood remains the main goal of a woman's life.

There is, however, one story in particular, from the *Discords* collection, which implies that motherhood does not in itself make women saintly and self-sacrificing. 'Wedlock' was the most notorious of the tales from the second volume, in part because it takes alcoholism and murder as its themes, and in part because it does so with a commitment to a quasi-naturalistic explanatory framework in the discourse of degeneration. The presentation, though, is anything but naturalistic, again taking place elliptically. The story begins with the conversation of two builders who are working in a London suburban neighbourhood who observe as they work the domestic ruin in one of the families in the new houses. The mother of that family is a drunk and the younger of the two builders finds her vice insupportable: if she were his wife, he would beat her. The older man, however, argues from his own experience that alcoholism is an inherited disorder, and that we should not leap to conclusions about how or why a woman becomes a drunk. His own wife, he tells us, is a drinker. It comes from her family history, and he describes in detail the steps he has taken to care for her, and to protect his children from her vice. He is speaking in terms that may not quite seem enlightened to us, but which represent the 'best' thinking of the 1890s on such subjects.

The woman whose drunkenness they observe, however, is not quite so easily explained, or explained away, as a congenital alcoholic – her reasons are not purely biological, but are also clearly sociological. She is married to a brutal man who beats her, and who has broken his promise to her to let her illegitimate daughter live with them, to be brought up amongst his own children from a previous marriage, for whom the woman is to act as stepmother. Yearning mother-love is part of the explanation for the woman's 'weakness' in relation to drink and for her domestic failure. Her husband's children, 'keen-eyed London children with a precocious knowledge of the darker sides of life' (Egerton 1983, 124), are the victims of this precarious arrangement. When the stepmother discovers that her daughter's sickness and death have been kept from her by her husband, she returns home to re-enact Tess's murder of Alec D'Urberville amidst the very ordinary suburban world of modern London:

> Upstairs in a black room in the silent house a pale strip of moonlight flickers over a dark streak on the floor, that trickles slowly from the pool at the bedside out under the door, making a second ghastly pool on the top step of the stairs – a thick sorghum red, blackening as it thickens, with a sickly serous border. Downstairs the woman sits in a chair with her arms hanging down. Her hands are crimson as if she had dipped them in dye. A string of blue beads lies on her lap, and she is fast asleep; and she smiles as she sleeps for Susie [her dead daughter] is playing in a meadow, a great meadow, crimson with poppies, and her blue eyes smile with glee, and her golden curls are poppy-crowned … and her tiny waxen hands scatter poppies, blood-red poppies, in handfuls over three open graves. (Egerton 1983, 144)

The outcome of the story shows Egerton radically subverting the ideologies of motherhood and femininity. When Tess takes revenge on her lover, she is justified by the events that have led to that point. But when Susan kills her stepchildren in revenge for the loss of her own daughter, she is committing the worst crime that can be imagined in a woman – child murder. One of the defamiliarizing elements of the story is that we are given no clue about how to read this story. We do not know whether we are supposed to sympathize with her, or to judge her, and the writer evades the Victorian necessity for giving us moral guidance. It has dealt with shocking issues – alcoholism, male violence and most shockingly, female violence; the one voice of reasoned sanity and advanced thinking in the text comes from a working-class bricklayer, a man who in terms of the usual conventions of fiction, has no authority. New Woman writing in this instance is the representation of unpalatable subject matter, by a woman writer, without the clear moral perspective given by realist narrative and usually required by Victorian ideals. No wonder texts such as these caused a scandal when they were published.

The New Woman beyond the nineties

> … this strange disease of modern life,
> With its sick hurry, its divided aims,
> Its heads o'ertaxed, its palsied hearts … (Arnold 1993, 99, ll. 203–5)

Thus did Matthew Arnold define the condition of modern life in 'The Scholar Gypsy' (1853). He was not talking particularly about women, but about modernity generally. Nonetheless, those few brief phrases do define something about the way in which the New Woman was characterized in fiction and beyond. In Egerton's 'Wedlock', a minor part is played by a woman who lodges in the house where the tragedy takes place and who is clearly a New Woman writer. This woman tries to be kind and helpful to the 'fallen' sister who drinks and who fails at domesticity, but this second woman's life is also hard, and it is as if she has very little sympathy to spare. We see her in her lodging room, writing for money (Egerton 1983, 123–4). She forgets to eat in her anxiety to write. Her feet twitch, her fingers burn – she is a bundle of nerves. Although she tries to give good advice to her landlady, her sisterly gestures are futile, and before the tragedy of the child-murders unfolds, she moves on, discomfited by the vague feeling that the house is a place of gothic horror, haunted in advance by the feeling that 'she is facing one of those lurid tragedies that outsiders are powerless to prevent' (132). Her analytic mind makes her able to imagine the possible endings of this story. Like the sympathetic workman, she is sensitive to an oppressive domestic atmosphere, but she cannot act to prevent the unfolding of violence.

Women like this woman writer populate the pages of Egerton's stories; thin to the point of anorexia, the nervous women who hold emancipated views, but who are often powerless to put those views into action, proliferate. Schreiner's Lyndall is like them too; Evadne in *The Heavenly Twins* becomes like them; Sue Bridehead epitomizes the type: 'There was nothing statuesque in her; all was nervous motion. She was mobile, living, yet a painter might not have called her handsome or beautiful' (Hardy 1998b, 90). In Egerton's fictions such women are constructed as sexually attractive, as fascinating, bewitching, irresistible. Lyndall clearly has similar attractions; Jude cannot help himself with Sue. Perhaps even the wildly neurotic Evadne has a certain something, given the fact that George Galbraith cannot wait to marry and protect her. But fashions in types of female character, just as fashions in clothing, do change through time. In *Dracula*, Mina Harker is clearly a New Woman in that she has a career in her own right, and an acknowledged professional status in the part she plays in tracking down the monster. Mina, though, is 'healthy', evidenced in her diary by her own comments on her healthy appetite: 'I believe we should have shocked the "New Woman" with our appetites' (Stoker 1993, 118), she writes after a particularly gourmet tea, as if she is not a New Woman herself. Perhaps, then, as early as 1897 the fashion for nervy women was changing. Certainly Clara Dawes (*Sons and Lovers*) and Ann Veronica in Wells's New Woman novel are much more fleshy versions of femininity, physically healthier figures of female dissatisfaction. And if Ursula Brangwen (*The Rainbow*) and Hilda Lessways (*Clayhanger* and *Hilda Lessways*) are thin, that is because they are figures from an earlier age than the one in which they are being described.

But it is not just a question of fashion. The terms of the argument also began to change with the turn of the century. Although Suffrage writers whose main feminist aim was the gaining of votes for women, continued to use the Victorian discourse of purity well into the twentieth century, arguing that women needed votes because men could not be trusted, and producing wildly inflated statistics about rates of venereal infection amongst middle-class men, their activism was much more collectively than individually oriented. It demanded marching and speech making, and for the unlucky few, imprisonment, hunger strikes and forced feeding under the notorious 'Cat and Mouse Act' (1912). Such women might starve, but they did so as part of a self-conscious political campaign, not because they were nervous and had forgotten to eat. In the context of the suffrage campaign, facts became more important than fictions. The New Woman effort, which had always been diverse – written in fiction, but also in poems, plays, essays and pamphlets – concentrated far more on the kinds of evidence that legislators could not ignore. But most of all, the New Woman was co-opted into masculine fiction as a vehicle for masculine fantasy rather than for feminine emancipation. The advanced women did not go away, and some of them even got the vote in 1918, but the nineties name for them disappeared. The New Woman became old news, and feminism – indeed, activist politics of all kinds – separated from fiction.

As Ann Ardis argues, 'the critical establishment reacted hostilely to the success of [New Woman writers] ... Demanding in true Arnoldian fashion that the public recognize a distinction between "classics" and these "racy" new novels, conservative critics depoliticized "Literature" ... They began to valorize the kind of formalist aesthetic we associate with high modernism as they tried to steer readers away from these highly politicized and controversial works' (Ardis 1990, 4). Even the overtly political essay *A Room of One's Own* shows Virginia Woolf disavowing politics as a proper subject for literary practice, even as politics are shown to be essential to the processes of literary production. Woolf's essay makes no mention of the New Woman, argues that the vote is less important than her inheritance, and values above all those kinds of writing which remain resolutely outside the political sphere. In forgetting the fictions of Schreiner, Grand, Egerton and others, Modernism refused to acknowledge any debt to the generation of writers who had first pointed out the limitations of realism in expressing the conditions of modernity.

Notes

1. As a definition of the New Woman generally, Senf's description is very sound. In fact, though, Grand's essay 'The New Aspect of the Woman Question' focuses on men as being foolish and brutal, and the need of the superior moral training that women can offer them. The whole tone of the article depends on a very positive conception of maternity. Far from rejecting motherhood, Grand's New Woman will in fact 'mother' men into appropriate masculinity: 'now woman holds out a strong hand to the child-man, and insists, but with infinite tenderness and pity, upon helping him up' (Grand in Ledger and Luckhurst 2000, 90). In addition, Grand had certainly used the phrase before 1894. It occurs on a few occasions, uncapitalized and unemphasized, in *The Heavenly Twins*, for example, where Evadne is described as 'one of the new women who are just appearing among us, with a higher ideal of duty than any which men have constructed for women' (Grand 1992, 193).

2. Linton published most of these articles anonymously, and it is highly probable that most readers presumed that the writer was male.

3. Purity of language and purity of morals were often connected by novelists in the 1890s. In *The Heavenly Twins*, when Grand wishes to make it clear that Mrs Guthrie Brimston is not a respectable woman (as if her name were not enough), her narrator comments:

> Her conversation bristled with vain repetitions. She was always a 'worm' when asked after her health, and everything that pleased her was 'pucka'. She knew no language but her own, and that she spoke indifferently, her command of it being limited for the most part to slang expressions, which are the scum of language; and a few stock phrases of polite quality for special occasions. But she used the latter awkwardly, as workmen wear their Sunday clothes. (Grand 1992, 203)

Her linguistic practices are contrasted with those of the impossibly pure Evadne, who never uses slang, and whose morals can therefore clearly be seen as impeccable.

4. The novel makes it very clear, indeed, that Gregory Rose finds Em lacking precisely because she has no passion, and no idea that love might be sensual

or sexual in nature. She might embody an idealized version of femininity, but she also shows the extent to which ideals might just be rather hard to live with.

5. Working-class women, of course, had always worked. The Woman Question in this version of it was a profoundly bourgeois formulation.

6. Herminia Barton's story is obvious. Rhoda Nunn in *The Odd Women* evades a sexual relationship – but she certainly considers it for a while; Sue Bridehead has a sustained relationship with Jude that is outside the norms of married life; Hilda Lessways – victim of bigamy since Bennett did not wish her to be 'guilty' – gives birth to an illegitimate child, as does Helen Schlegel in rather different circumstances in *Howards End*. Paul Morel in *Sons and Lovers* achieves his first satisfactory sexual experiences with the emancipated Clara Dawes – though Lawrence cannot quite approve of Clara and returns her at the end of her novel to her Neanderthal husband, Baxter. And Ursula Brangwen battles for the New Woman's privileges of education and career, but ends *The Rainbow* having narrowly – and very mysteriously – avoided an unwanted pregnancy.

7. For a full narrative about the Contagious Diseases Acts and the purity campaigns for their repeal, see Walkowitz 1980.

8. Indeed, Tess is much more of an innocent victim than Angel is – her 'seduction' is really a rape, and Hardy tries to create her as much more sinned against than sinning.

9. Mary Elizabeth Braddon (1837–1915) was a writer of 'sensationalist' or railway fictions who enjoyed massive public success (though much less critical success) with novels about adultery, bigamy and attempted murder, notably *Lady Audley's Secret* (1861).

6   Conclusions?
Rainbow's End:
The Janus Period

The title of this chapter has several points of reference. In the first instance, it relates to the titles of novels by E. M. Forster and D. H. Lawrence, *Howards End* and *The Rainbow* respectively. But the rainbow's end is also a mythological place – it does not exist, but if it did, and you were ever to find it, there would be a pot of gold there. As I have argued, the usual history of the late Victorians, the Edwardians and the Georgians is one which presents the late Victorians as belated, more minor figures than their immediate forebears, and as much less significant than their inheritors. Modernism, the story goes, is the pot of gold at the end of the Victorian rainbow. Modernism, however, did not come from nowhere. Many of the conditions of modernity were Victorian in origin and the Victorians were the first to confront them. Although there may be a kind of Oedipal resistance to the acknowl- edgement of the influence wielded by the forefathers and foremothers of the Modernist novel and Modernist poetry, the story of Modernism's development is certainly one of transitions and continuities, not of sudden breaks with the past. Making it new depends absolutely on knowledge of the past. And the 1890s had already made it new, prolif- erating uses of the word 'new' as Holbrook Jackson demonstrated in 1913 (Jackson 1987, 23).

Forster and Lawrence do not at first sight seem like particularly comparable novelists. They came from very different backgrounds – both social and educational; and the aesthetics of the novels that they wrote are also worlds apart. Lawrence's *Sons and Lovers* (1913) and *The Rainbow* (1915) are set in the provincial English East Midlands, in a landscape of industry as much as of agriculture. His characters are often working class, distanced by material circumstances, geography and temperament from the attitudes of the capital. The Brangwens of *The Rainbow* are further up the social ladder than Paul Morel, the coalminer's son in *Sons and Lovers*; but the Brangwens are not the social equals of the Schlegels in Forster's *Howards End*, nor of the

Anglo-Indian community in *A Passage to India*. They have capital, but they could not live on it; they own land, but they have to work the land; they receive an education both from the state in the wake of the 1870 Education Act, and in a grammar school, for which their families must pay. That education, however, does not quite buy them the 'cultural capital' the Schlegels enjoy, with their rich European heritage derived from their intellectual German father, their artistic home, and their access to music and books. The Schlegels, as Forster is honest enough to admit, derive their outlook from very different conditions than these. As Margaret says to her women's group in London: 'so few of us think clearly about our own private incomes, and admit that independent thoughts are in nine cases out of ten the result of independent means' (Forster 1989a, 134). Lawrence, perhaps, was an example of the tenth case. His independence of thought leads to a distinctive iconoclasm in his fiction, where Forster, with more at stake in the social status quo, attempts to maintain some of the traditions of the past. Neither man, however, in their best fictions at any rate, makes the fictional world entirely anew.

One symptom of the relationship they each had with their immedi- ate predecessors as well as with their contemporaries is the continuity of the thematic concerns of their fictions with those that preceded them. Lawrence's *Rainbow* describes the effects of the Victorian expan- sions of industry and urban centres on the families at Marsh farm. *Howards End* is partially concerned with the creeping spread of sub- urban London which threatens to engulf the rural community that surrounds the edenic house from which the novel takes its title. As Lyn Pykett argues, in a phrase which belongs to a much earlier period of literary history, both novels are 'condition of England novels', a comment that surely also connects Lawrence and Forster to Bennett and Wells as well as the English novelists of the so-called 'Hungry' 1840s such as Gaskell, Disraeli and Kingsley. They describe a society in crisis, and they both – though very differently – return to explanatory models from earlier kinds of fiction to make their critique of contem- porary England. Degeneration theory might not be quite named in either book; but arguments about heredity, race and blood, underlie both of their accounts of modernity. The Schlegel sisters are half- German, and that half is their 'cultured half', the part of them that allows them to appreciate art, music and books. Ursula Brangwen might be bred and brought up on the Nottinghamshire–Derbyshire border, but as well as being the Anglo-Saxon daughter of that Brangwen soil, she gets part of her racial inheritance from her Polish grandmother and mother, which is an unspoken – but nonetheless potent – explanatory myth for her modernist sense of alienation from and restlessness within the landscape she lives in.[1]

Both novelists are partially also concerned with the figure of the New Woman. The Schlegel sisters attend a women's debating club for the improvement of their minds. Adela Quested who takes the passage to India is named as one of their friends who meets them in such activities and who is similarly hysterical. Similarly, Ursula Brangwen, as both Dorothea Brooke in *Middlemarch* and Sophia Baines in Bennett's *Old Wives' Tale* had done before her, wishes to 'do' something with her life, rather than settle into the old conventional mould of marriage and family imaged in her mother who 'was so complacent, so utterly fulfilled in her breeding'.

And Imperialism, that most 'Victorian' of discourses, is also present in both works, though slightly offstage in both *The Rainbow* and *Howards End*. In *Howards End*, the guests at Evie Wilcox's wedding include some rather appalling colonial types of the sort who would be more ruthlessly and thoroughly dissected in *A Passage to India* (1924). Paul Wilcox cannot marry Helen – even if he wanted to – because he must go and do the work of Empire in Nigeria. *The Rainbow* describes the alienating effects of Anton Skrebensky's tour of duty in Africa during that imperialist war, the Boer conflict (1899–1902), and he discovers that Africa is indeed a Heart of Darkness (Lawrence 1995, 413). He ends up in India, presumably enjoying the social life of the Anglo-Indian that Forster satirized in his later novel, and that is also part of the dissolute backdrop of Ford's *The Good Soldier*.

In addition, both novels are basically realist in technique. In *Howards End* and *The Rainbow*, the stories are told with an eye to their message; a point is being made through narrative which can be largely recuperated through paraphrase: we are not seeing steadily or whole, and the manner of the narrative does not always tell in a clear way. But the 'decent' values of a cultured liberal humanism are nonetheless preached by Forster; the more revolutionary concepts of emotional and sexual refashionings are part of Lawrence's message. In the works of both novelists, characters remain the sum of environment, heredity and experience as well as of any intrinsic personality; explanations for their motivations and behaviour are offered with varying degrees of straightforwardness. These are transitional texts which face, as it were, both ways, Janus-like, drawing on both fictional pasts and futures.

Time and character in *The Rainbow*

In a very famous and much-quoted letter to Edward Garnett in June 1914, Lawrence defended his conception of character in the novel that was to become *The Rainbow*. He wrote:

> You mustn't look in my novel for the old stable *ego* – of the character. There is another *ego*, according to whose action the individual is unrecognisable, and passes through, as it were, allotropic states which it needs a deeper sense than any we've been used to exercise to discover are states of the same single radically unchanged element. (Like as diamond and coal are the same single element of carbon. The ordinary novel would trace the history of the diamond – but I say, 'Diamond, what! This is carbon.' And my diamond might be coal or soot, and my theme is carbon.) (Lawrence 1962, 282)

One cannot say of Lawrence's characters, to paraphrase Woolf, that they are simply 'this or that'. The influence of Freudian psychoanalysis, even though explicitly disavowed by Lawrence as a reductive reading in discussions of *Sons and Lovers* in his letters, permeates his fictional people, arguing for a complexity in the making of personality that cannot be reduced to social factors.[2] The life of instinct – of the body, of sexual appetite – is formative in *The Rainbow*, not in opposition to the realist explanations of character, but in relation to them. The conception of character in *The Rainbow* looks both backwards and forwards. Lawrence in part makes use of realist conception, constructing his novel on the ideas of social causes and their social consequences, in much the same way as earlier fiction writers had done. But for Lawrence, both causes and consequences depend on a radically different way of seeing character. Something of the old bourgeois individual survives in this conception, but it is destabilized – hence Lawrence's description of character in terms of the chemical properties of the allotrope, an element (and therefore unchangeable) that can exist in two or more different forms.

The reasons for a different mode of characterization are embedded in a different conception of the effects of time in the novel. For traditional realist fiction, events unfold chronologically and therefore logically until an endpoint is reached from which explanations can be safely furnished, but in Lawrence's novel, time itself is multiple, and furnishes no simple superstructure. In *Howards End*, Margaret comes to realize 'the chaotic nature of our daily life, and its difference from the orderly sequence that has been fabricated by historians' (Forster 1989a, 115). Lawrence's novel works on a much bigger scale than Forster's, and dramatizes the complications of the relationships between time and telling. At its simplest, Lawrence's work evades simplistic chronology. *The Rainbow* has a broadly chronological organization in that each generation is dealt with in its turn; but it also organizes itself thematically, narrating events out of their proper order, circling backwards and forwards in a structure which dramatizes the presence of the past.

Thus, although in many ways *The Rainbow* is constructed on the realist foundations of telling causes and effects, it locates causes rather differently. In the traditional realist novel, the most common construction is of a story focussed on an individual character placed within a specific social, geographical, economic and cultural milieu. For the Lawrence of *Sons and Lovers*, as for Bennett and Wells before him, the fictional universe he wished to portray was not known in the traditional realist way, at least partly on the simple basis of the fact that he, like them, describes a different social milieu from that most common in Victorian and Edwardian fiction. *Sons and Lovers*, as Sagar notes, opens 'with a socio-economic history of Eastwood, followed by a meticulous placing of the Morel household within the industrial landscape'. He does this because 'he cannot assume that typical novel-reader would know anything about "small homes"; still less about miners' (Sagar 1985, 77).

The Rainbow opens in a similar way, though the language is more lyrical and less grounded in either the declarative structures of realism or the mechanical precision of its construction of causal sequences. It offers slightly but importantly different explanatory mechanisms. It opens with a description of the traditional way of life of a particular farming family living in the English East Midlands. In that opening – 'The Brangwens had lived for generations on the Marsh Farm' (Lawrence 1995, 9) – the timescale is non-specific. It is impossible to say with certainty *when* the story opens because Lawrence suggests in his opening that the Brangwens' way of life had been the same since before time could be measured. Official time, the measured time of clocks, calendars and history, changes people and brings them painfully to individuality and self-consciousness. Tom Brangwen, representing the first generation of Brangwen men to live with the effects of industrialization, urbanization and the mechanistic regulation of clock time, is also the first Brangwen to be represented as an individual with a personal history in this family saga. The notion of significant events in time having their effects on particular human beings is a direct inheritance from the realist tradition.

Time, however it is measured, is a central preoccupation of modern consciousness, and became therefore a central preoccupation of modernist aesthetics. It is no accident that clock time is the regular beat that pitilessly organizes Woolf's *Mrs Dalloway* (1925) – a novel that was originally to be called *The Hours*; nor that clocks striking nine and five regulate the flow of the crowds over the London bridges in T. S. Eliot's *The Waste Land* (1922). For Lawrence, too, time is far more complex than a clock or calendar, or even an historical epoch, can measure. *The Rainbow* conflates various measures of time as part of the attempt to explain the crisis of modernity. The Brangwens are farmers and are therefore 'naturally' and explicitly associated with the natural cycles of the seasons:

> They felt the rush of the sap in spring, they knew the wave which cannot halt, but every year throws forward the seed to begetting, and, falling back, leaves the young-born on the earth. They knew the intercourse between heaven and earth, sunshine drawn into the breast and bowels, the rain sucked up in the day time, nakedness that comes under the wind in autumn, showing the birds' nest no longer worth hiding. Their life and inter-relations were such ... (Lawrence 1995, 9–10)

Seasonal time is repetitive time, or continuous time. Every spring, there is the rush of sap, every autumn the dying away of life. The cycle is always the same. In his description of this kind of time, with its insistently sensual and sexual metaphors, Lawrence associates natural or cyclical time with fecundity and fulfilment, though it is a narrow fulfilment, dependent on narrowed horizons. All the same, no one can be immune to the forces of history as they approach the farm in the railway, the canal and the expanding town.

Alongside historical (or progressive, linear) time and natural (cyclical, seasonal) time, *The Rainbow* also places its events into other time frames. One is the frame of evolutionary time. In the course of the novel, the focus shifts from Marsh Farm to the new generations of Brangwens living first in the village of Cossethay, and finally in a red-brick house in Ilkeston – an evolutionary movement from primeval slime to 'civilization', if a red-brick house in Ilkeston counts as civilization. Evolution – just like historical movements – does not necessarily imply progress: degeneration is a powerful if scarcely articulated fear in the text.

The other important time frame is mythical time, expressed through the continuing references to the Book of Genesis. Lawrence had a 'mythic method', in which he too 'manipulated a continuous parallel between contemporaneity and antiquity' before Joyce did, and before T. S. Eliot described Joyce's method in his essay '*Ulysses*, Order and Myth' in 1923 (Eliot 1975, 177). Myths are shared stories expressing the continuity of communal values and providing explanatory contexts for the observed world and for lived experience. In this context, the Bible has a particular resonance for the Bible stories are also regulatory myths, describing a way of life and an ethical system that not only does continue, but one that *should* continue, timelessly as it were, because its final reference point is the eternal time of God. In a novel called *The Rainbow*, the symbol of God's promise never again to destroy his creation in flood, the Genesis story is a backdrop of continuity to the historical changes the fiction recounts. In this frame, far from being Primeval slime, Marsh Farm is an Eden in which man and nature are in perfect harmony, and where woman – like Eve – is vaguely dissatisfied, presented in her ambition for knowledge and a wider horizon than the farm can provide.

The three generations with which the novel deals – Lydia and Tom, Will and Anna, and Ursula and Skrebensky – represent continuity in the sense that the same battles are played out between husbands and wives, and between parents and children through the different generations. Husbands and wives fight for individual needs until they learn to complement each other; children rail against parental authority. But where Anna escapes Tom's parenting through her marriage to Will, her daughter escapes Anna's parenting through work, education, and a secret sexual life without the benefit of clergy: the times, they were a-changing. Anna's escape is one sanctioned by her community. Ursula's escape is based on individualism, on breaking free – eventually in *Women in Love*, from 'the "nets" which enfold characters in *The Rainbow*: the nets of custom, family and loyalty between a single man and a single woman' (Torgovnick 2001, 41). In other words, there is repetition with difference. The cyclical and repetitious nature of human relations are modified by their contact with history rather more than they are modified by the individual temperaments of the different individuals in each generation.

One of the changes wrought by large historical forces on local individual circumstances is the failure of the Polish rebellion which makes Lydia Lensky and her daughter into refugees, and which brings them into the orbit of Marsh Farm. This historical event is presented in

terms of its local effects. Their arrival in Cossethay is the decisive new
element which alters the Brangwens. The Lenskys are culturally and
politically sophisticated aristocrats; Lydia is half-German and half-
Polish – a distinctive new bloodline in the Brangwen gene pool the
narrative implies. Poland, which had disappeared off the map as an
independent state in the eighteenth century is a kind of 'non' place,
often used in English fiction as a shorthand for very different, often
temperamental, romantic and unstable, unEnglish people. Lydia and
Tom fight as well as love each other, their battle based on the traditional, organic stable values of English life (which may also be stultifying) represented by Tom and the sophisticated European values and
insights of the uprooted Lydia. The couple reaches an accommodation
with each other by valuing and accepting the differences between
them, mostly based on Lydia's compromise. She has suffered much
from the instability of Polish values, is tired of travelling and rootless-
ness epitomized by her husband, and recognizes the good in stability at
Marsh Farm on that basis. Lydia's intense grief when Tom is drowned is
symptomatic of the balance they have found in their relationship, a
balance between masculine and feminine, stability and flux, also
expressed in Tom's drunken speech at Anna's wedding, where he
describes – comically but sincerely – the complementarity of husband
and wife in the composite figure of the angel (129).

It is in the next generation that the battle between the sexes
becomes particularly bitter, in Anna and Will's marriage. Neither
member of this couple has a secure anchor in tradition and continuity.
Will's family might be Brangwens, but they are 'Nottingham
Brangwens' who have left the land and gone to live in the town. Anna
is by birth, if not by upbringing, a foreigner, deracinated from the traditions of her own family by death and emigration. She finds in Tom a
wonderful surrogate who can comfort her by reference to his own natural element – the natural world. But in leaving the family home, she
also leaves behind her tenuous rootedness. Her marriage to Will –
whose name is certainly not accidental; he is wilfulness personified –
is based on conflict. Each of them battles for dominance over the
other, whereas the parents' generation had battled towards equilib-
rium, not for victory. They are diametrically opposed in terms of temperament, signalled by reference to their opposing attitudes towards
organized religion and the art that symbolizes it. Will's relationship
with God is spiritual, not intellectual – he never listens to the sermons,
Anna says (149), but he glories in church architecture. Anna in contrast
has a practical attitude, resenting Will's transports of aesthetic pleasure

in part because they exclude her, and in part because, not feeling them herself, she believes they are a sham.

The contested narratives of Lawrence's evolving present clearly have specific pasts. One kind of past we all share, though we obviously share it very differently, is our personal past of childhood. In his depiction of Ursula, which makes up the bulk of *The Rainbow*, Lawrence presents an acutely realized description of what it is like to be a child. Childhood is a period of multiple repetitions in a context of change. The developing child experiences routines of family life as both comfort to nestle in and as a controlling structure to evade. In multiple vignettes of family life, Ursula's developing consciousness is described. Her relationship with her father – special and meaningful – is evoked as both passion and failure, for example in her failed attempts to help him plant potatoes in the garden. She tries hard, but 'the grown-up power to work deliberately was a mystery to her' (207). She is incompetent in this small task, and her disappointment at her failure, out of all proportion with its cause, is nonetheless precisely what a small child would feel.

Just like Stephen Dedalus in *A Portrait of the Artist as a Young Man*, Ursula has flights of fancy in which she escapes from mundane existence into romantic fantasy (*The Idylls of the King* in her case) but from which she must always return with a bump. The discovery that dreams cannot be lived in is made repeatedly, though never quite realized by Ursula. The grammar school is a place of dreams until she discovers that her fellow pupils are not romantic maidens but catty adolescent girls. The university feeds a similar kind of romantic Medieval fantasy in which the professors 'were black-gowned priests of knowledge, serving forever in a remote hushed temple' (400), until she is forced to recognize its mercantile basis as 'a little apprentice-shop where one was further equipped for making money ... a little slovenly laboratory for the factory' which is not redeemed by its 'spurious Gothic arches, spurious peace, spurious Latinity ... spurious naïveté of Chaucer' (403). For a while, Skrebensky makes a pretty good substitute for Sir Lancelot, until she realizes that being with him means acquiescing in the social world she despises, which turns her love into contempt. Ideals provide a framework which is repeatedly dismantled by experience, though experience does not stop Ursula from dreaming.

The process of growing up in Ursula's case is a process of both discovering relationships between causes and effects – seeds die if you tread on them when you are a child; much later, you fail your exams if you spend all your time with your lover – and deciding that such things do not matter much. And this is the real difference between Lawrence's conception of time and character and that found in other earlier novelists. Growing up for most people, and for the people in most realist fiction, is the process of accepting causal relationships and learning to live with them; for Ursula, maturity comes when she refuses the connection, a position the novel itself validates. Against the backdrop of her miserable teaching career (also very impressively realized), her university education, her love affairs with Winifred Inger and Anton Skrebensky, her rejection of both of them, and her discovery that she is pregnant, Ursula is shown breaking away from the conventions or 'nets' of her own society. She tests out the various roles that tradition has bequeathed her: good daughter, apt pupil, teacher, possible wife and mother, and finds them all wanting. In those conventional terms, at the end of *The Rainbow*, her life is a failure. She has tested out new social roles – become a New Woman, indeed – and found them wanting; she has fought her parents and her lover; she has failed her university course, and she is pregnant with her lover's child. She is adrift. Her experiences have not led to the usual conclusions about how to live life and 'new' conclusions are not quite forthcoming in this novel – they will be played out in *Women in Love*. Whatever lessons she has learned, she has not learned for all time. It is perfectly possible that she will continue to relive those problems in slightly different forms (and the battles with Birkin in the later novel are not very dissimilar from those with Skrebensky), suggesting a conception of character which is cyclical in its development rather than straightforwardly linear or progressive. Just as Will and Anna's accommodation of each other is cyclical – periods of calm and contentment followed by periods of brutal conflict – Ursula's life threatens to be a repetitive failure: repetitive in the sense that it might just replicate the old patterns inherited from the previous generations, and in the sense that she might just keep making the same mistakes.

But in a daring act of falsification as irresponsible – though not as cheerful – as anything to be found in Wells's unearned conclusions to his novels, Lawrence fabricates a happy ending, projected onto the future as a happy beginning, for Ursula. For no reason that is explained to the reader unless it is that she has been frightened by horses, she discovers that she is not, after all, pregnant. Pregnancy would certainly be one of the nets that might keep Ursula earthbound. Instead, Lawrence gives her the vision of the rainbow, a contemporary Ark of the Covenant promising a better future. As Ursula recovers from her miscarriage she sits expectantly to watch a new creation, having discovered through her experiences that she need not relive the old models of the past, particularly the models of coupledom her parents and grandparents

represented. Watching colliers and their wives as they cross the countryside, in a passage which clearly owes a great deal to the ending of
Zola's naturalist novel *Germinal* (1885), she sees a new life, not realized, but in potential: 'In the still, silenced forms of the colliers she saw
a sort of suspense, a waiting in pain for the new liberation: she saw the
same in the false hard confidence of the women. The confidence of the
women was brittle. It would break quickly to reveal the strength and
patient effort of the new germination' (458). And then she sees the
rainbow, and like Lily Briscoe in Woolf's *To the Lighthouse*, has her
vision. Sadly, just as with Lily, the vision is frankly vague, despite the
sonorous biblical cadences in which it is expressed. It is a vision of
the sweeping away of modernity – the houses and collieries disappearing in an apocalypse that will leave people free. Quite how this is
to come about is not described or imagined: enough that the vision
has been vouchsafed. But in the next narrated episodes of Ursula's
life in the opening chapters of *Women in Love*, the cycle of repetition
recurs, and she comes back to earth with a bump. The collieries and
the colliers have not been swept away, not here, not yet, probably not
ever. Realizing this, Ursula and her sister leave their roots, conditioned
by them, reacting against them, but not accepting their limitations.

Forster's connections

> The reality that lends itself to narrative representation is the conflict
> between desire and the law. (White 1987, 12)

Forster's fiction is much less iconoclastic than Lawrence's and it shares
neither the mystical attempt to break free from the past and the present in its thematic concerns, nor the sense of straining form in which
Lawrence partially articulates his vision. *Howards End* and *A Room
With a View* (1908) are far closer to Galsworthy than to Woolf not least
because Forster's fictions accept, as Lawrence's do not, at least a mini-
mal ethical requirement for the individual to take into consideration
the individuality of others. In other words, there is a conventional
acquiescence to the condition of maturity as the acceptance of limitations on freedom of personal action. In the terms of the Hayden White
quotation, the conflict between desire and duty, or desire and the law,
is best resolved in Forster's fiction by deferring to others. For Forster
though, 'the law' is a dangerous abstraction; the others to whom one
must defer are personal others – friends and lovers, not nation state,
not impersonal propriety, not unexamined conventions – a position

stated in *Two Cheers for Democracy* (1951) as the belief that given the choice between betraying one's country (an abstraction) and betraying one's friend (a person), the proper choice is to betray one's country. For Helen Schlegel, as for the Emersons in *A Room with a View*, 'personal relations are the important thing for ever and ever, and not this outer life of telegrams and anger' (Forster 1989a, 176). At the same time, though, Margaret responds to contradict her sister. The Wilcoxes might well be part of the outer world, but – and this the point of 'connection':

> If Wilcoxes hadn't worked and died in England for thousands of years, you and I couldn't sit here without having our throats cut. There would be no trains, no ships to carry us literary people about, no fields even. Just savagery… More and more do I refuse to draw my income and sneer at those who guarantee it. (Forster 1989a, 177–8)

Making that connection between material circumstances and the labour which produces them eventually makes Margaret a heroine. She rescues her sister from her impetuousness, and Mr Wilcox from his inhuman obtuseness about human relations. It is a small, local and individual victory over the kind of futility and anarchy that Eliot refers to (Eliot 1975, 177). Its smallness is a function of the domesticated nature of this particular fiction, and it shows the limitations of Forster's vision. All the same, I do not see any reason to think that Forster's vision is less significant than Woolf's or Lawrence's, the former equally limited in social reach, and the latter unrealizable.

But Forster also knew that his vision was limited, and in *A Passage to India*, the last novel he published in his lifetime, he set out to test its limitations against a broader canvas. India cannot be the kind of knowable community represented by the village at Howards End. And what becomes of personal relationships if the conditions under which they operate are not conditions of fairly basic equality and freedom? Or, to put it another way, Aziz and his friends enter the novel in 'a very sad talk … they were discussing as to whether or no it is possible to be friends with an Englishman' (Forster 1989c, 33). The answer at the end of the novel is 'not yet … not there' (316); personal relationships do not survive, but that is an argument that the conditions, in this case the conditions of imperialism in India, must be changed, not that the basic principle of personal relationships is wrong.

The Indian setting provides a powerful backdrop for the examination of alternative identities and positions, radically destabilizing the known and knowable conditions of England. India is presented as a space of epistemological crisis, where everything is a mystery or a muddle, but Forster's is not a nihilistic view, because he holds open the possibility that sense can be made of all of this even as he registers the absence of coherence from his own narrative project. *A Passage to India* has the most modernist credentials in Forster's fiction. In his adaptation of the title of a poem by Walt Whitman as his title for the book – from 'Passage to India' to *A Passage to India* – Forster's addition of the indefinite article signals that what is to be presented is one version of events amongst many possible versions. The novel's central event, the assault on Miss Quested in the Marabar Caves, may or may not have happened at all. As Fielding puts it to Adela, there are four possibilities, each of which has internal evidence for its own validity as an account of what actually happened: 'Either Aziz is guilty, which is what your friends think; or you invented the charge out of malice, which is what my friends think; or you had an hallucination' (240). The fourth possibility is that it was 'somebody else' (242). No definitive answer is ever given, and none of the principles can give a coherent account of the event, if indeed it was an event. One of the central questions we are accustomed to ask about novels – the sign of the declarative purpose in the realist tradition – is 'what is it about?' We are accustomed to be able to answer that question in terms of simple paraphrase. Typically in modernist writing, however, that question becomes more difficult to respond to, and Forster's novel is 'modernist' at least to the extent that it evades the clear telling of a story.

The setting is similarly unstable. The limited geographical reach and small social groupings of the knowable community do not apply to India. Over and over again characters on both sides of the racial divide describe the vastness and diversity of the subcontinent, seeing it very unsteadily and not at all whole, inassimilable by any individual mind. There is no one order of reality which is *the* truth about India, no single entity which represents the 'real' India that Adela Quested wishes to discover. This point is emphasized from the novel's first page. Chandrapore, the city in which the action (such as it is) is set, cannot be defined or adequately described. Its geography defies the classifications which a realist novelist takes for granted in creating solidity of specification. The town is radically non-specific, described largely through negatives: it 'presents nothing extraordinary', except for the Marabar Caves, but no one can explain why they are special. The Ganges, holy river of India, 'happens not to be holy there.' 'The streets are mean, the temples ineffective.' It is only when the perspective of distance is introduced that the city has anything remarkable about it, and even perspective does not give certainty of judgement.

If events and setting are unstable, then character is also problema-
tized, dependent on context, on racial and social grouping, and on the
responses of others to the individual, at least as much as on any intrinsic or essential qualities. In that first conversation between Aziz and
his friends when they ask the all-important question about friendship
with an Englishman, Mahmoud Ali, who has never left India, says it
is not possible. His experience of Englishmen tells him that they are
dictatorial and unpleasant. Hamidullah, educated in England, says it is
possible – but only in England.

Forster's presentation deliberately presents the world of feeling and
instinct as preferable to that of rules and empirical evidence. Sympathetic characters, notably Mrs Moore and Fielding, are defined as
'oriental', because they act on feelings not on rules. The struggle of
the Anglo-Indians is to impose their own version of reality on the multiple groupings of subject peoples. As part of the matrix which maintains power, it is not permissible for them ever to admit they are wrong.
They present themselves as figures of enlightenment and empirical
evidence, bringing law and education to the benighted savages. As
such, they are rule-bound, conventional, utterly dependent on a concept of observable 'facts' for their interpretation of India, in contrast
to the Indians who are presented as instinctive and feeling beings.[3]
Throughout the novel, then, and specifically with regard to the 'evidence' concerning Aziz's alleged guilt, Forster mounts a devastating
critique of realism's presumption that facts speak for themselves, and
that there is only ever one possible version of events. For all their insistence on the facts, the English have responded emotionally to an idea
(that a 'young girl, fresh from England' has been assaulted), rather than
dispassionately to highly circumstantial evidence.

The readers outside the text, however, know that each of the pieces
of evidence against Aziz is open to more than one interpretation. The
trip to the caves was conceived not out of lust for the white woman,
whom Aziz anyway thinks is ugly, but out of shame that he cannot
invite anyone to his house which is unswept and dirty. We know too,
that Aziz did not plan that his other guests would miss the train and
was distressed by Godbole and Fielding missing the train, spoiling his
hospitable purpose. We also know that although Aziz gave orders for
the English ladies' servant to be left behind, it was at their request, not
with any malicious purpose. Mrs Moore did not accompany them to
the fateful final cave because she felt unwell, not because Aziz plotted
to leave her behind. The vaunted logic of Europe is submerged in herd
instinct: 'All over Chandrapore [the day of the alleged assault], the
Europeans were putting aside their normal personalities and sinking

themselves in their community. Pity, wrath, heroism, filled them, but the power of putting two and two together was annihilated' (175). Ironically it is Aziz's Indian friend Hamidullah who thinks in Western terms: '[He] loved Aziz and knew he was calumniated; but faith did not rule his heart, and he prated of "policy" and "evidence" in a way that saddened [Fielding]' (181).

Fielding is the only character who can actively see 'both sides'. The English as a group, though far less sympathetically portrayed, are not so very dissimilar to the Indians, presented as 'better' in part because they are subjected not rulers of their own destiny. If the Anglo-Indians see all Indians as the 'same', the Indians perform similar acts of stereotyping on their colonial rulers: 'Turtons and Burtons are all the same' (266) says Aziz in the aftermath of the trial. The surnames are similar, virtually indistinguishable. This is the Indian version of the white racist comment 'they all look the same to me'. Fielding refuses any such simplistic seeing and is active in putting forward a philosophy that the two sides must meet. He comes to India, we are told, with a public role as a teacher, and, unlike Ronny, as an experienced man. When he is introduced, we are told:

> This Mr Fielding had been caught by India late. He was over forty when he entered that oddest portal, the Victoria terminus at Bombay, and – having bribed a European ticket-inspector – took his luggage into the compartment of his first tropical train. The journey remained in mind as significant. Of his two carriage companions, one was a youth, fresh to the East like himself, the other a seasoned Anglo-Indian of his own age. A gulf divided him from either: he had seen too many cities and men to be the first or to become the second. (Forster 1989c, 79)

Fielding is in all senses of the phrase a man of the world: he has travelled widely, and he has had wide experience (including sexual experience, we are told). He is unmarried, and so has no personal baggage to encumber him on his journey east, no girl fresh from England to protect with manly but unthinking vigour. As he tells Aziz, he travels light. But he also trusts his emotions, finding friendship and ties based on mutual affection more important than allegiance to abstract ideals such as country or social set. To use a metaphor from reading, Fielding does not see the world in black and white: 'The remark that did him most harm at the club,' comments the narrator, 'was a silly aside to the effect that the so-called white races are really pinko-grey' (80). The shades of grey are important for they are what connect disparate and oppositional world views. Also, unlike any other character in the novel, with the possible exception of Miss Quested, he has no faith in God. Consequently, he has no faith to lose – and it is loss of faith in her 'poor little talkative Christianity' which disables Mrs Moore as a power for active good in the text (161). But lack of religious allegiance also means inclusiveness. There may be many mansions in the Christian heaven, but Christianity 'must exclude someone from [its] gathering' (58), as Islam also does. Hinduism comes close to embracing the universe, but also excludes certain elements and even Professor Godbole cannot include inanimate matter in his scheme of heaven. Fielding does not much care about inanimate matter, but he can include all people in his view of a world based on trust and affection. Circumstances defeat him. His only regret over supporting Aziz is that it will now be possible for people to label him a 'pro-Indian' or as anti-British, and on the basis of that label, they will exclude him from their gatherings.

In the end, the single individual cannot alter the force of history. Fielding wants to be Aziz's friend, but is disabled by historical circumstance. The novel ends with a kind of rainbow-like promise for a better future. If Aziz cannot be friends with Fielding here and now, perhaps his children can be friends with Fielding's children then and there, when the world has changed again, and when India has achieved its independence. The poem from which the novel takes its title, Whitman's 'Passage to India', is a celebration of modernity:

> Singing my days
> Singing the great achievement of the present,
> Singing the strong light works of engineers,
> Our modern wonders, (the antique ponderous Seven outvied,)
> In the Old World the East the Suez canal,
> The New by its mighty railroad spann'd,
> The seas inlaid with eloquent gentle wires
> (Whitman 1975, 429)

These achievements make connection across racial and national divides possible – English men and Indian men can only be friends if they can meet. As yet, though, this modernity is an ambivalent gift. The remarkable technological feats of the Suez Canal, of the building of the railroad across the United States, and of the spanning of the Atlantic with the telegraph cable, all speak of a world defined by a communication revolution, at least to the West. Native Americans, Indians and Egyptians, amongst others though, certainly had reason to feel much more uncertain that technological advance represented progress.

What the West saw as advancement, it also saw as evidence of its superiority, and without equality there cannot be friendship.

To return, then, to the rainbow's end of Modernism. The aesthetics of Modernism, the attempt to make it new, to tear down the old conventions and find alternative modes of being in the world, and to find new ways of describing the world, represent a very attractive proposition. No one wants to be an old stick-in-the-mud in the primeval slime at Marsh Farm. Taking flight from those old certainties, which were never that certain anyway, though, leaves fictional characters – and in a modified way, their readers – at sea. What is being assented to when Molly Bloom ends her soliloquy in the final pages of *Ulysses* (1922) with an apparently triumphant 'yes'? What does Lily Briscoe's 'vision' amount to in *To the Lighthouse* (1927)? Is Ursula Brangwen really on the threshold of a better life in either of her two fictional endings? When T. S. Eliot glosses 'Shantih, Shantih, Shantih' as the peace that defies understanding in his notes to *The Waste Land* (1922), is it supposed to be comforting?

At the end of Fielding's tea party in *A Passage to India*, Professor Godbole sings a strange and haunting song: 'At times there seemed rhythm, at times there was the illusion of Western melody. But the ear, baffled repeatedly, soon lost any clue, and wandered in maze of noises, none harsh or unpleasant, none intelligible' (95). The Professor offers to explain 'in detail':

> It was a religious song. I placed myself in the position of a milkmaiden. I say to Shri Krishna: 'Come! Come to me only.' The God refuses to come. I grow humble and say: 'Do not come to me only. Multiply yourself into a hundred Krishnas, and let one go to each of my hundred companions, but one, O Lord of the Universe, come to me.' He refuses to come. This is repeated several times … I say to him, Come, come, come, come, come, come, come. He neglects to come. (Forster 1989c, 96)

His explanation is as baffling as the song itself. In its evasion of telos – in the absence of that structured ending that Western narratives usually provided – it appears to be a narrative without a point, expressive of the muddle or mystery of India rather than explanatory or elucidatory. A request is made and is not answered. The kinds of answer that come from neatly tied up endings in those realist narratives against which Modernists railed are obviously falsifications, not least because real lives do not begin and end so neatly. But I'm not always convinced that those other endings described in Modernist writing aren't just as false and misleading. The world did not change after all on the basis of the individual epiphanies that fictional characters experienced. The old illusions and the new illusions still really saw the same old world even if they saw it differently.

Notes

1. By the same token, degeneration explanations are at the heart of *Sons and Lovers*. It is surely not accidental that the family's name is Morel – a name they share with one of the foremost thinkers of degeneration theory, Bénédicte Augustin Morel (1809–73). The reasons for William Morel's death – the split in him between the cultured life his mother aspires to and the life of the body epitomized by his father – are part of a Lamarckian scheme. Lamarck (1744–1829) had suggested that the acquired characteristics of parents could be passed down to their children in a kind cultural hereditarian schema. William inherits two incompatible tendencies and cannot support the contradiction.

2. Complexes, he wrote, are 'vicious half-statements … When you've said Mutter complex [mother complex], you've said nothing … A complex is not simply a sex relation: far from it – My poor book: it was, as art, a fairly complete truth: so they carve a half lie out of it and say "Voilà". Swine!' (qtd in Sagar 1985, 93–4).

3. This, of course, is one of the problems of the book. The schema Forster establishes is dangerously close to inscribing an essentialist concept of race based on what Edward Said calls 'orientalism'. This idea refers to the habit of the western academy – scholars, artists, anthropologists, novelists and poets – to find in the 'East' (a mythical place that is not Europe or the US), the ideas and feeling that they expected to find there. Orientalism leads to essentializing stereotyping in the representation of non-white, non-Western peoples. See Said 1991 and 1994 for these arguments. Sara Sulieri's *The Rhetoric of English India* takes up Said's theme and develops it further.

Selective Chronology 1865–1925

Births and deaths	Principle publications	Cultural and scientific events	Historical and political events
1865			
W. B Yeats born; Arthur Symons born; Rudyard Kipling born; Elizabeth Gaskell dies; Palmerston dies.	John Ruskin, *Sesame and Lilies*; Matthew Arnold, *Essays in Criticism*; Lewis Carroll, *Alice's Adventures. in Wonderland*	Mendel's *Law of Heredity*; Elisabeth Garrett qualifies as a doctor (under licence from the Society of Apothecaries).	American Civil War ends; Lincoln assassinated. Liberal government under Russell in Britain.
1866			
H. G. Wells born.	Algernon Charles Swinburne, *Poems and Ballads*; George Eliot, *Felix Holt, the Radical*; posthumous publication of Gaskell's *Wives and Daughters*.		The Second Reform Act; Second Contagious Diseases Act (first passed in 1864); petition for female suffrage presented ; to Parliament Derby becomes prime minister.
1867			
Arnold Bennett born; John Galsworthy born.		Lister uses antisepsis in operating theatres; Queensberry rules for boxing.	
1868			
	Robert Browning *The Ring and the Book* (finishes publication in 1869); Wilkie Collins, *The Moonstone*.	Typewriter patented; last public execution in Britain and transportation of criminals ended; Telegraph system nationalized in UK.	Disraeli prime minister followed rapidly by Gladstone.

Births and deaths	Principle publications	Cultural and scientific events	Historical and political events
1869	John Stuart Mill, *On the Subjection of Women.*	Girton College (for the higher education of women) founded at Hitchin (moved to Cambridge, 1873); Josephine Butler founds Ladies National Association to campaign against the CD Acts.	Suez Canal opens; Third Contagious Diseases Act; Women ratepayers given the vote in local elections.
1870 Charles Dickens dies.	George Eliot's *Middlemarch* begins part publication (to 1871).		Forster Education Act; Franco-Prussian War begins.
1871	Lewis Carroll, *Through the Looking Glass*; Thomas Hardy, *Desperate Remedies.*	Charles Darwin, *The Descent of Man*; Football Association founded and the English FA cup competition begins.	Unification of Germany; Bank Holidays introduced; University 'tests' of religious conformity abolished; purchase of army commissions abolished.
1872	Hardy, *Under the Greenwood Tree.*	Edison's refined duplex telegraph invented.	
1873 John Stuart Mill dies.	Walter Pater, *Studies in the History of the Renaissance*; J. S. Mill, *Autobiography.*		Irish Home League Association established.
1874	Thomas Hardy, *Far From the Madding Crowd.*		Disraeli prime minister.

Births and deaths	Principle publications	Cultural and scientific events	Historical and political events
1875	Anthony Trollope, *The Way we Live Now*.	London Medical School for Women founded.	Cross Act – gives powers to local authorities for slum clearance.
1876	Eliot, *Daniel Deronda*; Henry James, *Roderick Hudson*.	Alexander Graham Bell invents the telephone; Sophia Jex Blake qualifies as a doctor.	Victoria takes title Empress of India.
1877		Thomas Edison's phonograph; tennis at Wimbledon; Charles Bradlaugh and Annie Besant tried for obscenity for publishing information about contraception.	
1878	Thomas Hardy, *The Return of the Native*.	London University admits women to degree conferments; Salvation Army founded; Ruskin-Whistler lawsuit.	
1879 E. M. Forster born.	Ibsen, *A Doll's House*.		
1880 George Eliot dies; Lytton Strachey born.	Eliot, *The Mill on the Floss*.	Electric light bulb independently invented by Edison in the US and Swan in Great Britain.	
1881 Thomas. Carlyle dies; Benjamin Disraeli dies; Pablo Picasso born.	Henry James, *Portrait of a Lady*; Ibsen, *Ghosts*.	D'Oyly Carte builds the Savoy Theatre – first to be lit by electricity; *Tit-Bits* founded by George Newnes.	

Births and deaths	Principle publications	Cultural and scientific events	Historical and political events
1882 Charles Darwin dies; Anthony Trollope dies; Virginia Woolf born; James Joyce born.	Robert Louis Stevenson, *Treasure Island*.		Married Woman's Property Act.
1883 Karl Marx dies.	Oliver Schreiner, *The Story of an African Farm*; Robert Louis Stevenson, *Treasure Island*.		
1884	Anthony Trollope, *An Autobiography*.	Maxim machine gun invented; Oxford English Dictionary begins publication.	Berlin Conference on the division of African territories; Third Reform Act.
1885 D. H. Lawrence born; Ezra Pound born.	Walter Pater, *Marius the Epicurean*; H. Rider Haggard, *King Solomon's Mines*	Internal combustion engine invented – Benz makes his first petrol engine; Leslie Stephen begins preparation of *Dictionary of National Biography*; Pasteur's vaccine against rabies. 'The Maiden Tribute of Modern Babylon' published in *Pall Mall Gazette*; Zola publishes *Germinal*.	Criminal Law Amendment Act (criminalizes homosexuality).
1886	George Gissing *Demos*; Stevenson, *Dr Jekyll and Mr Hyde*; first English translation of Marx's *Capital* published; Thomas Hardy,		Repeal of the Contagious Diseases Acts; defeat of the Irish Home Rule Bill; Gladstone loses election;

Births and deaths	Principle publications	Cultural and scientific events	Historical and political events
	Mayor of Casterbridge; James, *The Bostonians*.		Salisbury prime minister.
1887			
	H. Rider Haggard, *She*; *Allan Quatermain*; Arthur Conan Doyle, *A Study in Scarlet*; Pater, *Imaginary Portraits*; Hardy, *The Woodlanders*.	Goodwin invents celluloid film; the speed of light measured for the first time.	Victoria's Golden Jubilee; Bloody Sunday takes place in Trafalgar Square.
1888 Matthew Arnold dies; T. S. Eliot born; Katherine Mansfield born.	Rudyard Kipling, *Plain Tales from the Hills*.	Vizetelly tried and imprisoned for publishing translations of Zola; Kodak no. 1 camera and roll film invented and marketed; Forth Rail Bridge completed.	The Jack the Ripper Murders in London's East End.
1889 Robert Browning dies; Gerard Manley Hopkins dies; Constance Naden dies.	Yeats, *The Wanderings of Oisin*; Charles Booth, *Life and Labour of the People in London* begins publication (ends 1903); Pater, *Appreciations*; Wilde, 'The Decay of Lying' (*Fortnightly Review*).	First London performance of Ibsen's *A Doll's House* (1879); Eiffel Tower built.	London Dock Strike.
1890	Wilde, *The Picture of Dorian Gray* serialized; William Booth, *In Darkest England and the Way Out*; J. G. Frazer, *The Golden Bough* begins publication (completed in 1914).	Discovery of tetanus and diptheria viruses; William James, *Principles of Psychology*.	

Births and deaths	Principle publications	Cultural and scientific events	Historical and political events
1891	Wilde, 'The Soul of Man under Socialism' (*Fortnightly*); Doyle, *The Adventures of Sherlock Holmes* begins publication in *The Strand*; Gissing, *New Grub Street*; Hardy, *Tess of the D'Urbervilles*; William Morris, *New from Nowhere*.		
1892 Walt Whitman dies; Alfred Tennyson dies.	Rudyard Kipling, *Barrack-Room Ballads*; Wilde, *Lady Windermere's Fan*; Doyle, *The Adventures of Sherlock Holmes* (book version).	Diesel's internal combustion engine invented.	
1893 Wilfred Owen born.	Wilde, *A Woman of No Importance* and French version of *Salomé*; Yeats, *The Celtic Twilight*; Gissing, *The Odd Women*; Sarah Grand, *The Heavenly Twins*; George Egerton, *Keynotes*; Arthur Wing Pinero, *The Second Mrs Tanqueray*.	Henry Ford's first cars manufactured; the flashbulb (for photography) invented.	Independent Labour Party founded.
1894 Walter Pater dies; Robert Louis Stevenson dies.	Wilde, *Salomé* translated; George Moore, *Esther Waters*; Kipling, *The Jungle Book*; Arthur Morrison, *Tales of Mean Streets*;	*The Yellow Book* founded; Emile Berliner invents the gramophone disc.	

Births and deaths	Principle publications	Cultural and scientific events	Historical and political events
	George Moore, *Esther Waters*; Mona Caird, *The Daughters of Danaus*; George Bernard Shaw, *Arms and the Man*.		
1895 T. H. Huxley dies.	Wilde, *The Importance of Being Earnest* and *An Ideal Husband*; Symons, *London Nights*; Hardy, *Jude the Obscure*; Conrad, *Almayer's Folly*; Wells, *The Time Machine*; Allen, *The Woman Who Did*.	English translation of Max Nordau's *Degeneration*; London School of Economics founded; Röentgen discovers x-rays; Marconi invents wireless telegraph; Lumière brothers invent the cinematograph; Gillette safety razor.	Oscar Wilde tried and imprisoned. Jameson Raids in the Transvaal.
1896 William Morris dies.	A. E. Housman, *A Shropshire Lad*; Morrison, *A Child of the Jago*.	*The Savoy* founded and *The Daily Mail* begins publication as the first modern 'tabloid'; Becquerel discovers radioactivity; London School of Economics opens to students; Ramsay discovers helium; Rutherford publishes on the detection of electrical waves.	
1897 Eleanor Marx-Aveling dies.	Yeats, *The Secret Rose*; Bram Stoker, *Dracula*; Wells, *The Invisible Man* and *The War of the Worlds*; Gissing, *The Whirlpool*;	Tate Gallery opens; Victoria's Diamond Jubilee; J. J. Thomspon discovers the electron.	

Births and deaths	Principle publications	Cultural and scientific events	Historical and political events
	Conrad, *The Nigger of the 'Narcissus'*; Sarah Grand, *The Beth Book*; Richard Marsh, *The Beetle*.		
1898 Aubrey Beardsley dies; Lewis Caroll dies; William Gladstone dies.	Wilde, *The Ballad of Reading Gaol*; Arnold Bennett, *A Man from the North*; Hardy, *Wessex Poems*; James, *The Turn of the Screw*.	*Country Life* founded.	
1899 Grant Allen dies.	Kipling, *Stalky and Co*; Conrad, *Heart of Darkness* serialized; Yeats, *The Wind Among the Reeds*; Arthur Symons, *The Symbolist Movement in Literature*.		Boer War begins (till 1902).
1900 Ruskin dies; Nietzsche dies; Wilde dies.	Conrad, *Lord Jim*; Symons, *The Symbolist Movement in Literature*; Yeats, *The Shadowy Waters*.	Max Planck publishes his theories of quantum physics; Freud publishes *The Interpretation of Dreams*; the Kodak Brownie camera introduced.	
1901 Queen Victoria dies.	Kipling, *Kim*.	Marconi transmits radio waves across the Atlantic.	Edward VII accedes.
1902 Cecil Rhodes dies; Samuel Butler dies; Zola dies.	Bennett, *Anna of the Five Towns*.	William James, *Varieties of Religious Experience; Times Literary Supplement* founded.	Boer War ends.

Births and deaths	Principle publications	Cultural and scientific events	Historical and political events
1903 Whistler dies; Gissing dies; W. E. Henley dies; George Orwell born.	Samuel Butler, *The Way of All Flesh*.	The Wright Brothers succeed in flying; Henry Ford starts Ford Motors.	Pankhurst founds the Women's Social and Political Union.
1904	Conrad, *Nostromo*.	Rutherford discovers radioactivity in radium; Freud, *The Psychopathology of Everyday Life*.	
1905	Wilde, *De Profundis* (expurgated version); Wells, *A Modern Utopia* and *Kipps*; Forster, *Where Angels Fear to Tread*.	Einstein describes the special theory of relativity; Freud, *Three Essays on Sexuality*.	Liberal Administration takes over England on a platform of radical reform.
1906 Samuel Beckett born; Henrik Ibsen dies.	Galsworthy, *The Man of Property*.		Self-government granted to Transvaal and Orange colonies in South Africa.
1907 W. H. Auden born.	Conrad, *The Secret Agent*; Synge, *The Playboy of the Western World*; Forster, *The Longest Journey*.	Picasso exhibits *Les Demoiselles d'Avignon*; first Cubist exhibition in Paris; Baden Powell founds the Boy Scout movement.	
1908 'Ouida' dies.	Bennett, *The Old Wives' Tale*; Wells, *Tono-Bungay*; Forster, *A Room with a View*.		

Births and deaths	Principle publications	Cultural and scientific events	Historical and political events
1909 Swinburne dies; George Meredith dies; John Davidson commits suicide; Synge dies.	Wells, *Ann Veronica*.	Blériot flies the Channel.	
1910 Edward VII dies; Leo Tolstoy dies.	Forster, *Howards End*; Bennett, *Clayhanger*; Wells, *The History of Mr Polly*; Yeats, *The Green Helmet and Other Poems*.	Roger Fry mounts the post-Impressionist Exhibition in London.	George V accedes to the throne.
1911	D. H. Lawrence, *The White Peacock*; Ezra Pound, *Cantos*; Rupert Brooke, *Poems*; Wells, *The New Machiavelli*; Bennett, *Hilda Lessways* and *The Card*; Katherine Mansfield, *In a German Pension*.	Amundsen reaches the South Pole; Rutherford publishes *Theory of Atomic Structure*.	House of Lords partially reformed by Liberal Government; National Insurance measures (for pensions provision and healthcare) announced.
1912		C. G. Jung, *The Theory of Psychoanalysis*.	The *Titanic* disaster.
1913	D. H. Lawrence, *Sons and Lovers*.	Vitamin A isolated for the first time by McCollum.	Panama Canal opens.
1914	James Joyce, *Dubliners*; Yeats, *Responsibilities*.		Archduke Franz Ferdinand of Austria assassinated, precipitating the beginning of the Great War.

Births and deaths	Principle publications	Cultural and scientific events	Historical and political events
1915 Henry James dies.	D. H. Lawrence, *The Rainbow* (suppressed for obscenity later that year); Virginia Woolf, *The Voyage Out*.		Allies try to invade Turkey via Gallipoli and are defeated; zeppelins bomb London; sinking of the *Lusitania* begins process of bringing the US into the war. Coalition government of National Unity established in Britain.
1916 Henry James dies.	James Joyce, *A Portrait of the Artist as a Young Man*; Arnold Bennett, *These Twain*; Wells, *Mr Britling Sees it Through*.		The Battle of the Somme – first use of the tank, and massive casualties; Easter Rising in Dublin.
1917	T. S. Eliot, *The Lovesong of J. Alfred Prufrock*; Yeats, *The Wild Swans at Coole*.	Freud, *Introduction to Psychoanalysis*.	US enters the war. Russian Revolution overthrows the Tsars under the leadership of Lenin.
1918			End of the Great War; process of negotiating peace begun at Versailles; in Britain, the vote extended to all men over 21, and to women over 30 – first woman elected to British parliament is Constance Markiewicz, Sinn Fein.
1919			Treaty of Versailles formalizes the peace;

Births and deaths	Principle publications	Cultural and scientific events	Historical and political events
			influenza epidemic spreads across Europe and the US; Prohibition era begins in US.
1920 Olive Schreiner dies.	Katherine Mansfield, *Bliss and Other Stories*; John Galsworthy, *In Chancery*		National Socialist Party (Nazi) publishes its manifesto in Germany.
1921	John Galsworthy, *To Let*.	Einstein wins the Nobel Prize for Physics.	Red Army defeats the White Russians (Tsarists) in Russian Civil War.
1922	T. S. Eliot, *The Waste Land*; Virginia Woolf, *Jacob's Room*; Mansfield, *The Garden Party and Other Stories*; Yeats, *Michael Robartes and the Dancer*.	The BBC makes its first transmissions.	Irish Free State established; Mussolini establishes fascist dictatorship in Italy.
1923 Katherine Mansfield dies.	Arnold Bennett, *Riceyman's Steps*.	W. B. Yeats awarded the Nobel Prize for Literature.	Matrimonial Bill passed allowing wives to divorce husbands on more equal terms.
1924 E. Nesbit dies; Joseph Conrad dies.	E. M. Forster, *A Passage to India*.		Lenin dies; first British Labour government (a minority administration) under Ramsay MacDonald.
1925	Virginia Woolf, *Mrs Dalloway*.	John Logie Baird first practicable television set.	Hitler publishes *Mein Kampf*.

Annotated Bibliography

Anderson, Linda R. *Bennett, Wells and Conrad: Narrative in Transition.* Basingstoke: Macmillan, 1988.

As well as providing the kind of sensitive and intelligent readings that Bennett and Wells are seldom accorded, Anderson's text also goes to considerable lengths to describe and define the traditions of realism in English fiction, thereby making the connection between an aesthetic vision which appears 'Victorian' and one – in Conrad – which is distinctively modern or even Modernist. A highly recommended read.

Beckson, Karl *London in the 1890s: A Cultural History.* New York and London: W. W. Norton and Co. 1992.

A wide-ranging history of London culture in the 1890s. Beckson describes the whole gamut of cultural activity from Socialist clubs to the discourses of Empire, from the New Woman to homosexual subcultures, and from commerciality in publishing to the aesthetic isolationism of Celts and self-styled decadents. This is a really useful sourcebook for contextualizing the 1890s and beyond.

Carey, John *The Intellectuals and the Masses: Pride and Prejudice among the Literary Intelligentsia, 1880–1939.* London: Faber and Faber, 1992.

This book caused major ripples in the literary pond when it was first published since it makes a very strong case for describing literary modernism as elitist and even proto-fascist in its origins and development. It is passionately argued, and is one of the few relatively recent books to put an alternative view of the late-nineteenth to early-twentieth-century period. It acts as a useful corrective to the uncritical perception of Modernism as a 'good thing' in the words of Sellar and Yeatman and makes a strong case for Arnold Bennett as an important novelist.

Childs, Peter *Modernism*. New Critical Idiom. London: Routledge, 2000.

Part of a series which aims to provide introductory texts on key literary and cultural concepts, Childs's *Modernism* does exactly what it promises: it introduces the key concepts of Modernism. I've chosen it for inclusion here over other such guides that exist because of its contextualization of Modernism, and its careful location of Modernist origins in nineteenth-century thought. It is a very lucid introduction, but is also broadly informative – highly recommended as a place to begin.

Dijkstra, Bram *Idols of Perversity: Fantasies of Feminine Evil in Fin-de-Siècle Culture*. New York and Oxford: Oxford University Press, 1986.

From the bizarre to the macabre to the faintly comic ('Brenn and his share of the plunder', by Paul Joseph Jamin, 1893, combines all three elements), this book documents the history of pictorial art in the late nineteenth century and beyond from the point of view of its representations of women. Some of Dijkstra's descriptions are a little odd on occasion, but this richly illustrated book is an important resource for visualizing one aspect of culture in the period.

Edel, Leon and Gordon N. Ray, eds. *Henry James and H. G. Wells: A Record of Their Friendship, their Debate on the Art of Fiction, and their Quarrel*. London: Rupert Hart-Davis, 1959.

On first sight, this is perhaps a slightly unusual choice for an annotated bibliography. However, in the correspondence between Wells and James that is documented here, one finds the basis of the quarrels between aesthetic and practical considerations of literary practice that solidified in the modernist characterization of realism as naïve. Edel and Ray's introductory matter and scholarly apparatus is very helpful for situating the arguments – but modern readers need to bear in mind their presumption that James was right and that Wells was wrong, a presumption that the documents themselves do not necessarily support. Along with the letters the two novelists wrote to each other, there are also critical essays they each wrote in the press, essays which also state the differences between sociological fictions and the 'aesthetic' or psychological novel. This is a necessary supplement to reading Woolf's essays on fiction, suggesting some of the genesis of her ideas as well as the grounds for her disapproval of Bennett–Wells–Galsworthy.

Ellmann, Richard *Oscar Wilde*. Harmondsworth: Penguin, 1988.

Not only an excellent biography of Wilde, Ellmann's book is a tour de force in its evocation of the 'Wilde period', providing multiple and detailed perspectives on the 1880s and 1890s. There are problems with, not least its wholly inadequate index, and its misattribution of a photograph purporting to be of Wilde in drag, but actually of a German opera singer. But these are small details in an otherwise essential piece of period reading.

Greenslade, William *Degeneration, Culture and the Novel*. Cambridge: Cambridge University Press, 1994.

This book should be read alongside Daniel Pick's *Faces of Degeneration* (1989), which gives more detail about the historical development of degeneration theories in the earlier parts of the nineteenth century. What's particularly useful about Greenslade's book, however, is that it provides interesting readings of texts familiar and unfamiliar through the lens of such theories. In doing so, it demonstrates that this highly dubious pseudo-scientific Victorian discourse had an extremely long afterlife in post-Victorian culture. Greenslade argues, for example, that Woolf's *Mrs Dalloway* is degenerationist text. As such, it makes the case that there are observable continuities between Victorian values and Modernist aesthetics.

Heilmann, Ann *New Woman Fiction: Women Writing First-Wave Feminist Fiction*. Basingstoke: Macmillan, 2000.

It is rather invidious to single out one of the recent plethora of books taking New Woman writing as its theme, and readers are also recommended to look at Ardis 1990, Pykett 1992, Ledger 1997, and Richardson and Willis 2001. I've chosen Heilmann's book here partly because it is a very lucid exposition of the feminist politics of the New Woman writing; and partly because it reproduces in glorious detail large numbers of the cartoon and other images of the New Woman that proliferated in the 1880–1910 period, thereby providing a rich visual context for understanding the complexity that adhered to this multifarious cultural figure.

Jackson, Holbrook *The Eighteen Nineties* [1913]. Intro. Malcolm Bradbury. London: The Cresset Library, 1987.

Written by a near-contemporary, Jackson's *The Eighteen Nineties* gives useful period detail, and also describes how the immediately succeeding period saw the nineties. Jackson covers most of the major figures and most of what we would now see as the major cultural trends. The differences between his vision of the Beardsley–Wilde era and our own visions of it illuminate the changing preoccupations of literary and cultural criticism.

Keating, P. J. *The Haunted Study: A Social History of the English Novel, 1875–1914*. London: Secker and Warburg, 1989.

Less polemical and passionate than Carey's text, Keating's study of prose fiction in an 'age of transition', is indispensable reading, considering in detail the material conditions of literary production in the period. As well as offering readings of novels both obscure and canonical, it sets out to explain their provenance and aesthetics in terms of the economic and social conditions usually relegated to the footnotes of other kinds of study. It contains a wealth of detail not available elsewhere, in a very readable form.

Kern, Stephen *The Culture of Time and Space, 1880–1918*. Cambridge, Mass.: Harvard University Press, 1983.

Kern's underlying argument is that nineteenth-century technological advances radically altered the ways in which it was possible to view the world, in particular in relation to concepts of time (which seemed to be moving faster) and space (modified by the new concept of speed). These advances had discernible effects on the literary aesthetics of high culture (Modernism) across Europe and the United States, as well as fundamentally changing modes of popular culture. It is a dense and sometimes difficult read because the concepts it deals with are complex. But it is very rewarding and important all the same and perseverance is recommended.

Leavis, Q. D. *Fiction and the Reading Public* [1932]. London: Bellew Publishing, 1990.

Many of the value judgements that underlie this study are precisely those called into question and excoriated by Carey, and reading it is an occasionally uncomfortable experience. Nonetheless, Leavis's description and production of a sociological method for understanding the book market is a very valuable period piece, filled with gems of information about the book market and the formation of public taste in the early years of the twentieth century. Read in conjunction with Keating, it tells a lot about materiality of literary culture, and a lot about changing perceptions of literary value between 1932 and 1989.

Ledger, Sally and Roger Luckhurst, eds. *A Reader in Cultural History, c. 1880–1900*. Oxford: Oxford University Press, 2000.

A very useful anthology of extracts from contemporary documents in the period. This text has sections dealing with degeneration theory, social conditions, the city, the New Woman, Socialism and Anarchism, science and anthropology amongst other relevant concepts, written by contemporaries, and charting the nature of such debates in the period. Most of these texts are either extracts from books long out of print, or are only to be found in their original journal publication – making them available to general readers is a very useful enterprise.

Leighton, Angela and Margaret Reynolds, eds. *Victorian Women Poets: An Anthology*. Oxford: Basil Blackwell, 1995.

The final third of this volume is the place to begin to get a flavour of women's poetry in the late nineteenth century. As I note in the text, the process of canon formation for New Women poets is at an early and underdeveloped stage. Leighton and Reynolds cover all the important names, give excellent basic bibliographical and biographical contexts, and notes for further reading. This is a really helpful book.

Showalter, Elaine *Sexual Anarchy: Gender and Culture at the Fin de Siècle.* London: Bloomsbury, 1991.

The parallels Showalter draws between the Victorian fin de siècle and the twentieth-century millenarianism are not all always completely satisfying, but this book does a very good job of describing the cultural and political anxieties about gender in both periods, and examining the ways in which those anxieties were reflected in the variety of literary and artistic production. The book also has a very readable style, making theoretically inflected readings available to all kinds of readers.

Showalter, Elaine, ed. *Daughters of Decadence: Women Writers of the Fin-de-Siècle.* London: Virago, 1993.

This anthology of New Woman short fiction will perhaps soon be superseded by a forthcoming selection edited by Angelique Richardson. Its disadvantage is the uncritical use of the word decadence in relation to New Women writers who would certainly have disavowed the word in relation to their own project. Its advantage is that it has been constantly in print since its publication, making rare stories by Vernon Lee, George Egerton, Sarah Grand and Olive Schreiner available to student readers – and for that I am very grateful. It also provides biographical information about the writers, which is helpful context.

Stokes, John *In the Nineties.* Hemel Hempstead: Harvester Wheatsheaf, 1989.

Stokes's book gives a slightly different view of the late nineteenth century, based on the detailed consideration of cultural thematics as they were elucidated in the pages of the contemporary press – the New Journalism of the period. He considers the economics of journalism, its conventions, including the new form of the interview and the passing of journalistic anonymity, the letters pages of the popular press, and thence relationships between newspaper economics and the formation of literary aesthetics. It is a fascinating read.

Walkowitz, Judith *City of Dreadful Delight: Narratives of Sexual Danger in Late-Victorian London.* London: Virago, 1992.

This historical and cultural survey of London's seamier side provides an important contextual background for readers seeking to understand the literary representation of the city in the late Victorian and early modernist periods. The oxymoron of the title speaks of the ambivalence that many commentators felt about the city – dreadful conditions, especially for the working classes of the East End memorialized in the sociological surveys and fictions of the period, existed side-by-side with a city in the process of being rebuilt as a consumerist paradise. The Ripper murders of 1888 which provoked horror and grisly fascination in equal measure are one of the elements of that oxymoron. This is both gripping and queasy reading, for Walkowitz also demonstrates that we cannot judge the Victorians honestly if we do not admit that we are more like them than we wish to think.

Williams, Raymond *The English Novel from Dickens to Lawrence.* London: The Hogarth Press, 1984.

A recent critic has suggested quite rightly that Williams's book 'pivoted on loose assertions and bold general statements' that are not really substantiated (O'Gorman 2002, 159). All the same, Williams's responses to *fin-de-siècle* and proto-Modernist fictions in the last half of this book have been influential because they are intelligent responses to the materials. The book has a quasi-Marxist underpinning, and is, in parts, a simplified rewriting of some of the material from Williams's earlier book, *Culture and Society.* Key phrases about 'knowable communities' and about 'border countries' do help to make sense of the changes in English fiction from 'Victorian' to Modern, and they provide food for further thought and development.

Williams, Raymond *Keywords: A Vocabulary of Culture and Society* [1976]. London: Fontana Press, 1988.

This book is a dictionary of important words. It reminds us that key concepts, which we have a habit of taking for granted, actually have a history, and that the history of words is formative of their most recent meanings. In mini essays, Williams describes the changing usages of words like 'class', 'culture', 'aesthetics', 'intellectual', 'labour', 'literature' and 'industry', to choose a few random – but not insignificant – examples. Since the period of this book is a period in which meanings shifted, *Keywords* is recommended as a reminder that our vocabulary comes from specific historical circumstances.

Bibliography

Alford, Norman. *The Rhymers' Club: Poets of the Tragic Generation.* Basingstoke: Macmillan, 1997.

Allen, Grant. *The Woman Who Did* [1895]. Intro. Sarah Wintle. Oxford: Oxford University Press, 1995.

Allott, Miriam. *Emily Brontë, Wuthering Heights: A Casebook.* Revised edition. Basingstoke: Macmillan, 1992.

Altick, Richard D. 'Publishing'. In Valentine Cunningham, ed. *A Companion to Victorian Literature and Culture.* Oxford: Basil Blackwell, 1999, pp. 289–304.

Anderson, Linda R. *Bennett, Wells and Conrad: Narrative in Transition.* Basingstoke: Macmillan, 1988.

Arata, Stephen D. *Fictions of Loss in the Victorian Fin de Siècle.* Cambridge: Cambridge University Press, 1996.

Arata, Stephen D. 'The Occidental Tourist: *Dracula* and the Anxiety of Reverse Colonization'. In Glennis Byron, ed. *Dracula: Contemporary Critical Essays.* New Casebook Series. London: Macmillan, 1999, pp. 119–44.

Ardis, Ann. *New Women, New Novels: Feminism and Early Modernism.* New Brunswick and London: Rutgers University Press, 1990.

Armstrong, Isobel. *Victorian Poetry: Poetry, Poetics and Politics.* London and New York: Routledge, 1993.

Arnold, Matthew. 'General Report for the Year 1852'. In Sir F. Sanford, ed. *Reports on Elementary Schools, 1852–1882.* London: Macmillan, 1889.

Arnold, Matthew. *Selected Poems and Prose.* Ed. Miriam Allott. London: Dent, 1993.

Baldick, Chris. *The Social Mission of English Criticism, 1848–1932.* Oxford: The Clarendon Press, 1983.

Baldick, Chris. *In Frankenstein's Shadow: Myth, Monstrosity and Nineteenth-Century Writing.* Oxford: The Clarendon Press, 1987.

Bartlett, Neil. *Who Was That Man? A Present for Mr Oscar Wilde.* London: Serpent's Tail, 1989.

Batchelor, John. *The Edwardian Novelists.* London: Duckworth, 1981.

Battersby, Christine. *Gender and Genius: Towards a Feminist Aesthetics.* London: The Women's Press, 1989.

Bayley, John. *Housman's Poems.* Oxford: The Clarendon Press, 1992.

Beal, Anthony. *D. H. Lawrence.* London: Oliver and Boyd, 1961.

Becker, George (ed.) J. *Documents of Modern Literary Realism.* Princeton: Princeton University Press, 1963.

Beckson, Karl (ed.). *Oscar Wilde: The Critical Heritage*. London and New York: Routledge and Kegan Paul, 1970.

Beckson, Karl. *London in the 1890s: A Cultural History*. London and New York: W. W. Norton and Co., 1992.

Belsey, Catherine. *Critical Practice*. London and New York: Routledge, 1980.

Bennett, Arnold. *The Journals of Arnold Bennett*. 3 Volumes. Ed. Newman Flower. London: Cassell and Co., 1932.

Bennett, Arnold. *Anna of the Five Towns* [1902]. Intro. Frank Swinnerton. Harmondsworth: Penguin, 1936.

Bennett, Arnold. *Hilda Lessways* [1911]. London: Methuen, 1951.

Bennett, Arnold. *Clayhanger* [1910]. Ed. Andrew Lincoln. Harmondsworth: Penguin, 1989.

Bennett, Arnold. *The Old Wives' Tale* [1908]. Ed. and Intro. John Wain. Harmondsworth: Penguin, 1990.

Bergonzi, Bernard (ed.). *H. G. Wells: A Collection of Critical Essays*. New Jersey: Prentice Hall, 1976.

Bergonzi, Bernard (ed.). *Poetry, 1870–1914*. London: Longman, 1980.

Blain, Virginia. ' "Michael Field: The Two-Headed Nightingale": Lesbian Text as Palimpsest'. *Women's History Review*. V, ii (1996), 239–57.

Botting, Fred. *Gothic*. London: Routledge, 1996.

Bradbury, Malcolm (ed.). *E. M. Forster: A Passage to India – A Selection of Critical Essays*. London: Macmillan, 1970.

Bradfield, Thomas. 'A Dominant Note of Some Recent Fiction'. *Westminster Review*. Volume 142 (1894), 537–45.

Brake, Laurel. *Walter Pater: Writers and their Work*. Plymouth: Northcote House, 1994a.

Brake, Laurel. *Subjugated Knowledges: Journalism, Gender and Literature in the Nineteenth Century*. Basingstoke: Macmillan, 1994b.

Brantlinger, Patrick. *Rule of Darkness: British Literature and Imperialism, 1830–1914*. Ithaca and London: Cornell University Press, 1988.

Bristow, Joseph. *Empire Boys: Adventures in a Man's World*. London: HarperCollins Academic, 1991.

Bristow, Joseph. *Effeminate England: Homoerotic Writing After 1885*. Buckingham: Open University Press, 1995.

Bronfen, Elisabeth. 'Hysteric and Obsessional Discourse: Responding to Death in *Dracula*'. In Glennis Byron, ed. *Dracula: Contemporary Critical Essays*. New Casebook Series. London: Macmillan, 1999, pp. 55–67.

Butler, Josephine. *The Education and Employment of Women* [1868]. Reprinted in Harriet Devine Jump, ed. *Women's Writing of the Victorian Period, 1837–1901: An Anthology*. Edinburgh: Edinburgh University Press, 1999, pp. 158–65.

Butler, Josephine. *An ... Appeal ... on Prostitution* [1869]. Reprinted in Harriet Devine Jump, ed. *Women's Writing of the Victorian Period, 1837–1901: An Anthology*. Edinburgh: Edinburgh University Press, 1999, pp. 163–8.

Butler, Samuel. *Ernest Pontifex or, The Way of All Flesh: A Story of English Domestic Life* [1903]. Ed. Peter Raby. London: Dent, 1993.

Byron, Glennis. *Dracula: Contemporary Critical Essays*. New Casebooks Series. London: Macmillan, 1999.

Carey, John. *The Intellectuals and the Masses: Pride and Prejudice Among the Literary Intelligentsia, 1880–1939*. London: Faber, 1992.

Carroll, Lewis. *The Annotated Alice: Alice's Adventures in Wonderland and Through the Looking Glass*. Ed. Martin Gardner. Harmondsworth: Penguin, 1970.

Clark, Colin (ed.). *D. H. Lawrence: The Rainbow and Women in Love – A Selection of Critical Essays*. Casebook Series. London: Macmillan, 1969.

Conrad, Joseph. *Letters from Joseph Conrad, 1895–1924*. Ed. Edward Garnett. New York: Bobbs-Merril, 1928.

Conrad, Joseph. *Heart of Darkness* [1899, 1902]. Ed. Paul O'Prey. Harmondsworth: Penguin, 1985.

Conrad, Joseph. *Lord Jim* [1900]. Ed. Robert Hampson. Intro. Cedric Watts. Harmondsworth: Penguin, 1986.

Conrad, Joseph. *The Secret Agent: A Simple Tale* [1907]. Ed. Martin Seymour Smith. Harmondsworth: Penguin, 1986.

Coustillas, Pierre. 'Gissing's Feminine Portraiture' [1963]. Reprinted in J. P. Michaux, ed. *George Gissing: Critical Essays*. London: Vision Press, 1981, pp. 91–107.

Coustillas, Pierre and Colin Partridge (eds). *George Gissing: The Critical Heritage*. London: Routledge and Kegan Paul, 1972.

Cox, R. G. (ed.). *Thomas Hardy: The Critical Heritage*. London: Routledge and Kegan Paul, 1970.

Craft, Christopher. ' "Kiss me with those red lips": Gender and Inversion in Bram Stoker's *Dracula*' [1984]. Reprinted in Glennis Byron, ed. *Dracula: Contemporary Critical Essays*. New Casebooks Series. Basingstoke: Macmillan, 1999, pp. 93–118.

Cunningham, Gail. *The New Woman and the Victorian Novel*. London and Basingstoke: Macmillan, 1978.

Cunningham, Valentine (ed.). *A Companion to Victorian Literature and Culture*. Oxford: Basil Blackwell, 1999.

Danson, Laurence. *Wilde's Intentions: The Artist in his Criticism*. Oxford: Clarendon Press, 1997.

D'Arch-Smith, Timothy. *Love in Earnest: Some Notes on the Lives and Writings of English Uranian Poets, 1889–1930*. London: Routledge and Kegan Paul, 1970.

Dellamorra, Richard. *Masculine Desire: The Sexual Politics of Victorian Aestheticism*. Chapel Hill and London: University of North Carolina Press, 1990.

De Vere White, Terence. *A Leaf from the Yellow Book: The Correspondence of George Egerton*. London: The Richards Press, 1958.

Dickens, Charles. *Hard Times* [1854]. Ed. David Craig. Harmondsworth: Penguin, 1985.

Dijkstra, Bram. *Idols of Perversity: Fantasies of Feminine Evil in Fin-de-Siècle Culture*. New York and Oxford: Oxford University Press, 1986.

Dollimore, Jonathan. *Sexual Dissidence: Augustine to Wilde, Freud to Foucault.* London: Oxford University Press, 1991.

Doyle, Arthur Conan. *The Penguin Complete Sherlock Holmes.* Harmondsworth: Penguin, 1981.

Eagleton, Terry. *Saint Oscar.* Derry: Field Day, 1989.

Edel, Leon, and Gordon N. Ray (eds). *Henry James and H. G. Wells: A Record of Their Friendship, their Debate on the Art of Fiction, and their Quarrel.* London: Rupert Hart-Davis, 1959.

Egerton, George. 'A Keynote to *Keynotes*'. In John Gawsworth, ed. *Ten Contemporaries: Notes Towards their Definitive Bibliography.* London: E. Benn, 1932.

Egerton, George. *Keynotes and Discords* [1893, 1894]. Intro. Martha Vicinus. London: Virago, 1983.

Eliot, George. *Adam Bede* [1859]. Ed. Stephen Gill. Harmondsworth: Penguin, 1980.

Eliot, George. *Middlemarch* [1870–71]. Ed. Rosemary Ashton. Harmondsworth: Penguin, 1994.

Eliot, T. S. *Collected Poems: 1909–62.* London: Faber and Faber, 1963.

Eliot, T. S. *Selected Prose of T. S. Eliot.* Ed. Frank Kermode. London and Boston: Faber and Faber, 1975.

Eliot, T. S. 'Rudyard Kipling'. Introduction to *A Choice of Kipling's Verse.* London: Faber and Faber, 1988, pp. 5–36.

Ellmann, Richard (ed.). *Edwardians and Late Victorians.* New York: Columbia University Press, 1957.

Ellmann, Richard. *W. B. Yeats: The Man and the Masks* [1948]. Harmondsworth: Penguin, 1979.

Ellmann, Richard. *Oscar Wilde.* Harmondsworth: Penguin, 1988.

Emig, Rainer. *Modernism in Poetry: Motivations, Structures and Limits.* Harlow: Longman, 1995.

Felski, Rita. *The Gender of Modernity.* Cambridge, Mass. and London: Harvard University Press, 1995.

Fernihough, Ann (ed.). *The Cambridge Companion to D. H. Lawrence.* Cambridge: Cambridge University Press, 2001.

Field, Michael. *Wild Honey from Various Thyme.* London: T. Fisher Unwin, 1908.

Flanegan-Behrendt, Patricia. *Oscar Wilde: Eros and Aesthetics.* Basingstoke: Macmillan, 1991.

Fletcher, Ian (ed.). *Decadence and the 1890s.* Stratford-Upon-Avon Studies 17. London: Edward Arnold, 1979.

Fletcher, Ian (ed.). *British Poetry and Prose, 1870–1905.* Oxford: Oxford University Press, 1987.

Flint, Kate. *The Woman Reader, 1837–1914.* Oxford and New York: Oxford University Press, 1993.

Ford, Ford Madox. *The Good Soldier* [1915]. *A Norton Critical Edition.* Ed. Martin Stannard. New York: W. W. Norton and Co., 1995.

Forster, E. M. *A Room With a View* [1908]. Ed. and Intro. Oliver Stallybrass. Harmondsworth: Penguin, 1978.

Forster, E. M. *Howards End* [1910]. Ed. and Intro. Oliver Stallybrass. Harmondsworth: Penguin, 1989a.

Forster, E. M. *The Longest Journey* [1907]. Ed. and Intro. Elizabeth Heine. Harmondsworth: Penguin, 1989b.

Forster, E. M. *A Passage to India* [1924]. Ed. and Intro. Oliver Stallybrass. Harmondsworth: Penguin, 1989c.

Forster, E. M. *Aspects of the Novel* [1929]. Harmondsworth: Penguin, 1990.

Freud, Sigmund. 'The Uncanny' [1919]. *The Penguin Freud Library*. Volume 14. *Art and Literature*. Trans. James Strachey. Ed. Albert Dickson. Harmondsworth: Penguin, 1985, pp. 338–81.

Gagnier, Regenia. *Idylls of the Marketplace: Oscar Wilde and the Victorian Public*. Aldershot: The Scolar Press, 1987.

Galsworthy, John. *The Forsyte Saga* [*The Man of Property*, 1906; *In Chancery*, 1920; *To Let*, 1921]. Harmondsworth: Penguin, 1978.

Gawsworth, John. *Ten Contemporaries: Notes Toward Their Definitive Bibliography*. London: E. Benn, 1932.

Gerber, Helmut. 'The Nineties: Beginning, End, or Transition?' In Richard Ellmann, ed. *Edwardians and Late Victorians*. New York: Columbia University Press, 1957, pp. 50–70.

Gilbert, Sandra M. and Susan Gubar. *The Madwoman in the Attic: The Place of the Woman Writer in the Nineteenth-Century Literary Imagination*. London and Yale: Yale University Press, 1979.

Gilbert, Sandra M. and Susan Gubar. *No Man's Land: The Place of the Woman Writer in the Twentieth Century*. Volume 2. *Sexchanges*. New Haven and London: Yale University Press, 1989.

Gissing, George. *The Odd Women* [1891]. Intro. Margaret Walters. London: Virago, 1980.

Gissing, George. *New Grub Street* [1891]. Ed. and Intro. Bernard Bergonzi. Harmondsworth: Penguin, 1985.

Gissing, George. *The Nether World* [1889]. Ed. and Intro. Stephen Gill. Oxford: Oxford University Press, 1992.

Goode, John. *Thomas Hardy: The Offensive Truth*. Oxford: Basil Blackwell, 1988.

Goodwin, Michael (ed.). *Nineteenth-Century Opinion: An Anthology of Extracts from the First Fifty Volumes of the Nineteenth Century, 1877–1901*. Harmondsworth: Penguin, 1951.

Grand, Sarah. *The Heavenly Twins* [1893]. Intro. Carol A. Senf. Michigan: Ann Arbor, 1992.

Grand, Sarah. *The Beth Book* [1897]. Intro. Sally Mitchell. Bristol: Thoemmes Press, 1994.

Grand, Sarah. 'The New Aspect of the Woman Question' [1894]. Reprinted in Sally Ledger and Roger Luckhurst, eds. *The Fin de Siècle: A Reader in Cultural History, 1880–1900*. Oxford: Oxford University Press, 2000, pp. 88–90.

Grant, Michael (ed.). *T. S. Eliot: The Critical Heritage*. London: Routledge and Kegan Paul, 1982.

Greenslade, William. *Degeneration, Culture and the Novel*. Cambridge: Cambridge University Press, 1994.

Haggard, H. Rider. *King Solomon's Mines* [1885]. Ed. and Intro. Dennis Butts. Oxford: Oxford University Press, 1989.

Haggard, H. Rider. *Allan Quatermain* [1887]. Ware: Wordsworth editions, 1994.

Haggard, H. Rider. *She* [1886]. Ed. and Intro. Patrick Brantlinger. Harmondsworth: Penguin, 2001.

Hamilton, Susan (ed.). *Criminals, Idiots, Women and Minors: Victorian Writing on Women by Women*. Ontario: Broadview, 1995.

Hardy, Thomas. *The New Wessex Selection of Thomas Hardy's Poems*. Eds John and Eirian Wain. Intro. John Wain. Basingstoke: Macmillan, 1976.

Hardy, Thomas. *The Return of the Native* [1878]. Ed. and Intro. George Woodcock. Harmondsworth: Penguin, 1978.

Hardy, Thomas. *The Life and Death of the Mayor of Casterbridge: The Story of a Man of Character* [1886]. Ed. and Intro. Martin Seymour Smith. Harmondsworth: Penguin, 1978.

Hardy, Thomas. *The Mayor of Casterbridge: A Story of a Man of Character* [1888]. Ed. and Intro. Martin Seymour Smith. Harmondsworth: Penguin, 1978.

Hardy, Thomas. *Tess of the D'Urbervilles: A Pure Woman* [1891]. Ed. Tim Dolin. Intro. Margaret R. Higonnet. Harmondsworth: Penguin, 1998a.

Hardy, Thomas. *Jude the Obscure* [1895]. Ed. and Intro. Dennis Taylor. Harmondsworth: Penguin, 1998b.

Hardy, Thomas. *Far From the Madding Crowd* [1874]. Ed. and Intro. Rosemarie Morgan and Shannon Russell. Harmondsworth: Penguin, 2000.

Hardy, Thomas. 'Candour in Fiction' [1890]. Reprinted in Sally Ledger and Roger Luckhurst, eds. *The Fin de Siècle. A Reader in Cultural History, c. 1880–1900*. Eds Luckhurst. Oxford: Oxford University Press, 2000, pp. 111–20.

Hart-Davis, Adam. *What the Victorians Did for Us*. London: Headline, 2001.

Hart-Davis, Rupert. *Selected Letters of Oscar Wilde*. Oxford: Oxford University Press, 1979.

Heath, Stephen. 'Psychopathia Sexualis: Stevenson's *Strange Case*' [1986]. Reprinted in Lyn Pykett, ed. *Reading Fin-de-Siècle Fictions*. London: Longman Addison Wesley, 1996, pp. 64–79.

Heilmann, Ann. *New Woman Fiction: Women Writing First-Wave Feminism*. Basingstoke: Macmillan, 2000.

Henley, W. E. *Poems: A Book of Verses: London Voluntaries*. London: David Nutt, 1898.

Hepburn, James (ed.). *Arnold Bennett: The Critical Heritage*. London: Routledge and Kegan Paul, 1981.

Hewitt, Douglas. *English Fiction of the Early Modern Period, 1890–1940*. London and New York: Longman, 1988.

Hobsbawm, E. J. *The Age of Empire: 1875–1914*. London: Sphere Books, 1987.

Hopkins, Gerard Manley. *Poems and Prose*. Ed. and Intro. W. H. Gardner. Harmondsworth: Penguin, 1985.

Houghton, Walter E. *The Victorian Frame of Mind, 1830–1870*. New Haven and London: Yale University Press, 1957.

Housman, A. E. *Collected Poems and Selected Prose*. Ed. Christopher Ricks. Harmondsworth: Penguin, 1988.

Hunter, Jefferson. *Edwardian Fiction*. Cambridge, Mass.: Harvard University Press, 1982.

Jackson, Holbrook. *The Eighteen Nineties* [1913]. Intro. Malcolm Bradbury. London: The Cresset Library, 1987.

James, Henry. *The House of Fiction: Essays on the Novel*. Ed. Leon Edel. London: Mercury Books, 1962.

James, William. *Principles of Psychology* [1890]. 2 Volumes. New York: Dover Publications, 1950.

Joyce, James. *Dubliners* [1914]. Ed. Terence Brown. Harmondsworth: Penguin, 1992a.

Joyce, James. *A Portrait of the Artist as a Young Man* [1916]. Ed. Seamus Deane. Harmondsworth: Penguin, 1992b.

Jump, Harriet Devine (ed.). *Women's Writing of the Victorian Period, 1837–1901: An Anthology*. Edinburgh: Edinburgh University Press, 1999.

Keating, P. J. *New Grub Street* (Introduction). *English Literature in Transition*. 33 (1968), 9–16.

Keating, P. J. *The Haunted Study: A Social History of the English Novel, 1875–1914*. London: Secker and Warburg, 1989.

Kermode, Frank. *The Sense of an Ending: Studies in the Theory of Fiction*. Oxford and New York: Oxford University Press, 1967.

Kermode, Frank. *Romantic Image* [1957]. London: Ark Paperbacks, 1986.

Kern, Stephen. *The Culture of Time and Space, 1880–1918*. Cambridge, Mass.: Harvard University Press, 1983.

Kipling, Rudyard. *A Choice of Kipling's Verse*. Ed. and Intro. T. S. Eliot. London: Faber and Faber, 1988.

Lang, Andrew. 'Realism and Romance'. *Contemporary Review*. 52 (November 1887). Reprinted in Sally Ledger and Roger Luckhurst, eds. *The Fin de Siècle. A Reader in Cultural History, c. 1880–1900*. Oxford: Oxford University Press, 2000, pp. 99–104.

Lawrence, D. H. *The Collected Letters of D. H. Lawrence*. 2 Volumes. Ed. Harry T. Moore. London: Heinemann, 1962.

Lawrence, D. H. *Sons and Lovers* [1913]. Ed. Keith Sagar. Harmondsworth: Penguin, 1981.

Lawrence, D. H. *The Rainbow* [1915]. Ed. Mark Kinkead Weekes. Intro. Ann Fernihough. Harmondsworth: Penguin, 1995.

Leavis, Q. D. 'Gissing and the English Novel' [*Scrutiny* 7, June 1938: pp. 73–81]. Reprinted in R. P. Michaux, ed. *George Gissing: Critical Essays*. London: Vision Press, 1981, pp. 178–86.

Leavis, Q. D. *Fiction and the Reading Public* [1932]. London: Bellew Publishing, 1990.

Ledger, Sally. *The New Woman: Fiction and Feminism at the Fin-de-Siècle.* Manchester: Manchester University Press, 1997.

Ledger, Sally and Roger Luckhurst (eds). *The Fin de Siècle: A Reader in Cultural History, c. 1800–1900.* Oxford: Oxford University Press, 2000.

Ledger, Sally and Scott McCracken (eds). *Cultural Politics at the Fin de Siècle.* Cambridge: Cambridge University Press, 1995.

Le Gallienne, Richard. *The Romantic 90s* [1926]. London: Robin Clark Ltd, 1993.

Leighton, Angela. *Victorian Women Poets: Writing Against the Heart.* Hemel Hempstead: Harvester Wheatsheaf, 1992.

Leighton, Angela and Margaret Reynolds (eds). *Victorian Women Poets: An Anthology.* Oxford: Basil Blackwell, 1995.

Levenson, Michael (ed.). *The Cambridge Companion to Modernism.* Cambridge: Cambridge University Press, 1999.

Lilly, Mark. *Gay Men's Literature in the Twentieth Century.* Basingstoke: Macmillan, 1993.

Lodge, David. '*Tono-Bungay* and the Condition of England'. In Bernard Bergonzi, ed. *H. G. Wells: A Collection of Critical Essays.* New Jersey: Prentice Hall, 1976, pp. 110–39.

Lucas, John. *Arnold Bennett: A Study of his Fiction.* London: Methuen, 1974.

Lucas, John. 'Hopkins and Symons: Two Views of the City'. In John Stokes, ed. *Fin de Siècle/Fin du Globe: Fears and Fantasies of the Late Nineteenth Century.* Basingtoke: Macmillan, 1992, pp. 52–68.

Marsh, Jan. *Pre-Raphaelite Women.* London: Weidenfeld and Nicolson, 1987.

Marsh, Richard. *The Beetle* [1897]. Stroud: Alan Sutton, 1994.

Merrill, Linda. *A Pot of Paint: Aesthetics on Trial in Whistler v. Ruskin.* Washington and London: Smithsonian Institution Press, 1992.

Michaux, J. P. (ed.). *George Gissing: Critical Essays.* London: Vision Press, 1981.

Miller, Jane Eldridge. *Rebel Women: Feminism, Modernism and the Edwardian Novel.* London: Virago, 1994.

Moore, George. *Literature at Nurse, or Circulating Novels: A Polemic on Victorian Censorship* [1885]. Ed. and Intro. Pierre Coustillas. Facsimile Reprint. Sussex: The Harvester Press, 1976.

Morrison, Arthur. *A Child of the Jago* [1896]. Ed. Peter Miles. London: Everyman, 1996.

Nassaar, Christopher (ed.). *The English Literary Decadence: An Anthology.* Lanham, Maryland: University Press of America, 1999.

Nead, Lynda. *Victorian Babylon: People, Streets and Images in Nineteenth-Century London.* London and New Haven: Yale University Press, 2000.

Nicholls, Peter. *Modernisms: A Literary Guide.* Basingstoke: Macmillan, 1995.

Nord, Deborah Epstein. *Walking the Victorian Streets: Women, Representation and the City.* Ithaca and London: Cornell University Press, 1995.

Nordau, Max. *Degeneration* [1893, trans. 1895]. Ed. George L. Mosse. Lincoln and London: University of Nebraska Press, 1993.

Norquay, Glenda (ed.). *R. L. Stevenson on Fiction*. Edinburgh: Edinburgh University Press, 1999.

O'Gorman, Francis (ed.). *The Victorian Novel*. Oxford: Basil Blackwell, 2002.

Orwell, George. *Inside the Whale and Other Essays*. Harmondsworth: Penguin, 1957.

Parrinder, Patrick. 'The Comedy of Limitation'. In Bernard Bergonzi, ed. *H. G. Wells: A Collection of Critical Essays*. New Jersey: Prentice-Hall, 1976, pp. 69–82.

Pater, Walter. *The Renaissance: Studies in Art and Poetry, The 1893 Text*. Ed. Donald L. Hill. Berkeley, Los Angeles and London: University of California Press, 1980.

Pick, Daniel. *Faces of Degeneration: A European Disorder, c. 1848–c. 1918*. Cambridge: Cambridge University Press, 1989.

Pittock, Murray G. H. *Spectrum of Decadence: The Literature of the 1890s*. London: Routledge, 1993.

Powell, Kerry. *Oscar Wilde and the Theatre of the 1890s*. Cambridge: Cambridge University Press, 1990.

Power Cobbe, Frances. 'What Shall We Do With Our Old Maids?' [1862]. Reprinted in Susan Hamilton, ed. *Criminals, Idiots, Women and Minors: Victorian Writing By Women on Women*. Ontario: Broadview Press, 1996, pp. 85–107.

Pykett, Lyn. *The Improper Feminine: The Women's Sensation Novel and the New Woman Writing*. London: Routledge, 1992.

Pykett, Lyn. *Engendering Fictions: The English Novel in the Early Twentieth Century*. London: Edward Arnold, 1995.

Pykett, Lyn (ed.). *Reading Fin-de-Siècle Fictions*. London: Longman Addison Wesley, 1996.

Raby, Peter (ed.). *The Cambridge Companion to Oscar Wilde*. Cambridge: Cambridge University Press, 1997.

Richardson, Angelique and Chris Willis (eds). *The New Woman in Fiction and in Fact: Fin-de-Siècle Feminisms*. Basingstoke: Palgrave, 2001.

Riquelme, John Paul (ed.). *Dracula: Bram Stoker: Case Studies in Contemporary Criticism*. New York: Bedford Books, 2002.

Robbins, Ruth. ' "And Judas always writes the biography": The Many Lives of Oscar Wilde'. In Ruth Robbins and Julian Wolfreys, eds. *Victorian Identities: Social and Cultural Formations in Nineteenth-Century Literature*. Basingstoke: Macmillan, 1996, pp. 97–118.

Robbins, Ruth. 'Apparitions can be deceptive: Vernon Lee's Androgynous Spectres'. In Ruth Robbins and Julian Wolfreys, eds. *Victorian Gothic: Literary and Cultural Manifestations in the Nineteenth Century*. Basingstoke: Palgrave, 2000, pp. 183–200.

Robbins, Ruth and Julian Wolfreys (eds). *Victorian Identities: Social and Cultural Formations in Nineteenth-Century Literature*. Basingstoke: Macmillan, 1996.

Robbins, Ruth and Julian Wolfreys (eds). *Victorian Gothic: Literary and Cultural Manifestations in the Nineteenth Century*. Basingstoke: Palgrave, 2000.

Sagar, Keith. *D. H. Lawrence: Life into Art*. Harmondsworth: Penguin, 1985.

Said, Edward W. *Orientalism: Western Conceptions of the Orient* [1978]. London: Penguin, 1991.

Said, Edward W. *Culture and Imperialism* [1993]. London: Vintage, 1994.

Sanford, Sir F. (ed.). *Reports on Elementary Schools, 1852–1882*. London: Macmillan, 1889.

Schafer, Robert. 'The Vitality of George Gissing' [1935]. Reprinted in J. P. Michaux, ed. *George Gissing: Critical Essays*. London: Vision Press, 1981, pp. 37–57.

Schreiner, Olive. *The Story of an African Farm* [1883]. Intro. Dan Jacobson. Harmondsworth: Penguin, 1995.

Seiler, R. M. (ed.). *Walter Pater: The Critical Heritage*. London: Routledge and Kegan Paul, 1980.

Sellar, W. C. and R. J. Yeatman. *1066 and All That* [1930]. London: Methuen, 1984.

Senf, Carol A. Introduction to Sarah Grand, *The Heavenly Twins*. Michigan: Ann Arbor, 1992.

Showalter, Elaine. *A Literature of Their Own: British Women Novelists from Brontë to Lessing*. London: Virago, 1978.

Showalter, Elaine. *Sexual Anarchy: Gender and Culture at the Fin de Siècle*. London: Bloomsbury, 1991.

Showalter, Elaine (ed.). *Daughters of Decadence: Women Writers of the Fin-de-Siècle*. London: Virago, 1993.

Sinfield, Alan. *The Wilde Century: Effeminacy, Oscar Wilde and the Queer Moment*. London: Cassell, 1994.

Spencer, Robin. *Whistler: A Retrospective*. New York: Wings Books, 1991.

Spilka, Mark (ed.). *D. H. Lawrence: A Collection of Critical Essays*. Englewood Cliffs, New Jersey: Prentice-Hall, 1963.

Squillace, Robert. 'Bennett, Wells, and the Persistence of Realism'. In John Richetti, ed. *The Columbia History of the British Novel*. New York: Columbia University Press, 1994, pp. 658–84.

Stedman-Jones, Gareth. *Outcast London: A Study in the Relationship between Classes in Victorian Society* [1971]. Harmondsworth: Penguin, 1979.

Stein, Richard L. *The Ritual of Interpretation*. Cambridge, Mass. and London: Harvard University Press, 1975.

Stevenson, Randall. *Modernist Fiction: An Introduction*. Hemel Hempstead: Harvester Wheatsheaf, 1992.

Stevenson, Robert Louis. *The Strange Case of Dr Jekyll and Mr Hyde, and Other Stories*. Ed. Jenni Calder. Harmondsworth: Penguin, 1979.

Stevenson, Robert Louis. 'A Gossip on Romance'. *Longman's Magazine*. 1. (November, 1882). Reprinted in Glenda, ed. *R. L. Stevenson on Fiction*. Norquay. Edinburgh: EUP, 1999.

Stevenson, Robert Louis. 'A Humble Remonstrance'. *Longman's Magazine*. December 1884. Reprinted in Glenda Norquay, ed. *R. L. Stevenson on Fiction*. Edinburgh: EUP, 1999.

Stoker, Bram. *Dracula* [1897]. Ed. and Intro. Maurice Hindle. Harmondsworth: Penguin, 1993.

Stokes, John (ed.). *Fin de Siècle, Fin du Globe: Fears and Fantasies of the Late Nineteenth Century.* Basingstoke: Macmillan, 1992.

Stokes, John. *Oscar Wilde: Myths, Miracles and Imitations.* Cambridge: Cambridge University Press, 1996.

Strachey, Lytton. *Eminent Victorians: Cardinal Manning; Florence Nightingale; Dr Arnold; General Gordon* [1918]. London and Glasgow: Collins, 1959.

Stubbs, Patricia. *Women and Fiction: Feminism and the Novel 1880–1920.* London: Methuen, 1979.

Stutfield, Hugh E. M. 'Tommyrotics' [1895]. Reprinted in Sally Ledger and Roger Luckhurst, eds. *The Fin de Siècle: A Reader in Cultural History, c. 1880–1900.* Oxford: Oxford University Press, 2000, pp. 120–26.

Sulieri, Sara. *The Rhetoric of English India.* Chicago: Chicago University Press, 1992.

Swinburne, Algernon Charles. *Selected Poems of Swinburne.* Ed. Edward Shanks. London: Macmillan, 1950.

Symons, Arthur. *London Nights* [1895]. 2nd Edition. London: Leonard Smithers, 1897.

Symons, Arthur. *The Symbolist Movement in Literature* [1899]. New York: E. P. Dutton, 1958.

Symons, Arthur. *Silhouettes* [1892]. 2nd Edition. London: Leonard Smithers, 1986.

Thomson, E. P. *The Making of the English Working Class* [1963]. Harmondsworth: Penguin, 1980.

Thornton, R. K. R. *The Decadent Dilemma.* London: Edward Arnold, 1983.

Thornton, R. K. R. and Marion Thain (eds). *Poetry of the 1890s.* 2nd Edition. Harmondsworth: Penguin, 1997.

Torgovnick, Marianna. 'Narrating Sexuality: *The Rainbow*'. In Ann Fernihough, ed. *The Cambridge Companion to D. H. Lawrence.* Cambridge: Cambridge University Press, 2001, pp. 33–48.

Trollope, Anthony. *An Autobiography* [1883]. Ed. David Skilton. Harmondsworth: Penguin, 1996.

Trotter, David. *The English Novel in History, 1895–1920.* London: Routledge, 1993.

Trotter, David. 'The Avoidance of Naturalism: Gissing, Moore, Grand, Bennett, and Others'. In John Richetti, ed. *The Columbia History of the British Novel.* New York: Columbia University Press, 1994, pp. 608–30.

Tucker, Herbert F. *A Companion to Victorian Literature and Culture.* Oxford: Basil Blackwell, 1999.

Tydeman, William (ed.). *Wilde: Comedies: A Selection of Critical Essays.* London: Macmillan, 1982.

Wain, John. Introduction. *The New Wessex Selection of Thomas Hardy's Poetry.* Eds John and Eiran Wain. London and Basingstoke: Macmillan, 1976, pp. 10–18.

Walkowitz, Judith R. *Prostitution and Victorian Society: Women, Class and the State.* Cambridge and New York: Cambridge University Press, 1980.

Walkowitz, Judith R. *City of Dreadful Delight: Narratives of Sexual Danger in Late-Victorian London.* London: Virago Press, 1992.

Warner, Eric and Graham Hough (eds). *Strangeness and Beauty: An Anthology of Aesthetic Criticism, 1840–1910.* 2 Volumes. Cambridge: Cambridge University Press, 1983.

Watt, Ian. *Conrad in the Nineteenth Century.* Berkeley and Los Angeles: University of California Press, 1979.

Waugh, Arthur. 'Reticence in Literature'. *The Yellow Book.* Volume 1, April 1894, pp. 201–19.

Weeks, Robert P. 'Disentanglement as a Theme in H. G. Wells's Fiction'. In Bernard Bergonzi, ed. *H. G. Wells: A Collection of Critical Essays.* New Jersey: Prentice Hall, 1976, pp. 25–31.

Wells, H. G. *Tono-Bungay* [1909]. Ed. Bernard Bergonzi. Lincoln and London: University of Nebraska Press, 1978.

Wells, H. G. *Experiment in Autobiography* [1934]. 2 Volumes. London: Faber and Faber, 1984.

Wells, H. G. *Kipps: The Story of a Simple Soul* [1905]. Ed. Peter Vansittart. London: Everyman, 1993a.

Wells, H. G. *The History of Mr Polly* [1910]. Ed. Norman MacKenzie. London: Everyman, 1993b.

Wells, H. G. *The Island of Dr Moreau* [1896]. Ed. Brian Aldiss. London: Everyman 1993c.

Wells, H. G. *The Time Machine* [1896]. Ed. Michael Moorcock. London: Everyman, 1993d.

Wells, H. G. *Ann Veronica* [1909]. Ed. Sylvia Hardy. London: Everyman, 1993e.

White, Hayden. *Metahistory: The Historical Imagination in Nineteenth-Century Europe.* Baltimore: Johns Hopkins University Press, 1973.

White, Hayden. *The Content of the Form: Narrative Discourse and Historical Representation.* Baltimore: Johns Hopkins University Press, 1987.

Whitman, Walt. *The Complete Poems.* Ed. and Intro. France Murphy. Harmondsworth: Penguin, 1975.

Wicke, Jennifer. 'Vampiric Typewriting: *Dracula* and its Media'. In John Paul Riquelme, ed. *Dracula: Bram Stoker: Case Studies in Contemporary Criticism.* New York: Bedford Books, 2002, pp. 577–99.

Wilde, Oscar. *The Complete Works of Oscar Wilde.* Glasgow: HarperCollins, 1994.

Williams, Raymond. *The Country and the City.* Oxford: Oxford University Press, 1973.

Williams, Raymond. *Keywords: A Vocabulary of Culture and Society.* London: Fontana, 1976.

Williams, Raymond. *Marxism and Literature.* Oxford: Oxford University Press, 1977.

Williams, Raymond. *The English Novel from Dickens to Lawrence.* London: The Hogarth Press, 1984.

Williams, Raymond. *Culture and Society: Coleridge to Orwell* [1958]. London: The Hogarth Press, 1990.

Wilson, Harris (ed.). *Arnold Bennett and H. G. Wells: A Record of a Personal and Literary Friendship*. London: Hart Davis, 1960.

Wolfreys, Julian (ed.). *The Edinburgh Encyclopaedia of Modern Criticism and Theory*. Edinburgh: Edinburgh University Press, 2002.

Woolf, Virginia. *Moments of Being: Unpublished Autobiographical Writings*. Ed. Jeanne Schulkind. 2nd Edition. London: The Hogarth Press, 1985.

Woolf, Virginia. *A Woman's Essays: Selected Essays, Volume 1*. Ed. Rachel Bowlby. Harmondsworth: Penguin, 1992a.

Woolf, Virginia. *Mrs Dalloway* [1925]. Intro. Elaine Showalter. Ed. Stella MacNicholl. Harmondsworth: Penguin, 1992b.

Woolf, Virginia. *To the Lighthouse* [1927]. Intro. Hermione Lee. Ed. Stella MacNicholl. Harmondsworth: Penguin, 1992c.

Woolf, Virginia. *Between the Acts* [1941]. Ed. Stella MacNicholl. Intro. Gillian Beer. Harmondsworth: Penguin, 1992d.

Woolf, Virginia. *The Crowded Dance of Modern Life: Selected Essays, Volume 2*. Ed. Rachel Bowlby. Harmondsworth: Penguin, 1993a.

Woolf, Virginia. *Orlando: A Biography* [1928]. Ed. Brenda Lyons. Intro. Sandra M. Gilbert. Harmondsworth: Penguin, 1993b.

Woolf, Virginia. *A Room of One's Own and Three Guineas* [1928 and 1938]. Ed. Michèle Barrett. Harmondsworth: Penguin, 1993c.

Woolf, Virginia. *A Moment's Liberty: The Shorter Diary*. Ed. Anne Olivier Bell. London: Pimlico, 1997.

Wordsworth, William. *Selected Prose*. Ed. and Intro. John O. Hayden. Harmondsworth: Penguin, 1988.

Yeats, W. B. *Autobiographies*. London: Macmillan, 1955.

Yeats, W. B. *Collected Poems* [1950]. London: Macmillan, 1982.

Zola, Emile. 'The Experimental Novel'. In George J. Becker, ed. *Documents of Modern Literary Realism*. Princeton: Princeton University Press, 1963, pp. 162–96.

Index

Allen, Grant   126, 163
   The Woman Who Did   163, 164,
     191n
Altick, Robert   47
Anderson, Linda   50
Arata, Stephen   150, 153
Archer, William   106
Ardis, Ann   189
Armstrong, Isobel   13
Arnold, Matthew   7, 9, 10, 27, 28n, 37,
   81, 85, 100, 121, 123, 180, 187–8
Avril, Jane   98–9, 104n

Baldick, Chris   10
Bartlett, Neil   107–8, 127
Beardsley, Aubrey   179
Bennett, Arnold   19, 23, 27, 31, 33, 34,
   39, 62–73, 163, 193, 196
   Anna of the Five Towns   65
   Clayhanger   67, 71
   Hilda Lessways   189, 191n
   The Old Wives' Tale   66–71, 194
Besant, Walter   130
Binyon, Laurence   93
Black, Clementina   173
Booth, William   73n
Bourdieu, Pierre   147
Bowlby, Rachel   64
Braddon, Mary Elizabeth   125, 191n
Bradfield, Thomas   179–80
Bradley, Katharine   *See Michael Field*
Brake, Laurel   19, 13–14, 97
Brantlinger, Patrick   131, 132, 158n
Bristow, Joseph   107, 131
Bronfen, Elisabeth   151
Brontë, Emily   5, 28n
Browning, Robert   65, 75, 82
Burne-Jones, Edward Coley   1
Butler, Josephine   175
Butler, Samuel   105

Caird, Mona   167
Carey, John   66
Carroll, Lewis   109, 116
Chekhov, Anton   182
Cobbe, Frances Power   162
Coleridge, Samuel Taylor   81
Conrad, Joseph   17, 18–19, 33, 52, 126,
   128
   Heart of Darkness   17–18, 129, 146,
     155, 156
   The Secret Agent   18–19, 155
Contagious Diseases Acts   174–5, 176,
   191n
Cooper, Edith   *See Michael Field*
Corelli, Marie   126
Corot, Jean-Baptiste   18
Courthorpe, W. J.   12
Coustillas, Pierre   40
Cox, R. G.   19–20
Craft, Christopher   134, 157
cultural capital   147
culture   81
Cunningham, Gail   164

D'Arch-Smith, Timothy   127n
Darwin, Charles   138, 139
Davidson, John   83, 93
degeneration   138–45, 193–4, 197,
   209n
Dellamorra, Richard   15, 76
Dickens, Charles   44, 51
   David Copperfield   22, 63–4
Dollimore, Jonathan   115, 122
Douglas, Lord Alfred   105
Dowie, Ménie Muriel   167
Dowling, Linda   81
Doyle, Arthur Conan   16, 129, 135,
   144–5, 158n, 182
Dunne, Mary Chavelita   *See George
   Egerton*

Egerton, George [Mary Chavelita
    Dunne]   168, 179–87, 188, 190
Discords   180, 183, 185, 186–7, 188
Keynotes   179, 181–6
Eliot, George   8–9, 10, 19, 21, 22, 24, 58
Adam Bede   8, 21
Middlemarch   8–9, 24, 194
Eliot, T. S.   72, 75, 93, 102–3, 197, 198,
    202, 208
Ellmann, Richard   29n, 110, 119
Emig, Rainer   77

Felski, Rita   80
Ferrar, F. W.   41
Field, Michael   90–2
Flanegan-Behrendt, Patricia   127n
Flaubert, Gustave   68
Ford, Ford Madox   128
The Good Soldier   128–9, 153, 155–7,
    194
Forster, E. M.   24–6, 27, 28, 32, 33, 83,
    92, 128, 192, 202–9
A Passage to India   25, 129, 193, 194,
    203–8
Aspects of the Novel   24–5
Howards End   25–6, 55, 163, 191n,
    192, 193, 194, 195–6, 202, 203
The Longest Journey   26
A Room with a View   202, 203
Freud, Sigmund   24, 59, 126, 135, 141,
    146

Galsworthy, John   19, 33, 34, 39, 55–62,
    68, 71, 72, 202
The Forsyte Saga   55–6
The Man of Property   56–62
Garnett, Constance   182
Garnett, Edward   195
Gilbert, Sandra M and Susan Gubar
    173
Gissing, George   39–47, 49, 55, 63–4
Demos   40
The Nether World   40–1
New Grub Street   36, 41–7, 50, 62,
    63
The Odd Women   162–3, 191n
The Unclassed   40
Goode, John   22, 84, 164
Grand, Sarah   113, 159, 163, 164, 165,
    167, 168, 181, 190

The Beth Book   176, 178
The Heavenly Twins   176–9, 188, 190n

Haggard, H. Rider   129, 130, 132
King Solomon's Mines   132, 133–4,
    136, 146, 148, 155, 158n
She   136–7, 146, 148–9
Hamsun, Knut   181
Hardy, Thomas   19–23, 81–2, 84, 92,
    104n, 125
'Candour in Fiction'   20, 29n
Far from the Madding Crowd   19,
    21–2
Jude the Obscure   22, 33, 50, 163,
    164, 188, 191n
The Mayor of Casterbridge   22–3
The Return of the Native   20
Tess of the D'Urbervilles   20, 173–4,
    175–6, 178–9, 191n
Under the Greenwood Tree   19
Heath, Stephen   133
Heilmann, Ann   160, 165, 185
Henley, W. E.   79, 93–5, 100
Hill, Donald, L.   9, 28–9n
Hobsbawm, E. J.   147
Hopkins, Gerard Manley   15, 75–8, 92,
    103n
Housman, A. E.   3, 84–6, 92, 97, 104n
Hunt, William Holman
The Awakening Conscience   6
Huysmans, Joris-Karl   79
Hytner, Nicholas   108, 127n

Ibsen, Henrik   89
'Iota'   167

Jackson, Holbrook   192
Jackson, Russell   114
James, Henry   23, 25, 31, 32, 33, 53, 55,
    128, 130, 131
James, William   31, 35, 59
Johnson, Lionel   86, 96
Joyce, James   33, 39, 55, 63–4, 128, 182,
    198, 208
*A Portrait of the Artist as a Young
    Man*   72, 200
Jowett, Benjamin   16, 29n

Keating, P. J.   41, 63, 166
Keats, John   81, 82